Accounting and Distributive Justice

Routledge Studies in Accounting

Accounting and Distributive Justice

John Flower

Routledge
Taylor & Francis Group

LONDON AND NEW YORK

First published 2010 by Routledge

2 Park Square, Milton Park, Abingdon, Oxon OX14 4RN
52 Vanderbilt Avenue, New York, NY 10017

Routledge is an imprint of the Taylor & Francis Group, an informa business

First published in paperback 2012

Typeset in Sabon by IBT Global.

Library of Congress Cataloging-in-Publication Data
Flower, John, 1934–
  Accounting and distributive justice / John Flower.
    p. cm. — (Routledge studies in accounting ; 8)
  Includes bibliographical references and index.
  1. Distributive justice. 2. Accounting—Social aspects. I. Title.
  HB523.F62 2010
  657.01'1—dc22
  2010002145

ISBN13: 978-0-415-64563-8 (pbk)
ISBN13: 978-0-415-87177-8 (hbk)
ISBN13: 978-0-203-84746-6 (cbk)

Contents

Tables

Figures

Preface

The first impulse for this book came in 1993 when I did the English translation of the late Dieter Ordelheide's book on German financial reporting[1] and, for the first time, learned of the profit distribution function. I thought then and still think that this is a most important function of accounts and that the ignorance of the function by British and American accountants is much to be regretted.

The second impulse came when, in 2004, at the age of seventy, I started to study philosophy at the Open University and began to reflect on accounting's philosophical basis. I came to see the connection between the philosopher's concept of distributive justice and the distribution function of accounts that lies at the heart of this book.

The third impulse came when a draft article on the subject of this book which I submitted to a leading academic accounting journal was rejected. The peer reviewers gave two reasons: that the article was too long and that it was not 'academic' and had no place in an accounting journal. The first reason was fully justified; the second, in my opinion, less so. But I took this rebuff as a challenge to write a book that would solve the problem of length and would escape the censorship of peer reviewers.

Here is the book. It is addressed primarily at my fellow accountants. My sincerest wish is that it makes them think more profoundly about their discipline.

Acknowledgements

I would like to acknowledge the assistance that I have received from the following:

Dr Paul Harkin, my tutor at the Open University, on the nature of distributive justice

K. A. Siddiqui, BScEcon, a fellow student at the London School of Economics in the 1950s, now a Chartered Accountant and a German Wirtschaftprüfer, for invaluable information on the German financial reporting system

Dr Thorsten Sellhorn, MBA, Professor of External Accounting at the Otto Bensheim School of Management, for his very helpful suggestions concerning public utilities

Dr Axel Haller, Professor of Accounting at the University of Regensburg, for advice on sustainability

Dr Chris Lefebvre, Professor of Accounting at the Katholieke Universiteit, Leuven, for his continued support and encouragement

I would also like to express my appreciation of the helpful cooperation of the Global Reporting Initiative in granting permission to quote from the GRI G3 Guidelines. I would like to make clear that the comments and criticisms expressed in this book are my own and do not necessarily reflect the views of the Global Reporting Initiative.

1   The Wrong Paradigm

In this book I challenge the current paradigm[1] of accounting—more precisely the paradigm that underlies the financial reporting of firms.[2] I reject the current paradigm and propose a radical alternative. In this first chapter, I analyse the current paradigm and set out my reasons for rejecting it. The rest of the book is devoted to explaining and justifying my proposed alternative.

1.1. THE CURRENT PARADIGM OF FINANCIAL REPORTING

The nature of the paradigm that underlies the current practice of accounting may be gathered from the new conceptual framework that is being developed jointly by the International Accounting Standards Board (IASB) and the USA's Financial Accounting Standards Board (FASB), and which sets out the principles that these bodies intend to follow in setting the rules that govern financial reporting throughout much of the world.[3] In May 2008, the IASB and the FASB presented their proposals in the form of a common exposure draft (FASB 2008), which defines the objective of the financial reporting in the following terms:

> The objective of general purpose external financial reporting is to provide financial information about the reporting entity that is useful to present and potential equity investors, lenders, and other creditors in making decisions in their capacity as capital providers. (Paragraph OB2)

Later paragraphs develop further this objective:

> The Boards' mandate is to assist in the efficient functioning of economies and the efficient allocation of resources in capital markets by developing high-quality financial reporting standards. (Paragraph OB3)
> An entity's financial performance provides information about the return it has produced on its economic resources. In the long run, an entity must produce a positive return on its economic resources if it is to generate net cash flows and thus provide a return to its investors and creditors. (Paragraph OB19)

Financial reporting information helps capital providers make better decisions, which results in more efficient functioning of the capital markets and lower cost of capital for the economy as a whole. (Paragraph QC31)

These citations make clear that these bodies consider that the model that underlies their conception of accounting is capitalism and that the function of accounting is to meet the information needs of capitalists ('capital providers'). The IASB and the FASB are wedded to the paradigm of capitalism in the particular form of neo-liberalism, whose principal elements may be summarized as follows:

i. The objective of economic activity is to assure the highest possible material standard of living for mankind.
ii. The achievement of this objective requires the maximization of the output of goods and services.
iii. The maximization of output requires the optimal allocation of resources.
iv. The optimal allocation of resources will generally be achieved through the operation of market forces. Producers and consumers should have unrestricted freedom to buy and sell the goods and services of their choice on the market at prices determined by the interaction of supply and demand. They should be motivated solely by their own self-interest and, guided by Adam Smith's 'invisible hand', they will achieve the best result for mankind. For firms, the pursuit of self-interest implies the maximization of profits.
v. The most important factor of production is capital. Capital should be allocated to productive activities through the operation of the capital market, which brings together providers of capital and seekers of capital.
vi. Capital market participants should allocate capital to those productive activities that yield them the highest return.
vii. Hence capital market participants should be provided with accurate information concerning the returns from the outlay of capital.

According to the IASB and the FASB, the primary function of financial reporting is to supply this information. But are these bodies right in deciding that financial reporting should be based on the paradigm of neo-liberalism?

1.2 THE CASE FOR NEO-LIBERALISM

The neo-liberal paradigm is defended by its advocates on two main grounds:

a) Philosophy: The freedom of men and women to pursue their own good through economic activity should be restricted only when it

infringes the rights of others. Hence there is no moral obligation on sellers to sell at any but the highest prices and on buyers to pay more than the lowest price, because the people with whom they deal have no right to a different price.
b) Consequences: The neo-liberal paradigm works! The very substantial improvement over the last two centuries in the standard of living in Western industrialized countries and, more recently in China and India, has been brought about principally by allowing the free interplay of market forces.

I deal with the philosophical question in the next chapter, but first I consider whether, in fact, neo-liberalism works.

1.3. THE CONVENTIONAL CRITICISMS OF NEO-LIBERALISM

The neo-liberal paradigm has been criticized on the ground that principle iv is false. The market often does not achieve the optimal allocation of resources, for a variety of reasons:

i. Certain persons or firms may be so powerful that they can influence market operations to their own advantage (for example, monopolies).
ii. Certain goods and services may not be provided most efficiently through the operation of market forces, notably public goods, such as roads.
iii. Market participants, in pursuing their own immediate self-interest, ignore externalities; they do not take into account many of the adverse effects of their actions on others either in the present (for example through pollution of the environment) or in the longer term (for example the effect on future generations).

Most economists consider that these defects of neo-liberalism are so serious that the free play of market forces will not bring about the hoped-for improvement in the welfare of mankind. The state has to act to correct these market failures. Hence government intervention is necessary to control monopolies, to provide public goods, and to curb pollution. It would seem that private firms and institutions are incapable of acting on their own to moderate these shortcomings of neo-liberalism. For example the IASB has made no move to require private firms to report the costs to society of their activities (for example the harm done to outsiders by pollution created by the firm). According to the IASB, these costs should be reported only when they become the private costs of the firm (for example when the government levies a fine or forces the firm to clean up polluted land). The IASB considers that its task is to set standards for private firms operating within a framework (of laws, regulations, and so on) set by the state which seeks to mitigate the shortcomings of neo-liberalism. Within this framework, the private firm should seek to maximize its profits.

The IASB's attitude is defensible, and therefore it is necessary to find a further, more fundamental, criticism of neo-liberalism.

1.4 A MORE FUNDAMENTAL CRITICISM

However my criticism of neo-liberalism is more fundamental: neo-liberalism neglects society's most important problem. I consider that society is confronted with two fundamental economic problems:

1. The production problem: what goods and services to produce; how much to produce; who is to produce them; how to produce them most efficiently at the lowest cost.
2. The distribution problem: who gets what is produced; how output and income are divided (distributed) among society's members.

I consider that neo-liberal economics concentrates almost exclusively on the production problem and neglects the distribution problem. However the distribution problem is the more important for reasons relating to both production and distribution. I deal first with production.

1.5 THE PRODUCTION PROBLEM

I contend that mankind has largely solved the production problem. My contention is based on two arguments: (a) the analysis of mankind's needs and (b) the current level of production.

(a) The Analysis of Mankind's Needs

Eighty years ago, John Maynard Keynes predicted a world of plenty for his grandchildren: 'I draw the conclusion that, assuming no important wars and no important increase in population, the economic problem may be solved, or at least within sight of solution, within a hundred years' (Keynes 1930: 365–6). What reasons did Keynes give for believing that mankind would soon solve the production problem? He divided human needs into two classes: absolute and relative. Absolute needs are those a person feels irrespective of the situation of others; relative needs are those whose satisfaction depends on superiority over others. Keynes felt that it was impossible through economic activity to satisfy all relative needs and hence regarded their satisfaction as not an economic problem.

A generation after Keynes, John Kenneth Galbraith (1955) argued persuasively that the USA in the 1950s had already solved the production problem. Not only was output at a very high level but it increasingly consisted of goods and services that served no real need. The more recent work of Colin Hamilton (2005) confirms Galbraith's contention that the 'needs' of modern consumers in the world's richest countries are artificially created by sophisticated advertising techniques that appeal to man's baser instincts such as jealousy. Economists often claim that the role of the economic system is to satisfy the demands of consumers and that it is not the economist's role to question these demands: the consumer is sovereign. Hamilton (2003) emphatically rejects this doctrine. He considers that, in the present society dominated by consumerism, the 'needs' of consumers are created by the manipulative marketing techniques of multinational corporations. He argues that autonomous individuals should decide for themselves what is good for them and not allow themselves to be manipulated. Hamilton (2003: 12) likens the modern consumer who feels that he must have the latest (heavily promoted) gimmick to an alcoholic, commenting, '[A]n alcoholic would prefer more drinks, but we don't measure his wellbeing by the number of drinks that he has.'

Since Keynes, there has been much research on the relationship between a person's income and his level of self-reported happiness.[4] The following conclusions are well supported by the evidence and are accepted by most serious scholars:[5]

(i) In the major Western industrialized countries, there has been no increase in the general level of happiness over the past fifty years, despite very substantial growth in output, as measured by the gross domestic product (GDP). For example, in Japan, the GDP per head increased sixfold between 1958 and 1991, but there was no increase in self-reported happiness.

(ii) At the level of the individual, the correlation between the level of income and the level of happiness is positive but rather weak. At low income levels, an increase in income brings a significant increase in happiness but the effect is less marked at higher income levels. However, at all levels, following an increase in income, happiness reverts to its former level very quickly, as the individual becomes accustomed to her new income level—she adapts her aspirations to her current situation. Given this phenomenon of adaptation of aspiration levels, it is impossible for an individual to increase permanently her level of happiness by increasing her income. The implication is that human wants are insatiable; to maintain a certain level of happiness, the individual has to continually achieve an ever higher income—like Alice in *Through the Looking-Glass*, she has to run furiously just to stay where she is.

(iii) The individual, in assessing her level of happiness, makes, not an absolute judgement, but a relative judgement; she compares herself with other individuals, such as her work colleagues or neighbours—known as her reference group. If the income of the people in her reference group increases and her income remains unchanged, she becomes less happy; she is unable to 'keep up with the Joneses'. Easterlin (1994) demonstrates, using data from surveys in eleven industrialized countries, that the consequence of this human trait is that raising the incomes of all does not increase the happiness of all.

Happiness research provides a striking endorsement of Keynes's insight that human needs may be divided into two categories: relative needs which are generated by the individual comparing himself with other people, and absolute or basic needs which man needs to satisfy irrespective of his social position. Any attempt to satisfy man's relative needs through higher output is futile. After the basic needs of food, clothing, and shelter have been adequately satisfied, any further increase in GDP leads to no permanent improvement in mankind's happiness.

My argument that mankind has already solved the production problem is based on two claims:

1. Man's relative needs cannot be satisfied by greater output and hence their non-satisfaction is not part of the production problem.
2. The world's output is already sufficient to meet the basic needs of all the world's inhabitants. This claim will now be considered.

(b)   The Current Level of Output

The validity of the second claim will be considered with reference to mankind's most basic need: food. The United Nations' Food and Agricultural Organization (FAO) admits that 'the world currently produces enough food for everybody, but many people do not have access to it'.[6] This assertion may be validated using the FAO's own statistics. For the years 2000–02 (the latest for which statistics have been published), the world's supply of food was sufficient to provide every man, woman, and child with 2790 kilocalories per day.[7] The FAO estimates that, as a minimum, a person requires around 1800 kilocalories per day.[8] Hence, if the world's food were distributed equally among the world's population, it would provide everyone with a diet some 50% above the minimum. In fact the FAO estimates that, in 2009, there were over 1.02 billion chronically hungry people whose food intake was below the minimum.[9] These statistics confirm the presumption that, with food, the problem is not production but distribution. In many developed countries, agricultural surpluses are a major problem, with governments taking measures to reduce production, and much of the population suffers not from malnutrition but from obesity. Gary Stix (2007) has estimated that, in the year 2007, the number of over-nourished (a euphemism for obese) people world-wide exceeded the undernourished by several hundred million. The position with regard to food almost certainly applies to mankind's other basic needs for clothing, shelter, and so on. One may confidently conclude that the world's current output is sufficient to meet the basic needs of everyone.

(c) The Dangers of Economic Growth

Moreover, further increases in output are not only unnecessary; they may be positively harmful. More output now can lead to lower welfare in the longer run; hence the maximization of output is the wrong goal for mankind.

Throughout history, mankind has been able to achieve improvements in its standard of living by increasing the output of goods and services. However, in recent decades, increases in output have been running against constraints. There are two kinds of constraints:

(i) The exhaustion of the world's resources, and
(ii) The degradation of the earth's environment caused by man's past actions.

It is unrealistic to expect that man can increase output indefinitely; production entails using up the earth's resources (such as oil), which are finite; at some point these resources will be exhausted but, well before that point is reached, output will be constrained by shortages of raw materials. The aim of economic activity should not be to achieve the highest possible rate of economic growth, but instead to achieve a stable, sustainable level of output—that is, zero growth. It is significant that the neo-liberal paradigm was developed at a time when the earth's resources seemed unlimited and the impact of economic activity on the environment was imperceptible, but that time is long past. Essentially the neo-liberal paradigm is no longer relevant for today's world; in fact the striving for ever greater output may lead mankind to disaster.

This argument is highly controversial and contested. Since the writings of Thomas Malthus[10] in the early nineteenth century, there have been warnings that the world will run out of natural resources, but the threatened calamity has never materialized. So far mankind, using its natural talents for discovery and invention, has avoided the predicted disaster and has in fact succeeded in improving the average standard of living of the earth's population. However two recent developments cast doubt on whether mankind can maintain this feat for much longer.

(i) Energy prices: Over the past thirty years, there has been a long-run increase in the price of crude oil from less than $3 per barrel in 1970 to around $150 per barrel in 2008, a fifty-fold increase. Although recently the price has dropped to around $70 per barrel, this still represents over a twenty-fold increase. Moreover, the recent extreme fluctuations in the price of oil suggest that there is something seriously wrong with the neo-liberal economics paradigm. There is no dispute over the cause of the long-term price rise: the increased demand for oil, arising in particular from the explosive growth in the economies of China and India, coupled with natural physical limitations on supply. As Malthus predicted, at some point, the exponential growth of mankind's demands comes up against the indisputable fact that the world's resources are finite.

(ii) Global warming: It is now generally agreed that, unless there is a fundamental change in man's behaviour, there will be a significant increase in global temperatures over the coming century with catastrophic impacts on mankind's welfare. This global warming is directly attributable to mankind's economic activity over the past two centuries, notably the burning of fossil fuels, which is the direct outcome of the pursuit of ever-higher output. There is a general consensus among scientists on these central points. The best evidence of this consensus (which should persuade all but the most opinionated sceptics) is provided by the highly detailed and authoritative report of the United Nation's Intergovernmental Panel on Climate Change,[11] which sets out the research findings of over two hundred scientists.

Some economists claim that technical progress will solve all the problems of raw material shortages and climate change. As Hamilton (2003) points out technological change has, in some instances, greatly reduced the volume of resources that is needed to produce certain goods and services; for example silicon fibres have replaced copper wire, and much less aluminium is now needed to make a can. But, however great such progress, production will still use up a finite quantity of materials, and at some point in the future, the earth's resources will be exhausted, given that they are not infinite. As regards climate change, the reduction in man's output of CO_2 that is necessary to avert a catastrophic increase in global temperatures, is so great that it can be achieved only through a radical change in man's behaviour—at the very least a drastic cut in the rate of increase in output. There is no foreseeable technical fix to this problem.

Supporters of the IASB's approach may argue that, in order for mankind to tackle effectively the crisis arising from climate change and the exhaustion of the world's resources, it is necessary to ensure the most efficient allocation of resources (point iii in Section 1.1). There is an element of truth in this contention. Resources may be allocated so as to achieve most efficiently either a bad end (the maximization of output) or a good end (the preservation of the environment). But the IASB makes no reference to any end other than assuring a positive return on capital, and there is little doubt that virtually all the firms that currently adopt the IASB's standards are motivated by an urge to maximize their profits.

These developments support the conclusion that, for the two stated reasons (the exhaustion of the world's resources, and the degradation of the earth's environment) further increases in output are not in mankind's long-term interest.[12]

1.6 THE DISTRIBUTION PROBLEM

I contend that neo-liberalism and the IASB neglect the distribution problem: how the output of goods and services is distributed (divided) among the world's population. The importance of distribution for mankind's welfare may be illustrated with a highly simplified example. Assume that society consists of just two persons (George and Henry) and that output consists of just a single good (widgets). The total output of society (achieved through George and Henry working together) is ten widgets per period. Figure 1.1 shows how this output may be divided between George and Henry. George's share is shown on the y axis and Henry's on the x axis. The solid

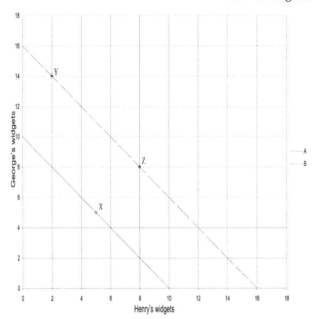

Figure 1.1 George and Henry.

line (A) shows all possible divisions of the ten widgets between the two: at the left end of the line, George has ten widgets and Henry no widgets; at the right end of the line, the reverse is the case. Assume that initially output is divided equally between the two, at point X in Figure 1.1. Now assume that there is a change in technology; George invents a machine that leads to an increase in output to sixteen widgets per period. The new possible division of this output is shown by the dotted line (B). However, as the inventor of the new machine, George is able to appropriate, for himself, a higher proportion of the total output; he gets fourteen widgets and Henry only two widgets (point Y). The change in technology has resulted in a change in both the level of the output and the distribution of the output.

Is the change from point X to point Y an improvement from the viewpoint of society as a whole (that is, for George and Henry combined)? According to the pure theory of neo-liberal economics, there is no reason for holding that the change from point X to point Y is undesirable. Neo-liberal economics is not concerned with how output is distributed; all points on the line A are equally desirable, as are all points on line B. Line B represents higher output; hence all points on line B are to be preferred to all points on line A. Hence point Y is to be preferred to point X.

However, most advocates of neo-liberal economics would be unhappy with this conclusion, as they would be disturbed by the high degree of inequality represented by point Y. They would not want to suggest that point Y is to be preferred to point X and would therefore seek arguments to prove that their theories do not lead to this conclusion. One possible argument is based on the first fundamental theorem of welfare economics, which states that the free play of competition brings about a competitive equilibrium which is Pareto optimal.[13] Pareto optimality consists of achieving a situation in which one person cannot be made better off without at least one other person being made worse off. All the points on line A fulfill this condition, and hence any point on this line might be reached through the interplay of market forces in perfect competition. The actual point reached would depend on such matters as the initial distribution of resources and the power relations between the parties. With the invention of the new machine, this competitive equilibrium is disturbed. The theorem assumes no change in technology and therefore is unable to shed any light on how the change in technology affects the distribution between George and Henry. The theorem simply states that, once equilibrium has been restored, it will be Pareto optimal. According to the theorem, the new equilibrium may be anywhere on the line B. Hence the movement from point X to point Y is fully compatible with the theorem. Feldman (1998) identified the basic limitation of the first fundamental theorem of welfare economics in the following terms: 'The most troubling aspect of the First Theorem is its neglect of distribution. Laissez-faire may produce a Pareto optimal outcome, but there are many different Pareto optima, and some are fairer than others.'

Other possible arguments are:

i. A move from point X to point Y is extremely unlikely in reality. Henry is likely to benefit from the increased total output, although probably not to the same extent as George, who invented the machine. This has been the general experience following past technological improvements.

ii. A move from point X to point Y would occur only through George employing illegitimate means, for example by enslaving Henry.

In fact both arguments strengthen my case, in that they are based on matters that are outside the theoretical framework of neo-liberal economics. The first argument refers to history and the second to moral (that is, non-economic) principles. The fundamental point is that the neo-liberal theory in its pure form is amoral. Within the terms of the theory, there is no way of distinguishing between behaviour that its advocates reject (such as George enslaving Henry) and those that they consider acceptable (such as George exploiting Henry's need in order to obtain the highest possible price). To cope with these problems, the theory's advocates have to appeal to other theories that do have a moral content. Hence neo-liberal economics, in its pure form, is an inadequate guide to proper behaviour.[14]

Figure 1.1 may be used to gain an insight into the problem of the proper distribution of the world's food supplies which was discussed in the previous section. Assume that the goods whose quantities are measured on the axes are not widgets but food, and that George and Henry represent not individuals but classes: Henry the class of undernourished people and George the class of over-nourished people. At present the world is at point Y: the Henrys of the world have too little food: the Georges too much. A move from point Y to point Z (an equal distribution of food) would surely lead to an increase in overall welfare. In fact it is arguable that a move from point Y to point X is desirable, even though it involves a fall in production. However, in order to reach these conclusions, it is necessary to make value judgements concerning the relative welfare of George and Henry—for example that the increase in Henry's welfare when his allocation is increased from two to five is greater than the reduction in George's welfare when his allocation is reduced from fourteen to five. Such evaluations are the domain of philosophy, which is the subject of the next chapter. The most that confidently can be concluded from this example is that the distribution of output has a major impact on welfare.

1.7 CUTTING THE CAKE

Implicit in my criticism of neo-liberalism is a certain view concerning the means by which the living standards of the most disadvantaged are to be improved. I hold that this is most effectively achieved by the more equitable distribution of the world's output. The advocates of neo-liberalism hold that a better way is to increase the world's output—that it is better to increase the size of the cake, giving everyone a bigger slice. It is my contention that it is no longer feasible to advocate increasing the size of the cake. Either it will prove impossible because of exhaustion of the earth's resources or it risks destroying the earth's environment.

However any move to stabilize the world's output or even merely to reduce the rate of increase must be accompanied by measures that assure a more equitable distribution. Many people at present live in poverty; they lack the minimum level of material goods that would enable them to live a worthwhile life. A constant sized cake or even one that grows more slowly will condemn these people to continued poverty. The biggest problem lies in the huge disparities in living standards between countries (for example between the USA and China). It is unrealistic, unreasonable, and, above all, unjust to expect that those countries with a lower standard of living should accept reduced economic growth. This implies that the richer countries should accept zero economic growth or even negative growth (a fall in living standards), whilst other countries catch up. For this to be feasible, the just and fair distribution of output within the developed countries assumes increasing importance.

1.8 CONCLUSION

On the basis of the preceding analysis, I conclude that the overriding aim of economic activity should not be the maximization of output, which is no longer essential and the pursuit of which may well lead mankind to disaster. Hence the IASB and the FASB, which base their approach to financial reporting on neo-liberalism, have chosen the wrong paradigm. I contend that the primary aim of economic activity should be to assure a just and fair distribution of output. I have still to define the meaning of the term 'a just and fair distribution'. That is the task of the next chapter.

2 Distributive Justice

The conclusion of the previous chapter was that, in the present circumstances, the principal objective of economic activity should be the just and fair distribution of output. This chapter discusses the meaning of a just and fair distribution (for example how to divide output between George and Henry), turning to the writings of philosophers for guidance.

The branch of philosophy that deals with the distribution of wealth and income among society's members is known as distributive justice.[1] For the purposes of this book, I propose the following definition: '[D]istributive justice is justice in the distribution of the costs and benefits of economic activity among the members of society.'[2] In general, philosophers do not accept the absolute supremacy of the economic objective of the maximization of the material standard of living. For example, the American philosopher John Rawls writes:

> It is a mistake to believe that a just and good society must wait upon a high material standard of life [. . .] great wealth is not essential. In fact, beyond some point it is more likely to be a positive hindrance, a meaningless distraction at best, if not a temptation to indulgence and emptiness.[3]

But, there is widespread agreement among philosophers that it is worthwhile to seek to improve the standard of living of the most disadvantaged. However there is much disagreement on the priority to be given to this objective. The source of this disagreement is a fundamental difference of opinion among philosophers as to the weight to be attached to two desirable social values: equality and liberty

2.1 EQUALITY VERSUS LIBERTY

2.1.1 Equality

The basic principle that underlies the concept of equality is that people who are similarly situated in morally relevant respects should be treated similarly.[4] The moral principle of equality does not require that Adolf Hitler and Mahatma Ghandi should have been treated identically, but it does require equal treatment when there is no moral basis for differentiating between people. There is a basic assumption that, in the absence of clear evidence to the contrary, all people are of equal moral worth; hence discrimination on the basis of race, gender, national origin, and other morally irrelevant characteristics is wrong. It is argued that many of the factors that lead to an unequal division of wealth are morally irrelevant: for example a person may have a good start in life, because he had rich and conscientious parents, or may be able to earn more than other people, because he is healthy and intelligent rather than sickly and mentally deficient; many argue that these are morally arbitrary factors, the outcome of the 'natural lottery', which do not entitle anyone to have more than his fellows. Hence it is argued that all people be given an equal share of the earth's wealth, since, with respect to people in general, there are no morally relevant reasons for unequal treatment. Others are of the opinion that other considerations, such as ability and effort, permit an unequal distribution.

2.1.2 Liberty

The basic principle that underlies the concept of liberty is that everyone should respect the autonomy of other people, who should be free to lead their lives in whatever way they choose. People have rights that others are obliged to respect. The clearest enunciation of this principle was given by John Stuart Mill:

> [. . .] [T]he sole end for which mankind are warranted, individually or collectively, in interfering with the liberty of action of any of their number is self-protection. That the only purpose for which power can be rightfully exercised over any member of a civilized community against his will, is to prevent harm to others.[5]

Clearly on occasions there is a conflict between liberty and equality. Some philosophers give priority to equality, others to liberty. This is the principal reason why there is no consensus among philosophers on the principles of distributive justice. In this chapter, I present a brief analysis of five of the more prevalent theories:

1. Egalitarianism
2. Libertarianism
3. Marxism
4. Utilitarianism
5. Justice as fairness

2.2 Egalitarianism

An egalitarian (an advocate of egalitarianism) gives precedence to equality over liberty. She gives priority to achieving an equal distribution of wealth and income among society's members, even at the cost of restricting the liberty of some, for example through redistributive taxation or, more controversially, by the expropriation of the wealthy's property. The philosophical basis of egalitarianism is the belief that the unequal division of society's wealth and income is the outcome of morally arbitrary factors. However, the egalitarian also claims that the following practical benefits are achieved by the redistribution of wealth and income from the rich to the poor.

1. The material living standard of the poorest is improved. This is clearly desirable when the poorest lack the material resources to live a worthwhile life, according to the society's norms.
2. All members of society (not just the poorest) benefit from a more equal distribution of income and wealth. Richard Wilkinson and Kate Pickett (2009) rank societies according to the level of inequality and according to unambiguous measures of welfare, such as life expectancy and infant mortality. There is clear evidence that the overall level of welfare is higher in the more equal societies.
3. There is less occasion for conflict between the classes. In theory everyone is happier. The poorest are no longer envious of the rich and the rich no longer feel threatened by the resentment of the poor. Many would regard this as a poor reason, as they consider envy to be a vice. However the same idea can be expressed in a rather more positive way: that the self-respect of poorer people is enhanced when the gap between them and the rich is reduced. A further reason why a more equal society may be more peaceful than an unequal society is that, in the latter, the rich may be able to maintain their privileged position only by oppressing the poor. Also people may be happier if the members of the reference group with which they compare themselves are not significantly better off than they are.[6]
4. It improves people's opportunity to participate equally in the political and social life of the community. Elizabeth Anderson (1999) argues that the most serious consequence of an uneven distribution of wealth is that it permits the more fortunate to dominate and oppress the less fortunate. The poorest suffer not only from less material goods but also from the erosion of their political rights. Given economic inequality, not all citizens are politically equal; for example the rich have far greater influence in the political process, even in so-called democratic countries, through their contributions to political parties. Anderson refers to the negative and positive aims of egalitarianism: 'Negatively, people are entitled to whatever capabilities are necessary to enable them to avoid or escape entanglement in oppressive social relationships. Positively, they are entitled to the capabilities necessary for functioning as an equal citizen in a democratic state.' The proper functioning of a democratic state depends on the elimination of excessive disparities in wealth.
5. A more equal distribution of wealth among the members of society promotes fraternity, a quality of society that tends to be neglected in

the contest between equality and liberty, but which is an absolutely essential feature of the good society[7].

Essentially, egalitarians argue that a society in which income and wealth are distributed evenly is more stable and cohesive than one with great disparities. All the aforementioned benefits are the consequences of equality; equality is sought not as an end in itself but as a means to other desirable ends. However certain philosophers, strict egalitarians, hold that equality is the sole criterion of a just society. Strict egalitarians are to be contrasted with pluralist egalitarians, who are prepared to accept less than complete equality in return for improvements along some other dimension. It is relatively easy to demonstrate that strict egalitarianism, when pushed to extremes, leads to irrational outcomes. This may be illustrated with the example of George and Henry.

When dealing with questions of distributive justice, it is appropriate to think of George and Henry as representing different classes, and the goods that are divided between them (described as 'widgets' in the previous chapter) as representing the total wealth of society. In Figure 2.1, the dotted 45° line (C) represents distributions between George and Henry that, according to strict egalitarians, are completely just. Distributions that do not lie on this line are unjust, the degree of injustice being indicated by the distance from the line. Hence the original distribution (point X) is just and the distribution of the increased output (point Y) is thoroughly unjust. The

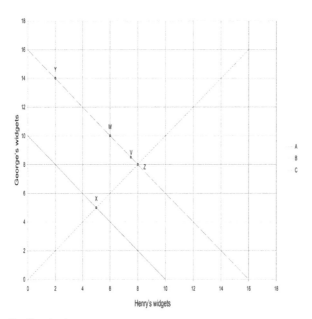

Figure 2.1   Egalitarianism.

injustice of the distribution represented by point Y compared to point X is not compensated for by the higher level of social output. The most just division of this increased output is given by the point Z: equal shares to George and Henry.

However, there is a practical problem. In practice, it may not be possible for society to reach point Z. George may not be prepared to put in the effort that is necessary to achieve the higher output, if he is not allowed to retain the lion's share. This is the incentive problem that complicates most theories of distributive justice (not just egalitarianism). Higher levels of social output may be achievable, only if those whose cooperation is necessary for the higher output keep a disproportionate share, leading to an increase in inequality. Suppose that George shares part of the increased output with Henry—as indicated by the point W (ten to George and six to Henry). In deciding whether the move from point X to point W is desirable and just, a pluralist egalitarian would compare the benefits to Henry (the increase in his income from five to six) with the disadvantages arising from the increased inequality, notably that George with his increased economic power is in a position to exploit and oppress Henry. It is certainly possible that a pluralist egalitarian would argue that point X should be preferred to point W, despite that fact that, at point X, both George and Henry are, in material terms, worse off compared with point W. Opponents of egalitarians accuse them of advocating 'levelling-down'; they are prepared to reduce living standards in the quest for greater equality.

A strict egalitarian would have no doubt that a move from point X to point W is undesirable as leading to an increase in inequality; in fact she would consider a move from point X to point V (8.5 to George and 7.5 to Henry) as wrong, because point V is less just than point X and, for her, the sole measure of justice is the degree of equality. Most rational people would consider such a judgement as absurd. The level of inequality at point V is trivial and very unlikely to lead to significant negative consequences.

For these reasons, strict egalitarianism makes little sense as a practical policy. However, given the undoubted benefits of increased equality, pluralist egalitarianism (which does not insist on complete equality) is a coherent and influential theory.

2.3 LIBERTARIANISM

Libertarianism lies at the opposite extreme to egalitarianism in the spectrum of theories of distributive justice. Libertarians give priority to liberty and place little or no value on equality. This section discusses first the rigorous version of libertarianism formulated by Robert Nozick.

2.3.1 Nozick's Entitlement Theory

Robert Nozick is an exponent of an extreme form of libertarianism. In his book *Anarchy, State and Utopia*, he presents the entitlement theory of justice. In complete contrast to egalitarians, Nozick has no interest in the pattern of holdings of wealth in a society—that is, how much each member of society owns. For Nozick, it is irrelevant whether all the wealth is owned by one person (complete inequality) or is spread evenly (complete equality). He is interested only in the process by which these holdings of wealth came about. According to his entitlement theory, a person is entitled to own something justly, if the process by which he acquired it was just. It is a backward looking or historical theory of distributive justice. What has happened in the past determines the justice of the present distribution. Nozick proposes three principles to determine the justice of holdings of wealth:

1. A person who acquires a holding in accordance with the principle of justice in acquisition is entitled to that holding.
2. A person who acquires a holding in accordance with the principle of justice in transfer, from someone else entitled to the holding, is entitled to the holding.
3. No one is entitled to a holding except by (repeated) application of 1 and 2.

The complete principle of distributive justice would say simply that a distribution is just if everyone is entitled to the holdings they possess.[8]

Nozick's theory of 'justice in acquisition' follows closely the defence of property in John Locke's Second Treatise of Government.[9] A person may appropriate to himself an unowned object by mixing his labour with it. Locke held that it was self-evident that a person owned his own body and therefore owned whatever he produced with his own labour. Thus a person who tilled a stretch of virgin ground was entitled to own that land permanently. Locke made the act of appropriation subject to only two conditions: that the new owner does not waste it and that he leaves enough and as good for others (that is, that at the time of the appropriation, other people are not made worse off, because there is enough unappropriated land left for them). Nozick gives fewer details of 'justice in transfer'; he condemns theft and fraud and states that a transfer is just even if one of the parties had no other option, as would be the case with a traveller in the desert who was dying of thirst and had to pay an exorbitant price for a glass of water from the owner of the only well.[10]

Once a person has acquired a just title to something, he has the right to use it in any way that he pleases; the only restriction on his use is that he may not use it to harm other people. The rightful owner of a gun may not use it to kill his rival but the rightful owner of the only well in the desert is under no obligation to supply other people with water at a price not of his choosing.[11] Hence the state is acting unjustly (violating a person's rights) when it confiscates part of a person's property in the form of taxation. Nozick is particularly critical of redistributive taxation (taxing the rich to help the poor) which he considers to be on a par with forced labour, on the grounds that the taxed person is forced to work for the benefit of some-one else.[12] Rather inconsistently, he accepts the justice of taxation to pay for the 'night-watchman state': the state that protects its citizens from aggression (both from their fellow-citizens and from foreign powers) and assures that contracts are honoured. But the state's role should be limited to these functions; any extension of its functions leads inevitably to a violation of the rights of individuals.

The kernel of Nozick's theory is the absolute right of a property owner to use his property as he pleases, subject only to respecting the rights of other people. For Nozick, rights consist only of negative rights: the right of the individual to be free of interference. He recognizes no positive rights: that is, rights that entitle the individual to benefits, such as the right of the traveller who is dying of thirst to be provided with life-saving water. According to Nozick, a person may not have an obligation imposed on him against his will, as this would be a violation of his rights.

Nozick draws a clear distinction between his entitlement theory and most other theories of distributive justice which he describes as 'patterned'. With a patterned distribution, the amount allocated to a person depends on some attribute of that person, for example her moral worth, her value to society, or her need. The equal distribution favoured by egalitarians is patterned in a very basic way: the sole criterion that determines whether someone participates in the distribution is that she should be a human being. Nozick claimed that his entitlement theory would not lead to a patterned distribution, because the free interplay of people acquiring and transferring holdings would inevitably lead to any pattern being broken up. It might be felt that this would be a serious shortcoming of the entitlement theory, that the resulting distribution would be haphazard with the ownership of property bearing no relationship to the merit or other morally relevant attribute of the owner. However Nozick argues that any attempt by some authority to impose a pattern inevitably leads to the violation of the rights of individuals. In a famous passage he uses the example of Wilt Chamberlain, a popular basketball player. He invites the reader to allocate money to people in accordance with her preferred pattern. But many people want to watch Wilt Chamberlain play and willingly use their money to do so. As a result, Wilt Chamberlain ends up with significantly more than other people, upsetting the initial distribution. In order to preserve the initial preferred distribution, 'society would have to forbid capitalist acts between consenting adults'.[13] It could be argued that the new distribution followed the pattern 'to each according to his ability to provide goods and services valued by other people'. Nozick accepts that, with the entitlement theory, the resulting distribution will manifest the influence of such patterns. However, he argues that the freedom of the individual to dispose of his property as he wills (donations to charity, bequests to children, and so on) means that any pattern is soon broken up.

A major reason for Nozick's rejection of patterned distributions is that he considers that they are based on the false idea that there already exists a quantum of wealth and that the main problem is how to distribute it justly—production and distribution are treated as two separate and independent issues. Nozick considers this is false, arguing:

> To think that the task of a theory of distributive justice is to fill in the blank in 'to each according to his ___' is to be predisposed to search for a pattern; and the separate treatment of 'from each according to his ___' treats production and distribution as two separate issues [. . .] The situation is not one of something getting made, and there being an open question of who is to get it. Things come into the world already attached to people having entitlements over them.[14]

Generally the people who are entitled to them are those who have incurred the costs of making them (in terms of effort, use of their property, postponement of consumption, and so on).

The implications of Nozick's entitlement theory can be illustrated with the example of George and Henry presented in Figure 1.1 in the previous chapter. Nozick would argue that the justice of the distribution identified by point Y (fourteen to George and two to Henry) is determined solely by the historical process that brought it about. If the process was just (for example George worked harder than Henry), then the distribution is just; if the process was unjust (for example it involved George violating Henry's rights, say by enslaving him), then the distribution is unjust. Nozick places no value on the actual pattern of the distribution.

2.3.2 Criticisms of Nozick

Nozick's theory has been criticized on a number of grounds of which two are particularly pertinent:

1. The theory denies people who are unable to provide for themselves (for example, the mentally ill and the handicapped) the right to be supported by society. Nozick argues that such people have no claim in justice on society. Many consider this to be an excessively narrow definition of justice.
2. It is abundantly clear that much of the property currently owned was acquired initially in an unjust fashion. For example the original title of much land in Britain goes back to the Norman Conquest, and clearly force is not a just method of acquisition. Nozick accepts

this point and concedes that a fourth principle of justice is necessary: the principle of rectification of injustice in holdings, which applies when present holdings violate his three principles of justice. However he is almost completely silent on how to apply this principle. Varian (1975: 227) comments:

> The impression that one gets from reading Nozick is that the problem of rectification is somehow minor. It seems to me that the reverse is the case: the problem of rectification is central to the issue of justice. We are interested in the question of justice precisely because we live in an unjust world; injustices have occurred in the past and are occurring now. The question is what we should do about them.

2.3.3 The Consequentialist Case for Neo-Liberalism

Nozick's entitlement theory of justice provides the most rigorous philosophical justification for the neo-liberal economic theory that was discussed in the previous chapter. Economic actors should have complete freedom in disposing of their property and their labour, subject only to respecting the equivalent rights of others.

However, most advocates of neo-liberalism, such as the Nobel Laureate Milton Friedman, whose views are analysed in the next chapter, base their support not on Nozick's rigorous philosophical analysis but on the more pragmatic ground that neo-liberalism leads to increased prosperity and higher economic growth. Like all libertarians, Friedman accepts that priority should be given to the liberty of the individual but also attributes value to other factors such as the material welfare of the individual.

2.3.4 The Moral Case for Neo-Liberalism

It is sometimes argued that, because neo-liberalism is based on the principle that each individual should single-mindedly pursue his own selfish interests, it is for this reason immoral or at least amoral. Libertarians strenuously refute this charge, particularly in relation to distribution. Milton Friedman writes: 'The ethical principle that would directly justify the distribution of income in a free market society is, "To each according to what he and the instruments he owns produces".'[15] He argues that it is ethical that the distribution of wealth among members of society should be determined by the contribution that each has made to the creation of that wealth. Libertarians reject the implicit assumption of the egalitarians that there exists a quantum of wealth ('a pie') and the principal problem is the division of this wealth (how the pie is to be divided). Libertarians argue that first the wealth has to be created, and those who contributed most to the creation of that wealth are entitled to the largest share. Certain libertarians define distributive justice *solely* in terms of contribution. Elaine Sternberg (1994), in writing about how much a firm should pay its workers, argues that 'the principle of distributive justice asserts that organisational rewards should be proportional to contributions to organisational ends'[16] and

> [R]ewarding anything other than contributions to long-term owner value [. . .] violates distributive justice [. . .] that a secretary is an unmarried mother with triplets may perhaps be a reason to sympathise with her plight [. . .] but it is no reason to grant her a pay rise: rises are earned by producing contributions to the business end, not by producing offspring.[17]

This quotation makes very clear the emphasis that libertarians give to the creation rather than the distribution of wealth. Actions and policies that interfere with the wealth creation process are wrong, not only economically inefficient but morally wrong.

There are two rather different arguments against basing the distribution of wealth on contributions:

1. People who contribute nothing to output receive nothing. The mentally ill, the chronically sick, and the very young would either starve or be forced to lead a precarious existence dependent on the benevolence of the economically productive. People who, although not completely unproductive, have lower than normal productivity (for example through lower mental or physical capabilities) would be condemned to a lower standard of living. Libertarians argue that the unproductive have no moral right to be supported by the productive and the productive are under no moral obligation to help them. Most people find this to be a profoundly unattractive philosophy, which clashes with their intuitions of morality.
2. It is difficult, perhaps impossible, to determine the contribution made by each member of society to total output. This might be possible in a primitive economy of one-man firms which occasionally exchanged goods,[18] but seems impossibly complicated in a modern economy, which is essentially a vast system of interconnected and interrelated parts. Consider the activities that contribute to a good finally arriving in the hands of a consumer: research, development, design, training, financing, production, marketing, transport, retailing, and so on. How is the contribution of each of these activities to be measured? According to the economic theory that underlies much libertarian thought, the wage to be paid to a worker in a firm should be equal to the value of the marginal product of the marginal worker, which is surely impossible to calculate in a modern firm of any size. Anderson (1999: 321–22) argues that the economy is a system of cooperative, joint production, explaining that 'by "joint production", she means

that people regard every product of the economy as jointly produced by everyone working together. From the point of view of justice, the attempt, independent of moral principles, to credit specific bits of output to specific bits of input by specific individuals represents an arbitrary cut in the causal web that in fact makes everyone's productive contribution dependent on what everyone else is doing.

I find Andersen's argument persuasive as far as it concerns people who actually work, including women who work in the home caring for children and the elderly, and who most certainly contribute to the total output of society. Andersen's concept of contribution is far removed from that of the libertarian, as the earlier quote from Sternberg makes abundantly clear. And it would seem to render even more problematic the measurement of the contribution of each member of society to total output.

2.4 MARXISM

According to Marxist philosophy, capitalism is inherently unjust. Society is divided between the proletariat (the workers) and the bourgeoisie (the capitalists). The capitalists own the means of production (factories, machines, and so on); the workers own no property apart from insignificant personal belongings. The capitalists employ the workers, paying them a wage agreed by contract. However the wage paid to workers is less than the value of what they produce. The workers are unable to extract a higher wage from the capitalists because of their weak bargaining position: they are dependent on the capitalists in that they can produce nothing without the use of the capitalists' means of production, and furthermore there exists 'a reserve army of the unemployed' of men willing to work for the going wage if the present workers hold out for a higher wage. Hence the capitalists are able to cream off 'surplus value' (in the form of profits, rents, and other returns to capital), being the difference between the wage paid to the worker and the value of what he produces (the selling price less the cost of materials and other items that do not represent returns on capital).

Karl Marx believed that capitalism was not only unjust but also inherently unstable; it contained internal contradictions that would result in it eventually being replaced by socialism. This transformation would occur when two historically inevitable developments coincided: man's productive forces had developed to the degree that the economy produced sufficient to meet all his needs, and the exploitation of the proletariat had become intolerable. Marx would have undoubtedly agreed with the conclusion of the previous chapter that, given the present level of the world's output, the most pressing problem facing mankind is not to increase that output further but to assure its just distribution.

However, given his belief that capitalism was a transient phenomenon, Marx gave no thought in his writings on how to make capitalism more just. He did sketch briefly how justice would be achieved in the forthcoming socialist utopia. He claimed that people should use their abilities to create useful goods and services which should be allocated on the basis of need, coining the seductive slogan 'from each according to his abilities, to each according to his needs'.[19]

Marx's prediction that capitalism would collapse and be replaced by socialism has not (so far) been realized. In fact, in the century and a half since Marx wrote, capitalism seems to have gone from strength to strength. World output is at an all time high, and the standard of living of the workers in the industrialized countries has increased substantially (and not declined as Marx predicted). It would seem that Marx's analysis of capitalism may have been (more or less) correct as to the economic system of mid-nineteenth century England, but not as to that of contemporary industrialized countries, whose economies have developed in ways that Marx did not foresee. These are no longer purely capitalist economies but are more accurately described as mixed economies. The state plays a far greater role in the economy than it did in Marx's day, in such areas as:

1. The state ownership of certain industries, for example the railways;
2. The regulation of other industries;
3. The management of the economy through fiscal and monetary policy with the aim of achieving stable growth and low levels of unemployment;
4. The provision of social benefits, such as pensions, through the welfare state.

It is not suggested that there are no problems with contemporary capitalism. The present (2009) financial crisis is the latest example of capitalism's tendency to suffer severe cyclical fluctuations and, in most industrialized countries, there is a hard core of the long-term unemployed who are excluded from the primary labour market. Both developments are fully consistent with Marxist philosophy. However, there is no sign of capitalism's imminent collapse. It may reasonably be assumed that industrialized countries, such as Britain and the USA, will continue to have reasonably successful mixed economies for the foreseeable future. As already mentioned, Marx himself wrote nothing that was directly relevant to the question of how to achieve justice in such economies. However contemporary Marxist philosophers have applied Karl Marx's basic ideas to the current situation; the work of one such philosopher, G. A. Cohen, is discussed in Section 3.5 of the next chapter.

2.5 UTILITARIANISM

2.5.1 The Principles of Utilitarianism

Utilitarianism is the philosophical system that argues (in the words of its founder, Jeremy Bentham) that 'the greatest happiness of the greatest number is the foundation of morals and legislation'. As this quote makes clear, utilitarianism is both a system for defining morals (including justice) and a method for guiding the actions of individuals and governments. The aim specified by Jeremy Bentham is incoherent, because it is not generally possible to achieve two aims simultaneously. Later utilitarians adopted the revised objective of achieving the single aim of the greatest happiness, that is, the sum total of the happiness of society's members,[20] The principal characteristics of utilitarian philosophy are:

1. It considers only one attribute of these individuals. According to Jeremy Bentham, this should be 'happiness'. Others have proposed alternative terms: well-being, welfare, satisfaction, and desire fulfillment. The economist's preferred term is 'utility'. All these terms refer to something that the individual desires or strives for. Utilitarianism leads to a patterned distribution of wealth, fundamentally different from that resulting from Nozick's entitlement theory.
2. What provides the individual with utility is decided by that individual; it is not dictated to him by authority. Hence, utilitarianism is essentially individualistic. What is important is the sum of the happiness of individuals, not of the community or any other group.
3. Utilitarianism is egalitarian. Each person's utility is given equal weight. Each person counts for one, but not for more than one.
4. It is forward looking. In deciding on the morality of any action, the individual or the government should consider only its likely impact on utility in the future. The past is irrelevant. Utilitarianism is a consequentialist philosophy: the rightness of an action is determined solely by the rightness of its consequences. This is another difference from the entitlement theory of Robert Nozick, although not so different from the approach of those pragmatic libertarians who emphasize the favourable consequences of neo-liberalism.

2.5.2 Utilitarianism's Assumptions

It is easier to explain the principles of utilitarianism, if one first makes the assumption that the utility experienced by an individual can be measured and compared with that of another individual. This assumption is completely unrealistic and is made only in order to facilitate the exposition. The implications of the unreality of this assumption for the validity of utilitarianism are considered later.

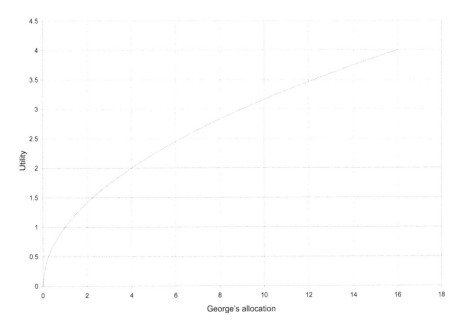

Figure 2.2 George's utility.

A further assumption is central to the utilitarian theory of distributive justice: that individuals experience diminishing marginal utility. As a person's allocation of goods increases, the increase in her total utility from each additional good is positive but declining. This is illustrated in Figure 2.2 which presents George's utility function. George's wealth (the number of widgets that he possesses) is measured on the x axis and the utility that he experiences from this wealth on the y axis. Note that George's utility is given a quantitative value, which ranges from zero to four. This follows from the assumption that utility can be measured. As George's wealth increases, his total utility increases but at a declining rate. The assumption of diminishing marginal utility is very plausible. If I give a loaf to a man without bread, there is an increase in his utility. If I give him a second loaf, there is a further increase in his utility. But this increase is likely to be less than that experienced from the first loaf. One can envisage situations in which diminishing marginal utility does not occur. If shoes were sold singly and not in pairs, the utility experienced from the second shoe could well be greater than that experienced from the first shoe. However this complication can be side-stepped by treating the relevant article as a pair of shoes and not a single shoe. With pairs of shoes, diminishing marginal utility surely occurs at some point. The utility experienced from the second pair of shoes is likely to less than that from the first pair. No reputable economist doubts that individuals in the real world experience diminishing marginal utility. Frankfurt (1987/2003) asserts that it is false. His arguments are interesting, but ultimately unconvincing. I feel that the case for diminishing marginal utility is strengthened by Frankfurt's failure to disprove it, since he is a reputable philosopher who expended considerable intellectual effort on the task.

One further assumption is necessary in order to develop the first theorems of the utilitarian theory of distributive justice: that all persons have identical utility functions. As applied to specific goods, this is clearly false; the utility experienced by a typical Frenchman in eating snails is almost certainly greater than that experienced by the typical Englishman. However, as applied to goods in general (wealth or money), it has more plausibility. Furthermore it seems a reasonable assumption to make by a statesman or a philosopher who seeks the best distribution of goods among the population, who assumes that each person is of equal moral worth and defines the 'best distribution' as that which yields the greatest sum of the individual utilities.

2.5.3 The Optimal Division of Wealth

With these assumptions, it is easy to prove that the greatest sum of utilities is achieved with an equal division of the available wealth, for if one man

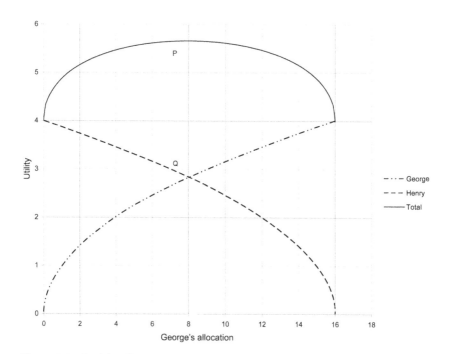

Figure 2.3 Social utility.

(A) has more wealth than another man (B), a transfer of wealth from A to B would increase B's utility by more than the decrease in A's utility. These transfers should continue until A and B have equal quantities of wealth. This point is illustrated in Figure 2.3, which shows the utility arising from the allocation of a fixed amount of wealth (sixteen units) between George and Henry. George's utility curve is copied from Figure 2.2. Henry's utility curve is drawn, taking into account the fact that, if George has x units of wealth, then Henry has (16–x) units. Hence Henry's utility function is the mirror image of George's, but, in all other respects, it is identical. In particular Henry's utility is measured in the same quantitative units as George's. This reflects the assumptions that the utilities experienced by different persons may be compared and that all people have identical utility functions. The total utility function is the sum of the individual utilities of George and Henry; it may be considered to be the utility function of society; the economists preferred term is social welfare function. It reaches its highest point (greatest social welfare) at point P, which is directly above point Q, where the utility functions of George and Henry intersect and which represents an equal division of the available goods.[21]

Figure 2.3 is the graphical demonstration of the intuition that €1000 spent on feeding starving persons generates more social benefits than if the money were spent on a second television set for an affluent person.

If the utility functions of George and Henry were not identical, then an equal division of wealth may not achieve the maximum social welfare.

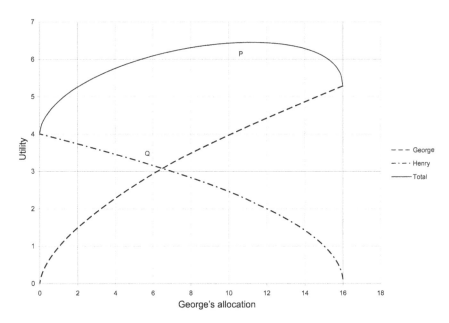

Figure 2.4 Differing utility functions.

Thus if, for a specific level of wealth, George experiences a higher utility than Henry, he is a 'more efficient utility machine'[22] than Henry and, in order to maximize total utility, he should be allocated a greater share of the available wealth. This is illustrated in Figure 2.4, which is the same as Figure 2.3 except that George's utility function rises more quickly than Henry's. The total utility function has a different shape and reaches a maximum at point P (around twelve units to George and four to Henry), which is very different from the division in Figure 2.3. This is a distribution of great inequality; not only is George allocated more units than Henry but he experiences significantly more utility (about 4.5 units compared with 2 units for Henry). George and Henry experience equal utility at point Q: 6.5 units to George and 9.5 units to Henry. Since Henry is a less efficient utility machine, he requires a greater allocation in order to reach the same level of utility as George. Utilitarians are not egalitarians and hence reject point Q. Since they maximize society's happiness, they choose point P.[23]

2.5.4 Unequal Divisions

The concept of the social welfare function may be used to tackle the problem illustrated in Figure 1.1 of Chapter 1, as to whether the distribution

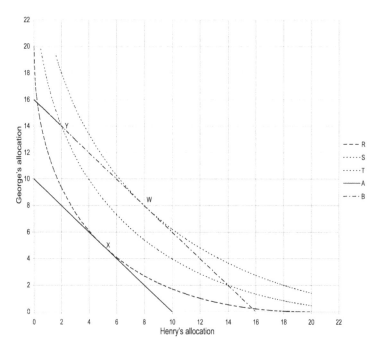

Figure 2.5   Indifference curves.

represented by point Y (fourteen to George and two to Henry) is to be preferred to point X (five to George and five to Henry). Figure 2.5 (in which the axes represent the same units as Figure 1.1) shows points X and Y, plus three indifference curves R, S, and T. These indifference curves join points of equal social welfare (equal total utility). R joins all points that have a social welfare equal to that of point X; S joins all points with a social welfare equal to point Y; and T joins all points with a social welfare equal to point W. The shape of these curves reflects the fact that, if George receives less, then Henry has to receive more in order that total social welfare should remain the same. They are based on the utility functions of George and Henry shown in Figure 2.3. Since these utility functions manifest diminishing marginal utility, the indifference curves that are derived from them are concave to the origin: as one party receives less and less, the other party has to receive ever greater amounts to ensure that the total social utility remains the same. Curve T represents a higher level of social welfare than curve R. This is obvious as curve T passes through point W which represents a higher level of welfare than point X, since at W both George and Henry enjoy higher amounts of utility than at point X. Curve S represents an intermediate level of social welfare. Using Figure 2.5, it is now possible to determine whether, according to the utilitarian theory of distributive justice, point Y is to be preferred (delivers greater distributive justice) than point X. The indifference curve that passes through point Y (curve S) represents a higher level of social welfare than the one (R) that passes through point X. Therefore the distribution represented by point Y (fourteen to George and two to Henry) is more just than that at point X (five to George and five to Henry).

2.5.5 Utilitarianism's Weak Point

Readers may be astonished at the conclusion that a distribution which manifests such extreme inequality should be considered more just. However this example is a good illustration of what the opponents of utilitarianism consider to be its greatest shortcoming: in determining the action that results in the greatest happiness, it is possible that some people (often a minority) are seriously harmed—the harm that they suffer is more than offset by the benefits enjoyed by others. This anomaly applies not only to questions of distributive justice but to moral issues in general as is illustrated by the following story told by the Jewish historian Josephus. In Jerusalem in the first century, the Jews rioted because a rumour had spread that a Roman soldier had desecrated the Temple. The riots spread and led to considerable loss of life and property. In order to stop the riots, the Roman governor selected a Roman soldier at random, announced to the Jews that he was the guilty person, and had him executed. The riots stopped at once. It may reasonably be calculated that the Roman governor's action saved the lives of hundreds of people (many of whom were innocent of any wrong-doing) at the cost of the life of a single person, who was equally innocent. It certainly can be argued that the Roman governor made the right decision according to the utilitarian calculus, notwithstanding that the governor's action was a grave violation of the soldier's rights and a breach of the categorical imperative of Immanuel Kant not to treat another person solely as a means.

The utilitarian calculus is likely to lead to persons being disadvantaged if they are significantly less numerous than those who benefit; thus if the class represented by Henry in Figure 2.5 is much smaller than that represented by George, then the harm that they suffer may not be given much weight in the calculation of social welfare. Rawls (1971/1999) criticizes utilitarianism on the grounds that it adopts a principle that is appropriate for an individual: the principle that he accept some disadvantage at some time during his life in order to achieve a greater advantage at another time. He argues that utilitarianism, in applying this principle to society as a whole, is wrong: the harm done to one individual may not be offset by the gain of another individual, commenting:

> The striking feature of the utilitarian view of justice is that it does not matter, except indirectly, how the sum of satisfaction is distributed among individuals any more than it matters, except indirectly, how one man distributes his satisfactions over time.[24]

Rawls considers that, in one important sense, utilitarianism is not individualistic because it does not take seriously the worth of the individual but only that of society as a whole.

If the utility functions of George and Henry were to manifest more rapidly declining marginal utility, then it is possible for the social welfare at point X to be greater than that at point Y. Whether point X or point Y is to be preferred is purely a question of the shape of the utility functions. However, one thing is certain: the distribution at point W is superior to both of them. In fact it represents the optimal distribution of the total wealth, being the point on the allocation line (the dotted line B which shows all possible divisions of the total wealth) that is tangential to the highest indifference curve (T).

2.5.6 Criticisms of Utilitarianism

Utilitarianism has been criticized on three principal grounds:

(a) Unrealistic premises.
(b) Implementation difficulties.
(c) Victimization of minorities.

(a) Unrealistic Premises

Many philosophers reject utilitarianism on the grounds that it is based on false premises. The utilitarian analysis presented in this section used three assumptions:

(i) That a person's utility can be measured;
(ii) That one person's utility can be compared with that of another person;
(iii) That all people have identical utility functions.

The third assumption clearly does not reflect reality. It was used in the analysis in this section to demonstrate its implications, which turned out to be important—that wealth should be divided equally between individuals. This assumption is not an essential element of utilitarianism, but when it is relaxed the analysis becomes much more complicated, as is illustrated in Figure 2.4. The first two assumptions are much more central. Some philosophers argue that it is theoretically impossible to measure a person's utility, which is a state of the person's mind that cannot be directly observed. I do not agree with them. Perhaps one day, a clever scientist will invent a 'utilitometer'[25] which, by observing a person's brain waves or other objective physical phenomena, measures the utility that he is experiencing. I accept that at present this is not possible.[26] However this does not mean that utilitarianism is of no use, either to the philosopher in developing theories of justice or to the statesman in deciding practical matters. Many subjects of philosophy are not measurable; Aristotle argued that rewards should be distributed according to the merit of the recipients, which is even less measurable than utility. The statesman who uses utilitarian analysis in policy decisions clearly has to make some rough and ready estimates of utility. However the fact that these estimates are rough and may on occasions be seriously wrong does not mean that utilitarianism has no practical value.

(b) Problems of Implementation

There is a vast literature on the practical problems of applying utilitarianism, which is well summarized in Bojer (2003: 32–35). Much attention has been given to three problems:

1. Expensive tastes: Suppose that to reach a satisfactory level of utility, Alfred needs a diet of caviar and champagne, whereas Bert, his frugal neighbour, reaches the same level of utility with a diet of bread and water. Does utilitarianism imply that Alfred should be given more of the world's scarce resources than Bert?
2. Differential needs: Charles is blind, whereas Dick is sighted. Charles needs a greater allocation of resources (a guide dog, a specially equipped flat, and so on) in order that he achieves the same level of

utility as Dick. Should Charles receive this bigger allocation? If 'yes', how can one distinguish Charles's greater need from Alfred's expensive tastes? Perhaps the source of Alfred's expensive tastes is a genetic disposition that is not essentially different from Charles's blindness. Although the answer in this example may be obvious, there are clearly borderline cases.

3. Anti-social preferences: Fred gets extreme pleasure from torturing Gus. Perhaps Fred's pleasure exceeds Gus's pain. This may well be the case where 'Fred' represents a group of people. Does utilitarianism provide a moral justification for Fred's actions? Similar considerations apply to racial and sexual discrimination.

My personal judgement is that these problems are not so severe as to render the application of utilitarianism impractical; it is generally possible to find pragmatic solutions, which, although not perfect, are acceptable to most people.

(c) Victimization of Minorities

The most cogent criticism of utilitarianism is that it can lead to one person (or a small group of persons) suffering harm so that others are provided with a higher level of utility—the case of the executed Roman soldier discussed in Section 2.5.5. Supporters of utilitarianism have made great efforts to counter this charge. Thus some argue for 'rule utilitarianism': that people should follow the rules that, if applied generally, would lead to the greatest happiness. It is argued that, in this case, there is less danger of minorities being victimized, as everyone would be aware that to do so would have negative consequences for the cohesion of society: people would lose confidence in the judicial system, if they perceived that a person could be harmed for reasons that were not related to his individual merit, and ultimately everyone would feel less secure.

In conclusion, my personal judgement is that the first two criticisms listed earlier (unrealistic premises and problems of implementation) are serious and have some substance, but are not fatal. They are not so serious that it is impossible both to develop a coherent philosophy of utilitarianism and to find ways of applying utilitarian principles in practice. The third criticism is more fundamental. In my opinion, the case of the executed Roman soldier shows that, for utilitarianism to be acceptable as a measure of justice, it needs to be tempered with principles imported from other philosophical systems. This is not to deny that utilitarianism offers profound and valuable insights into the nature of distributive justice, of which the most relevant is the argument for an equal distribution of wealth presented in Section 2.5.3.

2.6 JUSTICE AS FAIRNESS

2.6.1 An Alternative to Utilitarianism and Libertarianism

John Rawls in his book *A Theory of Justice*[27] sought to develop principles of justice that did not suffer from the defects of other theories, notably utilitarianism and libertarianism. He judged that utilitarianism was wrong for two reasons: (a) Individuals' concept of the good life varied so much that it was impossible to compare their utilities and that any attempt to do so would inevitably involve imposing the philosopher's scale of values on the individual. (b) Utilitarianism tended to lead to the situation where some persons suffered harm in order that others should benefit. He considered that this violated the Kantian categorical imperative, that no one should be treated solely as a means.

Rawls judged that libertarianism was wrong because it considered that formal equality of opportunity was a sufficient condition for the achievement of distributive justice.[28] Formal equality of opportunity is achieved when there is no legal bar to access to education, and all jobs and positions are filled on merit. Rawls believed that this was insufficient to achieve the level of equality that he considered to be right.

2.6.2 The Basic Structure

Rawls considered that society was a cooperative venture for mutual advantage; everyone gained, for the alternative was Hobbesian misery in which life was 'solitary, poor, nasty, brutish and short'[29] with, at best, everyone eking out a bare subsistence with his own unaided efforts. However the very existence of the greater wealth created by social cooperation brought with it conflicts because people were concerned as to how this wealth was to be distributed. This conflict explains the need for a set of principles of social justice, which (according to Rawls) 'provide a way of assigning rights and duties in the basic institutions of society and define the appropriate distribution of the benefits and costs of social cooperation'.[30]

Rawls's theory of justice applies to the basic structure of society. The basic structure is a difficult concept. It clearly includes the political constitution and the judicial system, and the outputs of these systems: laws and judgements. It also includes the basic economic system, such as competitive markets and private property in the means of production.[31] The basic structure also includes widely held and generally accepted beliefs, such as the rule of law, freedom of thought, and liberty of conscience. It is rather easier to define what is not part of the basic structure. Private dealings between individuals are not part of the basic structure and hence the principles of justice that apply to the basic structure do not necessarily apply to how individuals should treat each other. Also, they do not apply to relations between nations, but only to social arrangements within nations.

2.6.3 The Three Principles of Justice

Rawls set out three principles that should govern the basic structure:

1. Each person is to have an equal right to the most extensive scheme of equal basic liberties compatible with a similar scheme of liberties for others.
2. Social and economic inequalities are to be arranged so that they are attached to offices and positions open to all under conditions of fair equality of opportunity.
3. Social and economic inequalities are to be so arranged that they are to the greatest benefit of the least advantaged.[32]

The first principle refers to basic liberties. Rawls defines the basic liberties to include political liberty (the right to vote and to hold public office), freedom of speech, and liberty of conscience. He also includes as a basic liberty the right to hold personal property. The principles are listed in 'lexical' order, by which is meant that the first principle has priority over the later principles and must be achieved to the greatest extent possible, with no consideration to be given to its impact on the matters covered by the other principles (social and economic advantages). Therefore it is not permitted that equal liberties be compromised in order to achieve greater social and economic advantages. The first principle is strongly egalitarian: *each* person is to have *equal* rights to *equal* basic liberties. Nowhere in his book does Rawls present a convincing argument for this egalitarian stance; he seems to consider it be a self-evident truth.

The second and third principles refer to social and economic advantages. The fundamental idea is that these advantages should be distributed equally. However this distribution may not be Pareto optimal, in that everyone may benefit from an alternative distribution. For example, paying a skilled worker more than an unskilled worker (an inequality attached to an office and position) may result in an increase in output from which the unskilled worker also benefits. This is known as the difference principle.

2.6.4 The Difference Principle

The difference principle is that economic and social inequalities (differences in rewards, wealth, income, status, and so on) are justified if they are to the benefit of the least advantaged.

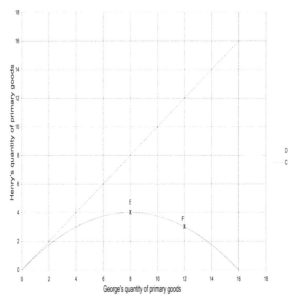

Figure 2.6   Rawls's analysis.

There is an underlying assumption that some degree of inequality in the distribution of the fruits of social cooperation may be necessary in order to create the output in the first place, because people will be unwilling to expend the required effort unless they are rewarded. This idea is presented graphically in Figure 2.6, which is adapted from a similar graph in Rawls's book.[33] The axes measure the primary goods held by George and Henry. The concept of primary goods is explained in the next section. For an appreciation of the difference principle, it is sufficient to understand that a person is 'better-off' the more primary goods he has. The origin 0 represents the position without social cooperation. The curve C indicates how the increase in output resulting from social cooperation is divided between George and Henry. It is assumed that George receives the larger share; the output curve C lies below the dotted 45° line which represents an equal division of output between George and Henry. However, Henry benefits to a certain extent. His benefit reaches a maximum at point E. Thereafter it declines; further increases in output can be achieved only at Henry's expense, perhaps because they are possible only in ways that harm Henry. Rawls's argument is that the move from 0 to E is efficient (Pareto optimal) but that moves beyond E are not. The move from 0 to E is permitted according to the third principle of justice: it leads to greater justice. The further move from E to F is not justified, as it is not to the benefit of the least advantaged. However a utilitarian would be in favour of a move from

E to F as it represents an increase in total primary goods (from twelve at point E to fifteen at point F).[34]

2.6.5 Primary Goods

Rawls rejects the notion of utility. He considers that it is unmeasurable and that any attempt to measure it would involve the measurer imposing his concept of the good life over that of the individual. Rawls, in a typical liberal fashion, insists that every individual should be free to choose and pursue his or her concept of the good life without interference, subject to the constraint of not harming other people. Instead of utility, Rawls allocates to every person a certain quantity of 'primary goods'. The 'well-offness' of George and Henry in Figure 2.6 is measured by the quantity of primary goods that they have. There are two great advantages in the concept of primary goods: in contrast to utility, primary goods can be objectively observed and measured, and the freedom of the individual to use his allocation of primary goods in whatever way he considers appropriate is not restricted.[35]

Rawls describes primary goods as follows: 'These goods normally have a use whatever a person's rational plan of life. For simplicity the chief primary goods are rights, liberties and opportunities, income and wealth.'[36] Later he defined them more fully as:

1. First, the basic liberties;
2. Second, freedom of movement and choice of occupation;
3. Third, powers and prerogatives of office and positions of responsibility;
4. Fourth, income and wealth;
5. Fifth, the social bases of self-respect.[37]

Rawls also states that the equalization of goods listed under 1. and 2. must be complete, given the lexical priority of the first principle of justice. However the difference principle allows the allocation of primary goods 3, 4, and 5 to vary from person to person. Since primary goods are made up of very different types of benefit, it is not a straightforward matter to calculate a quantity of primary goods, which is however necessary to apply Rawls's theory, both to identify the group that is least advantaged (which is measured by their allocation of primary goods) and to decide whether a proposed action is to their benefit (increases their allocation of primary goods). It is therefore necessary to construct an index of primary goods, in which the different goods are given appropriate weights. The construction of such an index is fraught with difficulties.[38] Hence, although the concept of primary goods is a neat way of resolving certain theoretical problems, it is difficult to apply in practice.

2.6.6 The Original Position and the Veil of Ignorance

Rawls justifies his three principles of social justice by appealing to a thought experiment. Free and equal human beings meet together to agree the principles of justice that would regulate the basic structure of the society in which they are to become members. Rawls terms this situation 'the original position'. Each person is self-interested: he wants the basic structure of society to be that which best satisfies his interests. However each person is completely ignorant of the position that he would hold in society: for example whether he would be rich or poor, have wealthy or impoverished parents, and so on. His ignorance would extend to his personal identity: his sex (male or female), race (black or white), genetic endowment (healthy or handicapped), and even his concept of the good life. Rawls terms this ignorance 'the veil of ignorance'. He reasons that, behind the veil of ignorance, persons would agree on principles that would be objective and take fully into account the interests of all people in society, even the most disadvantaged, because each person would appreciate that there was a chance that he would find himself in that position.

For Rawls the concepts of the original position and the veil of ignorance are techniques that enable his readers to free themselves from the prejudices and bias that stem from their present situation. He writes: 'At any time we can enter the original position, so to speak, simply by following a certain procedure, namely, by arguing for principles of justice in accordance with these restrictions.'[39]

Rawls argues that behind the veil of ignorance people would choose the first principle of justice and give it absolute priority, because they do not know their concept of the good life and it is only through securing the basic liberties that they can be assured that they will be free to lead the life of their choosing (for example there would be a chance that he would be a Muslim for whom an important element of the good life is the capability of praying five times a day). Rawls argues that each would choose the difference principle, because he appreciates that there is a possibility of his occupying the least advantaged position in society (for example a cripple born of impoverished parents) and that, in setting principles of justice for the basic structure, he is committing himself to the principles that will determine his life-time prospects.

There is a second argument for the difference principle that is based on the concept of Pareto optimality. If, from an initial position of equality, output can be increased by an alternative organization of society, so that no one is worse off and the least advantaged are better off, then it is in everyone's interests to adopt this alternative organization.

Using the intuitions gained from entering the original position, Rawls argues that many of a person's characteristics are morally irrelevant for distributive justice. The list is quite surprising:

1. The economic position of the person's parents: whether they were rich or poor;
2. A person's productive capacity in so far as it may be attributed to: (a) the better education bestowed on him by wealthy and attentive parents; (b) his superior genetic endowment (for example a high IQ); (c) his superior physique (for example in comparison with a blind person);
3. A person's sex, race, or religion.

On the basis of these considerations, Rawls argues for the equal distribution of primary goods. This initial equal distribution may be modified only if it is not Pareto optimal; that the least advantaged benefit from an alternative (unequal) distribution.

2.6.7 Justice as Fairness

Rawls argues that his principles achieve fairness in distributive justice because they are the outcome of a fair bargain. Referring to the original position, Rawls argues:

> [T]he principles of justice are the result of a fair agreement or bargain. For given the circumstances of the original position [. . .] this initial situation is fair between individuals as moral persons [. . .] and thus fundamental agreements reached in it are fair. This explains the propriety of the name 'justice as fairness': it conveys the idea that the principles of justice are agreed in an initial situation that is fair.[40]

In Rawls's philosophy, the concept of fairness is closely linked to the concept of equality. The principles of justice are fair, because they are agreed between equal persons, persons with equal bargaining power. According to the second argument for the difference principle, the unequal distribution is fair because it is derived from (and better than) an equal distribution. For Rawls, the concept of fairness is a way of respecting egalitarian intuitions whilst avoiding the defects of pure egalitarianism, notably the 'levelling-down' objection.

2.6.8 Criticisms of Rawls

In my opinion, it is impossible to prove or disprove Rawls's philosophy by logical reasoning. His arguments are rational and coherent. Many critics claim that Rawls is assuming an unreasonable degree of risk avoidance in arguing that people in the original position would choose the difference principle. Another criticism is that people who, through no fault of their own, suffer from bad luck (such as being born blind) are not given extra allocations of primary goods, unless they form the least advantaged group in society. A third criticism is that Rawls was wrong to limit his theory of justice to the basic structure: a comprehensive theory of social justice should also cover transactions and relationships between individuals. This third criticism is considered in more detail in the next chapter.

2.6.9 Evaluation of Rawls's Theory of Justice

Most commentators agree that Rawls's theory of justice as fairness represents an important contribution to the understanding of distributive justice. It represents a well-argued and ingenious theory that deals effectively with many of the defects of competing theories.

2.7 THE CONCEPT OF FAIRNESS

There is no general agreement among philosophers on the concept of fairness in distributive justice. Rawls's theory of fairness is only one of many. Varian (1975) presents an alternative theory based on envy: a person is envious of another person, if he would prefer that person's allocation of goods to his own. An allocation of goods is 'envy-free' if no one is envious of anyone else. However such a distribution can be a very unequal distribution. For example assume that Crusoe and Friday are marooned on a desert island and their total wealth consists of ten fish and ten coconuts. Crusoe has ten fish and four coconuts; Friday has only six coconuts. However assume that Friday obtains no utility from fish and hence does not prefer Crusoe's bundle of goods over his own. Hence this distribution is envy-free, but many would consider that a distribution of ten fish to Crusoe and ten coconuts to Friday would be fairer.[41] Hence a further condition is necessary to ensure that an envy-free distribution is fair. Varien (1975) argues that the concept of fairness is based on the principle of symmetry—no person is privileged over any other person. Hence the distribution where each person is given an identical allocation of goods is fair. It is also envy-free, because, as each person has the same bundle of goods, no one prefers another person's bundle. However, there are probably many other distributions that are fair and envy-free, and the equal distribution may not be efficient, in the sense of Pareto optimality. Such an efficient distribution would be achieved by people exchanging their goods at market prices, because, according to the first fundamental theorem of welfare economics, the resulting distribution would be Pareto optimal. The process of voluntary exchange at market prices does not destroy the twin characteristics of the initial distribution—that it was fair and envy-free. His procedure of modifying the initial equal distribution through market exchanges in order to reach a Pareto optimal distribution is remarkably similar to Rawls's second argument for the difference principle.

G. A. Cohen (2008) puts forward a rather different definition of fairness: '[A]n unequal distribution whose inequality cannot be vindicated by some choice or fault or desert on the part of (some of) the relevant affected agents is unfair, and therefore, pro tanto, unjust.'[42] Cohen assigns value to equality and contends that any deviation from equality must be justified; in particular differences that can be attributed to bad luck are unjust. Bad luck includes 'acts of god' such as being struck by lightning but also such factors as gender and race, as well as the nature of one's parents, which has an enormous influence on how successful a person is in life, through such factors as early upbringing, education, and the level of inherited wealth. None of these factors is morally relevant in determining distribution.

The following features are common to the concepts of fairness put forward by Rawls, Varian, and Cohen:

- An initial assumption of equality.
- Any deviations from equality must be justified.
- Deviations caused by morally irrelevant factors are not justified.

It is difficult to fault Nozick's argument that a person who has acquired something by a just process holds it justly. Hence the need to add that a distribution should be not only just but also fair.

2.8 CONCLUSION

All the theories of distributive justice discussed in this chapter have been developed by reputable and respected philosophers. They are all based on valid arguments, without logical errors. Hence the choice between them is largely a matter of judgement. Personally, in common with many other people, I find strict egalitarianism irrational. Also, I consider that Marxism is essentially a revolutionary philosophy and, in the absence of the hoped-for revolution, it has very little to offer towards the solution of the current practical problems of industrialized countries, such as Britain and the USA. Both libertarianism and utilitarianism seem to suffer from significant defects. Libertarianism seems to advocate a heartless and selfish society in which no one cares for his neighbour. Utilitarianism leads to the victimization of minorities. Rawls's theory of justice as fairness seems to offer the best compromise between egalitarianism and libertarianism. It has strong egalitarian roots, in that the principles of justice are formed by people who are fundamentally equal in the original position behind the veil of ignorance. It retains the better elements of liberalism, in that people are free to dispose of their allocation of primary goods as they will, subject to not harming other people. It is noteworthy that Rawls has been attacked, on the one hand, as being excessively egalitarian in not basing rewards on people's innate qualities, and, on the other hand, as being insufficiently egalitarian, in that his difference principle justifies inequalities on the condition that they provide some benefit to the least advantaged, even if this benefit is very small. These criticisms of Rawls from both extremes suggest to me that he got it about right!

However, I doubt whether any single theory of distributive justice can capture all the intuitions that people have on the subject. Personally I feel that utilitarianism, despite its acknowledged shortcomings, provides a very helpful insight with its theorem that a more equal distribution of wealth in a society leads to an increase in overall utility. Hence my approach to questions of justice is based on pluralism. Pluralism is not so much a specific philosophy, as the recognition that no single theory can capture the whole truth about justice. Gray et al. (1996: 27) argue that all theories have flaws but add 'this is not to deny their value or their insights; rather, all we deny is their perfection'. In the same spirit, in working out my own views on justice, I take the best element from different theories, where 'best' means that which most closely reflects my deeply held intuitions.[43]

On the basis of the analysis in these first two chapters, I set out the following conclusions, which will form the basis of the rest of this book. They contain a strong element of personal judgement, but this is inevitable in the field of distributive justice, in which there is no consensus:

- Society should aim to achieve a reasonable level of welfare for its members and should seek to improve the situation of those whose welfare falls below this level.
- Distribution is important because of its impact on the welfare of society's members.
- The interplay of market forces will not necessarily lead to a just and fair distribution of output.
- Therefore the achievement of distributive justice is not automatic; it requires action by responsible parties—the state, firms, and individuals.
- Since I am concerned at the level of welfare experienced by the members of society, I reject theories of distributive justice that neglect the pattern of distribution, notably libertarianism.
- I give more weight to welfare than to equality; therefore I reject strict egalitarianism.
- I value equality and do not give absolute priority to liberty over equality; in principle liberty may be constrained in the interests of equality, notably if this is necessary to improve the welfare of the most disadvantaged. However I follow Rawls in giving absolute priority to basic political liberties.
- I believe that, in general, more equality leads to more welfare; a society with a higher level of equality will manifest a higher level of welfare.

I believe that the analysis so far provides a solid basis for my claim that society's aim should be to achieve a just and fair distribution of wealth and output among its members. I now turn to the implications of this objective for the firm.

3 The Firm's Responsibility for Distributive Justice

The conclusion of the previous chapter was that, in the present circumstances, the overriding aim of society should be the achievement of distributive justice. Distributive justice has been defined as justice in the distribution of the costs and benefits of economic activity among the members of society. The subject of the present chapter is the role that the firm[1] plays in the achievement of distributive justice. As a first step, the impact of the firm's activities on distributive justice is analysed.

3.1 THE IMPACT OF THE FIRM ON JUSTICE

3.1.1 The Production Chain

The modern firm is a part of an extraordinarily complex economic system. The complexity of this system may be demonstrated by considering how many people are involved in supplying someone with a simple good, such as a loaf of bread: the shop assistant who sells the loaf to the customer, the baker who bakes the bread, the miller who supplies the baker with flour, the farmer who supplies the miller with wheat, the merchant who supplies the farmer with fertilizer, and so on. These people form a chain: the production chain. This list does not include the people who are only indirectly involved in the production chain, for example the petrol station attendant who supplies the farmer with fuel for his tractor, the workers in the oil company from which the petrol station acquires the fuel, including those engaged in refining, transportation, and exploration.

The modern economic system is a network of interrelated and interdependent parts. Assume the customer pays €2 for her loaf of bread. Over time, that sum will be divided among all the people in the production chain. Some part will go to the shop assistant and some part to the shop owner, and so on to all the people in the chain. It is the source of these people's income. It may be argued that the shop assistant is paid a wage, which is determined independently of sales. However the ultimate source of the shop assistant's wage is the revenue from the sales of bread to the final consumer. That reasoning applies equally to the farmer's profit and even to the salary of the oil company's geologist searching for new oil fields. Of course, given the complexity and magnitude of the economic system, the income of people located in the more remote parts of the production chain (such as the oil company's geologist) will be derived from the purchases of many millions of consumers of a myriad of consumer products.

In a capitalist economy, some part of the customer's €2 will go to the suppliers of capital, who play a vital role in the economy's functioning by enabling firms to bridge the gap between payments (for capital equipment, materials, and wages) and the receipts from sales. The payments to capital providers, in the form of rent, interest, and dividends, may initially be paid to financial institutions, such as banks, but these bodies are essentially intermediaries between the firms (which need capital) and those able to supply capital. This capital comes, in the end, from individuals, perhaps after transiting other financial intermediaries, such as pension funds.

Ultimately, the €2 paid by the customer for the loaf will end up in the pockets of people in the production chain.[2] The division of this €2 between these people is one aspect of distributive justice.

The consumer is clearly part of the chain. If, in the example, the customer were to pay €3 and not €2 for the loaf, then clearly the balance of justice between the consumer and the people in the production chain would be altered.

All the persons in the chain influence the level of the income of other people in the chain, and hence the justice that they experience. Consider a firm in the middle of the production chain, say the miller who buys wheat from farmers and sells flour to bakeries. The amount that he charges for the flour influences the income of persons higher up the chain, those who are 'downstream' of the firm: the people in bakeries and shops, plus the final consumers. The higher the price that the miller charges, the less there is available for these people. The firm's payments influence the distributive justice experienced by people lower down the chain: the firm's employees and people 'upstream' of the firm, such as farmers. These people's income is influenced by the price or wage that the miller pays. The miller's own welfare is strongly affected by his profit (the difference between his receipts and his outlays), and the level of his profit is certainly a matter of distributive justice.

So far the analysis has been in terms of the distribution of monetary amounts among people in the production chain: how much of the customer's €2 goes to the shop assistant and so on. However distributive justice is not solely a question of money income, which is an inadequate measure of a person's welfare. Other factors that contribute to welfare include:

- Leisure: An individual may place great value on leisure; for example, she may prefer to work thirty hours a week for a wage of €200 to working forty hours a week for €250. The welfare that she experiences from thirty hours of work (€200 plus the utility of an extra ten hours of leisure) is greater than that from forty hours of work.

- Working conditions: The conditions in which a person works have a strong influence on her welfare—in a comfortable office rather than in a cold and noisy factory. The shop assistant who starts work at 8.30 a.m. has a more comfortable life than the baker who has to start at 4 a.m.
- Work organization: The way in which a person's work is organized affects her welfare. A person whose working day consists of eight hours of doing nothing more than repeating a simple task on a production line may be less happy than someone with a job that enables her to more fully exercise her talents on a variety of tasks.
- Security: A person may place great value on security of employment. She prefers a permanent position to a temporary position at a higher wage.
- Health: A person's health is clearly an important component of her welfare, and often a worker's health is affected by her job. In certain dangerous occupations such as coal mining, the workers are subject to a great risk of harm from disease and accidents.

It is of course very difficult to express in quantitative terms the impact of the firm's activities on the welfare of other people in the production chain, and certainly the impact on many people is so slight as to be imperceptible. However there is no doubt that the firm's activities do influence the welfare of all people in the production chain and therefore have an impact on distributive justice.

3.1.2 People Outside the Production Chain

The impact of the firm's activities is not limited to people in the production chain. How the firm affects people outside the production chain will be considered under four headings:

- The environment
- The future
- Competitors
- The state

(a) *The Environment*

The firm's activities often have an impact on the environment. People living close to the firm's premises may suffer from the noise and the noxious gases resulting from the firm's operations. Air pollution caused by the firm may ultimately cause harm to all the world's inhabitants through its impact of global warming. The same is true of water pollution. Effluents may poison rivers, causing great harm to their natural life. Both air pollution and water pollution are aspects of the negative externalities mentioned in Chapter 1. They represent the firm's misuse of the 'free goods' of air and water. The firm may damage the environment in more direct ways. The farmer who sprays his crops with pesticide kills weeds and perhaps other more attractive forms of natural life such as butterflies. That raises the interesting philosophical question as to whether non-human life (such as butterflies) has intrinsic value and therefore should be protected for its own sake. Certain philosophers, such as Peter Singer,[3] argue that it does; others disagree and argue that only human life has value. Fortunately there is an easy practical way out of this disagreement. Provided that some people value butterflies and other features of the natural world, then these people suffer a loss in utility when the environment is harmed. Hence the environment should be preserved for the sake of people.

(b)   The Future

The firm's activities have an impact on the welfare of people in the future. This is clearly the case when the firm's operations cause the emission of greenhouse gases which contribute to global warming. Where a firm through its activities (perhaps in conjunction with other firms) causes the extinction of an entire species of animal or plant, then it is not just people presently living who suffer a loss, but all future generations. This is also the case when the firm uses up a non-renewable resource such as oil. The present generation benefits from the use of this resource but at the expense of future generations. Even if the present use of a non-renewable resource may have no immediate impact on the environment, it certainly has an impact on the welfare of future generations.

(c)   Competitors

The firm's competitors clearly are affected by the firm's activities and may be severely harmed by the firm's success. In the extreme case, the competitor may be forced out of business, causing hardship to its employees who lose their jobs and to its suppliers who lose their sales. This harm to competitors is a fact. Whether it is a factor which the firm or society as a whole should acknowledge and perhaps seek to alleviate is a difficult question that is considered later.

(d)   The State

The state is an important source of welfare for its citizens. It provides them with education and health services. It provides them with security, protecting them from attacks by foreign powers and from the aggression of their fellow citizens. It provides them with public goods, such as roads. It administers the judicial system, which is vital for the functioning of a capitalist economy. The firm benefits enormously from these activities of the state. However it also contributes, principally through the taxes that it pays. Through its taxes, the firm is contributing to the welfare of everyone in society. The determination of the size of this contribution (that is, the proper level of taxation) is a major theme of distributive justice.

3.2 IS THE FIRM RESPONSIBLE FOR DISTRIBUTIVE JUSTICE?

It is clear that the firm's activities have an impact on the welfare of many people both within and outside the production chain. With some people, for example the firm's workers, the impact may be considerable; with others the impact may be so slight as to be imperceptible. However, there is no dispute that the firm does influence the degree of justice experienced by many people. To cite the definition of distributive justice, the firm does have an effect on the distribution of the costs and benefits of its economic activity. Most of the impact is on people with whom the firm has direct dealings, such as its employees, its customers, and its suppliers; but, as pointed out in the discussion of pollution, it can have an impact on the welfare of people in distant countries. To what extent does the firm carry a moral responsibility for this impact? This is a highly controversial question, to which different thinkers have given very different answers. In the following sections, four different theories concerning the firm's responsibility for distributive justice are described and criticized.

3.3 THE LIBERTARIAN STANDPOINT

The main tenets of libertarian philosophy were analyzed in Section 2.3 of the previous chapter. The libertarian's view on the question of the firm's responsibility for distributive justice is set out rather brutally in a famous passage by the Nobel Laureate, Milton Friedman, who wrote:

> [T]here is one and only one social responsibility of business—to use its resources and engage in activities designed to increase its profits so long as it stays within the rules of the game, which is to say, engages in open and free competition, without deception or fraud.[4]

Friedman used two arguments to justify his position:

- Consequences: If businessmen maximize the profits of their firms without regard to the impact on justice, society will benefit more than if they attempt to achieve justice.

- Agency: The responsibility for achieving justice lies with the owners of firms. Where the managers are not the owners (which is the common position with larger firms), the managers are abusing the powers given to them by the owners when they do anything other than maximize the (owners') profits.

It is easy to question the first argument. It is based on the first fundamental theorem of welfare economics that, if all firms maximized their profits, the economy would reach a competitive equilibrium which would be Pareto optimal. There are two decisive counter arguments. Firstly, no economy in the real world fulfills the necessary conditions of the first fundamental theorem, which are: perfect competition (all firms are price takers; none is able to set the price for its products or influence the price of its inputs), perfect knowledge, no externalities (such as pollution), and no change in technology. Secondly, the theorem essentially ignores distribution. It simply states that a Pareto optimum will be achieved. However, as already pointed out in Chapter 1, there are infinitely many Pareto optima and some would be considered by most people to be unjust.

However the second argument is more difficult to refute. It is a fact that very many firms and almost all large firms in modern capitalist countries are corporations, such as limited companies. Under the law of these countries, the owners of the corporation are the shareholders. In accordance with the law, the shareholders appoint professional managers to run the corporation on their behalf. Generally these managers own only an insignificant proportion of the corporation's share capital. Hence there is almost complete separation of management from ownership. In such a situation, Friedman's argument runs as follows:

- It is the owners' responsibility to decide whether the firm should seek distributive justice.
- Typically the preference of the owners (shareholders) is that the firm should maximize profits.
- If, contrary to the owners' preferences, a manager seeks to achieve distributive justice at the expense of profits, the manager's behaviour is morally wrong: he is betraying the trust given to him by the owners. An individual should honour the commitments that he has voluntarily undertaken. When the manager has agreed with the owner to use the resources with which he has been entrusted, only in the ways specified by the owner, it is morally wrong for the manager to use them in any other way. Such an action would violate Kant's categorical imperative that one should not treat another person solely as a means. The manager is treating the owner solely as a means of achieving his own ends.[5]

Friedman's premises have been questioned, notably:

- That shareholders are interested solely in maximizing profits and are unconcerned about the achievement of distributive justice, which seems to be contradicted by the growth of ethical unit trusts.
- That an owner has an almost unrestricted right to use his property as he wills, which is contrary to recent developments in the law of property, which place limits on the owner's rights (see Honoré 1961).
- That the sole ethical obligation of a manager is to follow the instructions of the owner.

To be fair to Friedman, he recognizes these factors. He states categorically that the manager is justified in pursuing a charitable objective when so instructed by the owner and that the manager should stay within 'the rules of the game', which presumably means obeying the law and respecting generally accepted moral conventions. However, he is very vague as to the 'rules of the game' and he clearly thinks that most shareholders are interested only in financial gain. Like most libertarians he is suspicious of government intervention in business, which he considers should be kept to a minimum. The next section considers the ideas of a philosopher for whom the role of the government and, in particular of law, is a vital element of his theory of justice.

3.4 RAWLS'S PHILOSOPHY

John Rawls's theory of justice has already been presented in Section 2.6 of the previous chapter. Central to Rawls's theory is the basic structure. His concept of the basic structure is rather obscure but it certainly includes the law and other rules set by the government (see Section 2.6.2). According to Rawls, a society is just, if its basic structure is just. In these circumstances, the principal obligation of the individual is to support the basic structure, which is the most effective way of achieving justice in society; the individual should not substitute his judgement of what is just for that of a just society. The individual's primary duty is to obey the law. Rawls made his position very clear in the following passage:

> We start with the basic structure and try to see how the structure itself should make the adjustments necessary to preserve background justice. What we look for, in effect, is an institutional division of labour between the basic structure and the rules applying directly to individuals and associations[6] and to be followed by them in particular transactions. If this division of labour can be established, individuals and associations are then left free to advance their ends effectively within the framework of the basic structure, secure in the knowledge that elsewhere in the social system the necessary corrections to correct background justice are being made.[7]

The corrections that Rawls had in mind are taxes and subsidies; for example, inheritance taxes to prevent children benefitting from the efforts of their parents, for which there is no moral justification; income taxes to provide revenue to pay subsidies to the most disadvantaged—those with the lowest incomes who, according to the difference principle, should be helped. Rawls did not consider that it was practicable to tackle the problems of inequality through rules that governed the transactions of individuals. For example, he felt that the law of contract should be limited to such matters as the prohibition of fraud and duress. He argued that the alleviation of the lot of the most disadvantaged should be left to the state, writing, '[T]he difference principle applies to the announced system of public laws and statutes and not to particular transactions or distributions, nor to the decisions of individuals and associations.'[8] Rawls's reasons for not wanting to impose an obligation on the individual or the firm to strive for distributive justice are firstly that it was impractical, secondly that it would lead to inefficiency, and thirdly that individuals should be free to pursue their own chosen ends without excessive constraints.

Rawls's advocacy of a division of labour between the state and the individual is shared by many economists. The firm should be left free to maximize output. If the resulting distribution of the output is not just, the most effective way of rectifying the position is through the state's tax and subsidy policies. Any action by the state that interferes with the production processes of firms leads to a misallocation of resources and a fall in output. As there will be less to distribute, everyone (and especially the poor) will be worse off. Rawls was well aware of this danger and developed the difference principle as a way of achieving the two desirable objectives: a high level of output and the improvement of the lot of the poorest.

It is striking that Friedman, considered by many on the left as a right-wing libertarian, and Rawls, considered by many on the right as a left-wing liberal, should be in agreement on the important matter that the firm's principal moral duty in relation to society is to obey the law. No doubt Rawls and Friedman would have very different opinions on the nature of the laws that the state should enact: Rawls would be in favour of a law that required firms to pay a minimum wage to its workers. Friedman would be against a minimum wage law as causing a misallocation of resources. However, he acknowledges that firms should obey the law and does not advocate civil disobedience. Hence both Friedman and Rawls limit the firm's responsibility for distributive justice to obeying the law. However, as demonstrated in the next two sections, there are many who advocate a different approach.

3.5 COHEN'S CRITICISM OF RAWLS

Rawls's position that distributive justice should be limited to the basic structure has been criticized by several philosophers, most notably by G.

A. Cohen, who argues that individuals should also seek distributive justice in their dealings with other people. He argues that, for a society to be just (in practice and not solely in theory), it is insufficient that citizens obey the law; their actions should also governed by an ethos of justice.[9] Individuals should follow the difference principle in their dealings with other individuals. Rawls acknowledges that, for economic activity to be just, it should lead to an improvement in the position of the least advantaged. Cohen argues that this precept applies not only to the basic structure but also to the dealings of individuals, who should actively seek to improve the lot of the least advantaged. Cohen justifies his position with three arguments:

 (i) It is logical that the individual, who, according to Rawls, accepts that the difference principle should be a guiding principle for the state, should also base his private behaviour on the same principle. A person who believes in justice should practise justice in his personal dealings.

 (ii) Non-state institutions, such as the family, have a profound influence on the justice experienced by those involved with them. It is impracticable for the state, through its laws, to regulate the activities of these institutions in such detail that they achieve justice. This would require an unrealistically high degree of knowledge on the part of the state and would involve that the state intervene in the workings of these institutions to a degree that is incompatible with liberty. The persons involved in these institutions have a responsibility to complement the state's actions relating to justice.

 (iii) It is abundantly clear that the basic structure of many countries is not just. This is true even of advanced capitalist countries, such as Britain and the USA. Although there may be disagreement over the level of injustice, no one can deny that the basic structure of these countries is not completely just. When the basic structure is not just, the individual should do his best to bring about justice; there is no other way to bring about justice, except through the actions of individuals.

Cohen does not explicitly deal with the activities of firms in this book. His main concern is to analyze how the individual should behave. However his remarks about non-state institutions (see (ii) above) clearly apply to the firms. Cohen's thesis about the responsibility of the individual for justice applies to the individuals that make up the firm. Firms are composed of individuals; they are not impersonal machines. Hence Cohen provides a coherent and persuasive argument for why the firm has a responsibility to seek justice.

3.6 THE SOCIAL CONTRACT THEORY OF THE FIRM

An alternative argument for the moral responsibility of the firm to seek distributive justice is provided by the social contract theory of the firm.

This theory is explicitly derived from the social contract theory of the state that was developed in the seventeenth and eighteenth centuries by Thomas Hobbes and Jean-Jacques Rousseau. These political philosophers asked what life would be like in the absence of the state (in the state of nature) and envisaged the conditions that the state would have to meet for individuals to agree to create the state. The state is thus founded on a contract between rational individuals. It is important to appreciate that neither philosopher believed that there was an historical contract, that at some time in the past people came together to agree to form a state. The theory is based on a thought experiment, which provides insights on the conditions the state must fulfill in order for it to be morally legitimate (that citizens are morally obliged to obey the state's laws). Hobbes and Rousseau came to different conclusions. For Hobbes the state is legitimate if it protects its citizens from aggression; for Rousseau the state is legitimate if its laws reflect the general will.

The social contract theory of the firm follows the same sequence of reasoning: in the beginning there are no firms (each man produced the goods that he needed without the cooperation of other men); then the members of society came to an agreement to allow firms to be formed; the ethical obligations of firms are derived from the terms of this agreement. The social contract theory posits an implicit contract between the members of society and firms in which society grants firms the right to exist and carry on their business, subject to certain restrictions and in return for providing society with certain benefits.[10] The right to exist covers such points as limited liability for corporations and the right to hire other members of society as employees (a practice which did not exist in the state of nature). In return, society may reasonably demand that 'the benefits from authorizing the existence of productive organizations outweigh the detriments of doing so'. Firms should be required 'to enhance the welfare of society [. . .] in a way that relies on exploiting corporations' special advantages and minimizing disadvantages'.[11] Hasnas (1998) analyses the advantages of firms to society from the viewpoint of people as producers and as consumers. As producers (employees) they benefit from both an increased income and a more stable income. As consumers they benefit from a greater and more stable supply of more varied goods (the result of increased specialization). The disadvantages are that people, as employees, may suffer alienation and dehumanized working conditions, and, as consumers, may be harmed by the pollution of the environment and the depletion of natural resources. According to Hasnas, the people who are most affected by the existence and operations of firms are the firms' employees and customers. However, certain aspects of the firm's operations may affect society as a whole; for example, there is the possibility that the people's liberty may be endangered if firms grow too big and too powerful.

The social contract theory provides a reasoned argument for the following precepts:

- The firm should act to enhance the welfare of its customers, for example by supplying them with goods that provide the utility that they demand.
- The firm should act to enhance the welfare of its employees, for example by providing them with a steady adequate income and with humane working conditions.
- In respect of other stakeholders,[12] the firm should act so as to ensure that that the welfare of society as a whole is not harmed, for example by not polluting the environment.

It is important to understand that these obligations are imposed on the firm not through the laws of the state; they are moral obligations, which have their source in the social contract.

The social contract theory supplies the moral basis for the rights and duties of firms. Society demands that firms justify their existence and activities. These ideas were well expressed by the following authors:[13]

> Any social institution—and business is no exception—operates in society via a social contract, expressed or implied, whereby its survival and growth are based on: 1) The delivery of some socially desirable ends to society in general and 2) The distribution of economic, social or political benefits to groups from which it derives its power [. . .] An institution must constantly meet the twin tests of legitimacy and relevance by demonstrating that society requires its services and that the groups benefitting from its rewards have society's approval. (Shocker and Sethi, 1973)
>
> Every large corporation should be thought of as a social enterprise; that is an entity whose existence and decisions can be justified in so far as they serve public or social purposes. (Dahl, 1972)

The social contract theory has been criticized on two grounds:

- There is no actual contract. However, this is a misunderstanding of the nature of the thought experiment used in developing the theory. The social contract theory specifies the moral obligations of firms: what society may reasonably demand of them. It does not specify what firms are contractually obliged to do.
- Firms do not need the permission of society to exist and carry on their business. This criticism seems unfounded in the case of corporations, such as limited companies. In Britain, the approval of a government department (the Registrar of Companies) is necessary for the formation of a company, and the law (the Companies Act) specifies the company's rights and powers.[14] The law grants the company very valuable privileges of which the most important are limited liability and legal personality. In return for these privileges, the law places

certain obligations on the company, for example the requirement to publish accounts. In the USA, the Supreme Court has declared, 'The corporation is a creature of the state. It is presumed to be incorporated for the benefit of the public.'[15] In both countries, it would seem that, at least with respect to corporations, the law is based on the concept of benefits in return for obligations, which is the fundamental concept of social contract theory. The argument against this theory may have some force in the case of unincorporated businesses such as partnerships.[16] However, since all except the smallest businesses are corporations, this point is of no practical significance.

The social contract theory provides a persuasive basis for the proposition that the firm is under a moral obligation to achieve distributive justice.

3.7 TWO QUESTIONS

The last two sections have presented coherent and convincing arguments for the firm having a responsibility to seek distributive justice. The firm's responsibility is not limited to obeying the law and fulfilling its contracts, as claimed by Friedman and Rawls. It has a further responsibility to seek distributive justice in its actions. However, for this to be practicable, answers must be found to two fundamental questions:

(i) Who, within the firm is responsible for the achievement of distributive justice? As already argued in Section 3.5, firms are composed of individuals; all individuals have some personal responsibility for achieving justice, but which individuals have the principal responsibility?

(ii) In the case of the typical firm, the number of people whose welfare is affected by the firm's activities is enormous. The firm can hardly be expected to give equal consideration to the welfare of all these people. How is it to decide which group deserves the most consideration and how is it to decide on priorities when the interests of one group conflict with those of another?

I believe that answers to these questions are provided by the stakeholder theory of the firm.

3.8 THE STAKEHOLDER THEORY OF THE FIRM

The stakeholder theory of the firm is based on the concept of a stakeholder in a firm, which, in principle, is straightforward: a stakeholder is anyone who has a stake in the firm's success—who prospers when the firm does well and who suffers when the firm does badly. In practice, it appears that it is difficult to convert this concept into a precise definition, with various authors offering slightly different definitions. In this section, I set out my own version of stakeholder theory which I consider to be the most appropriate for analysing the firm's responsibility for distributive justice and to be consistent with the other theories presented in the literature.[17]

Stakeholder theory is based on a concept of the firm that is fundamentally different from that of neo-liberalism. Neo-liberal economic theory considers the firm to be an independent entity which buys factors of production (labour, materials, and so on) on the market, and transforms them into other goods and services, which it sells on the market. If the value of its output is higher than the cost of its inputs, the firm makes a profit. At the same time, the firm has converted resources with a certain market value into goods and services that have a higher market value—it has increased the total value of society's goods and services. For this reason, profit is a measure of the benefits that the firm has rendered society.

The stakeholder theory of the firm is based on a fundamentally different concept. It considers that the various parties with which the firm has dealings are not independent of the firm but are more or less closely associated with it. The firm is a nexus of relations between these parties who are given the generic title of stakeholders. For example, Evan and Freeman (1993), in presenting stakeholder theory, refer to the firm as 'a forum of stakeholder interaction' and 'a vehicle for coordinating stakeholder interests'. Clarkson (1995) defines the firm as 'a system of primary stakeholder groups'.

The stakeholders of a firm may be divided into two groups:

- Primary stakeholders: a narrowly defined group comprising all those who are vital to the firm's survival and/or success.
- Secondary shareholders: a wider group that comprises all those (other than primary stakeholders) who are affected by the firm's existence and activities.

3.8.1 PRIMARY STAKEHOLDERS

Clarkson (1995) offers the following definition: 'A primary stakeholder group is one without whose continuing participation the corporation[18] cannot survive.' The word 'group' is important. A firm can survive if it loses an individual customer, but not if it loses the group of customers. The following are the principal primary stakeholders.

i. Suppliers of capital (that is, shareholders and loan creditors), who provide the funds to finance the firm's assets.
ii. Suppliers of labour services (that is, employees), who operate the machines and other assets acquired with the capital.

   iii. Suppliers of raw materials and other inputs which go into the goods and services that are the firm's output.
   iv. Customers who buy the firm's output.
   v. The state, which in many ways may be considered a partner in the firm, taking a percentage of the profits in the form of taxation. The state is vital for the firm's operations as it both protects the firm from aggression and provides the legal framework which ensures that contracts are honoured.
   vi. The managers of the firm.

The relationship between the firm and these stakeholders is essentially one of mutually beneficial exchange. Suppliers of capital provide funds and receive dividends and interest; employees offer their skills, effort, and time, and receive wages; suppliers provide raw materials in exchange for cash; customers receive goods and services in exchange for cash. In many cases the exchange relationship is the subject of an explicit contract that is legally enforceable. But, even when there is no explicit contract, there will generally be a quasi contract that confers moral rights and duties. Furthermore a narrowly framed explicit contract may be supplemented by a wider quasi contract. For example an employee who has worked for the firm for thirty years and who has become dependent on his continued employment for his livelihood, may have a formal contract that permits the firm to dismiss him with one week's notice. However the continued relationship has generated a quasi contract; it would be unjust for the firm to attempt to enforce its legal right of dismissal, as it would also be for the employee to exercise his right to leave (where the firm has become dependent on his services). Quasi contracts are not only a moral concept. The courts of law in many countries have become increasingly prepared to recognize the legally binding character of implied contracts that have arisen from the behaviour of the contracting parties. Both the law and philosophy emphatically reject the economist's maxim 'bygones are forever bygones'. The thirty years' past service of the long-term employee may not be dismissed as irrelevant.

   The shareholders are clearly important stakeholders. In most countries, the law grants shareholders a privileged position. Under the law they appoint the managers who are required to manage the firm in their interests. According to neo-liberal economic theory, the firm should be managed so as to maximize profits, which, according to the law, belong to the shareholders. The stakeholder theory of the firm treats shareholders in a fundamentally different way. The interests of *all* stakeholders should be taken into consideration and shareholders should not be treated differently from other stakeholders. The principle is put very clearly by Donaldson and Preston (1995: 68) as follows: 'Stakeholder analysts argue that all persons and groups with legitimate interests participating in an enterprise do so to obtain benefits and that there is no prima facie priority of one set of interests and benefits over another.' There is no suggestion that shareholders have no rights or that all stakeholders should be treated equally, other than they all be treated with equal consideration.

Another important stakeholder group is the firm's management. The firm's managers are clearly primary stakeholders. Normally a manager has a contract with the firm by which he is obliged to provide labour services in return for a salary. However a manager is a very special type of stakeholder. In the words of Evan and Freeman (1993: 81), '[M]anagement has a duty of safeguarding the welfare of that abstract entity that is the corporation . . . [It] must look after the health of the corporation and this involves balancing the multiple claims of conflicting stakeholders.'

As pointed out in the preceding quotation, an important task of the firm's management is to balance the conflicting claims of stakeholders: employees want higher wages; shareholders want higher dividends; customers want a higher quality product or a cheaper product or preferably both. It is the management's task to keep the relationships among stakeholders in balance. When these relationships become unbalanced, the survival of the firm is in jeopardy. As Clarkson (1995, 106) points out: 'If any primary stakeholder group, such as customers or suppliers, becomes dissatisfied and withdraws from the corporate system, in whole or in part, the corporation will be seriously damaged or unable to continue as a going concern.' Stakeholders have conflicting interests but also common interests. They all want the firm to survive and prosper. The most successful and long-lasting firms are those where the management has ensured that the interests of one group of stakeholders have not prevailed over the interests of the firm as a whole.

When the other stakeholders have dealings with the firm, they invariably deal through the management. Essentially, from their point of view, the management *is* the firm. In the remainder of this book whenever references are made to decisions or actions of the firm, they should be interpreted as decisions or actions of the firm's managers. The managers are the personification of the firm. This approach provides a neat solution to certain problems in stakeholder theory:

(i) If the firm is defined as a nexus of relationships between stakeholders, the idea of a stakeholder (such as a supplier) having a relationship or a contract with the firm is problematic, since it suggests that a person can have a relationship with himself. But the idea of a contract between the supplier and the management is straightforward.

(ii) It makes clear that decisions are made by people and not by an anonymous entity, the corporation. The statement 'Mr. Smith, the CEO of the XYZ Corporation, has declared 1000 workers redundant' reflects more accurately and truthfully reality than the anodyne statement 'The XYZ Corporation has downsized its workforce by 10%'.

(iii) It makes operational the principle that the firm has a responsibility to achieve distributional justice. The firm's management is clearly the element in the firm that is responsible for achieving distributive justice.

The term 'management' is vague and impersonal. The people who are responsible are individual managers, each with a responsibility for justice in a particular area; for example, a foreman is responsible, within the degree of discretion given to him by higher management, for justice among the group of workers under his supervision. The firm's top management is responsible for the overall direction of the firm. The top management may consist of a single person, in which case there is no ambiguity over personal responsibility. Where it consists of an organ, such as a board of directors, each individual member of that organ carries personal responsibility.

The idea that the management *is* the firm is a moral principle and not a legal principle. In law, a corporation is a separate entity from its managers. The firm's assets are the legal property of the corporation and not of its managers. But how these assets are used is the moral responsibility of the managers who control them.

3.8.2 Secondary Stakeholders

This wider group of stakeholders covers all those whose welfare is affected by the firm's activities and who have a legitimate claim on the firm. They include all those who may experience actual benefit or harm (or may anticipate such benefit or harm) from the firm's actions or inactions.[19] Examples of such stakeholders are:

i. The local community in which the firm is located, whose welfare is often strongly affected by the firm's activities.
ii. Persons who are affected by pollution emanating from the firm. In the case of noise pollution this will include the local community, but in the case of air and water pollution it can include people on the other side of the globe.
iii. Persons in the production chain, who have only indirect dealings with the firm. For example, a baker buys flour from a miller, and, since there is a direct relationship, the miller may be considered to be a primary stakeholder of the baker. The miller buys wheat from the farmer. The farmer may be considered to be a primary stakeholder of the miller, but only a secondary stakeholder of the baker. The farmer's welfare can certainly be affected by the baker's actions. For example, if the baker (who is in a monopsony position) forces the miller to accept a low price, this may well have an impact on the price received by the farmer and hence on his welfare. For this reason the farmer is a secondary stakeholder of the baker; another secondary stakeholder is the customer.

Often the aforementioned groups overlap. An inhabitant of the local community may suffer from the firm's pollution and work for a firm in the production chain.

There are a number of problems with the concept of secondary stakeholder. The term 'stakeholder' is not ideal; some secondary stakeholders have no stake in the firm, and the term can lead to the secondary stakeholders being equated with the primary stakeholders, who clearly have a stake in the firm.[20] One problem is that, according to the definition, it would seem that competitors are stakeholders, since their welfare is clearly affected by the firm's activities, for example in drawing away their customers. John Stuart Mill considered this question and concluded that the claim of a competitor that he should not be harmed is not legitimate, commenting, '[S]ociety admits no right, either legal or moral, in the disappointed competitors, to immunity from this kind of suffering.'[21] The definition of secondary stakeholder given earlier includes the words 'and has a legitimate claim against the firm'. This phrase was included principally to exclude competitors from the group of stakeholders.

Sternberg (1997), in a spirited attack on stakeholder theory, claims that among the groups that are considered to be stakeholders are terrorists, vegetation, and generations unborn. The case for including terrorists was based on defining as stakeholders all those who can affect the firm, as proposed by certain authors.[22] The definition given previously does not include that group—it includes only those who are affected by the firm (the passive verb). However, a terrorist might be considered to be a secondary stakeholder, if the reason why he attacked the firm was that he was adversely affected by the firm's activities, for example he blew up a pipeline in protest at the pollution caused by an oil company. Perhaps he had a legitimate claim that he pursued by illegitimate means. I believe that it is appropriate to exclude from the concept of stakeholder, groups, such as terrorists, which can affect the firm but are not affected by the firm, when the objective is the assessment of distributive justice. For other purposes (for example in deciding how the firm should be managed to assure its survival), it may well be appropriate to include such groups in the definition of stakeholder.

Sternberg's second category, vegetation, is clearly not a stakeholder. Only people can be stakeholders. However, if people value the natural world, then the claims of these people to protect vegetation are not illegitimate solely because they relate to non-humans.

Sternberg's third category (generations unborn) presents a problem for stakeholder theory. It seems to maintain that persons who do not yet exist are current stakeholders of the firm. A principal source of the problem is the term 'stakeholder', which, as already noted, is not ideal. When analysing the firm's responsibility for distributive justice, it is necessary first to identify the people who are affected by the firm's activities, before deciding whether the firm has any responsibility towards them. If a person is unaffected by the firm's operations, then the firm has no responsibility towards that person. The purpose of specifying a group of 'secondary stakeholders' is to identify the group towards which the firm may have a moral responsibility. There is certainly a case for arguing that the firm has a moral obligation to consider the welfare of future generations; for example it would be wrong for the firm to use up all of a non-renewable resource and leave none for succeeding generations. Hence future generations are stakeholders.

The secondary stakeholders will often not have a contract (either explicit or implicit) with the firm and in some cases their interest in the firm is adversarial (their principal interest is in the harm caused by the firm). This is in sharp contrast to the primary stakeholders who are bound to the firm by contract (explicit or implicit) and by ties of mutual benefit (actual or potential).

3.9 THE FIRM'S MORAL OBLIGATIONS TOWARDS ITS STAKEHOLDERS

3.9.1 General Principles

What is the moral responsibility of the firm (that is, the management) towards its stakeholders? Most philosophers accept the fundamental rule that one should treat all people with respect, which is derived from the categorical imperative of Immanuel Kant that one should never treat another human being solely as a means but also as an end (that is, as being valuable in his or her own right). However, the firm, in carrying on its activities, is obliged to treat its stakeholders as means. Its suppliers are the means by which it acquires its materials; its employees are the means by which these materials are transformed into finished goods; its customers are the means by which the firm acquires the money with which to pay its suppliers and employees. Evan and Freeman (1993) argue that, when the firm treats a stakeholder as a means, it must also treat him as an end, which means respecting his autonomy: the firm must consider the stakeholder's viewpoint and ensure that the stakeholder accepts being treated as a means. The stakeholder is affected by the firm's decisions and, as an autonomous human being, has a right to participate in these decisions. Evan and Freeman (1993: 79) set out the moral obligation of the firm towards its stakeholders in the following terms: 'The corporation[23] and its managers may not violate the legitimate rights of others to determine their own future.'

They set out a second general principle that is based on the philosophical theory of consequentialism: 'The corporation and its management are responsible for the effects of their actions on others.'

These two general principles form a valid and rational basis for the proposition that the firm has some degree of responsibility towards its stakeholders. The second principle defines the persons to whom this responsibility is owed—those who are affected by its actions, which is identical to the definition of secondary stakeholder given earlier.

The first principle indicates the nature of this responsibility. It is rather vague. Evan and Freeman (1993: 82) expand it with two further principles, which they term management principles, as they are designed to guide the managers in their dealings with stakeholders:

- 'The corporation should be managed for the benefit of its stakeholders: its customers, suppliers, owners, employees, and the local community. The rights of these groups must be ensured, and, further, the groups must participate, in some sense, in decisions that substantially affect their welfare.'
- 'Management bears a fiduciary relationship to stakeholders and to the corporation as an abstract entity. It must act in the interests of the stakeholders as their agent, and it must act in the interest of the corporation to ensure the survival of the firm, safeguarding the long-term stakes of each group.'

The first management principle clearly states that managers should take into account the impact of their actions on the welfare of stakeholders, that is, with distributive justice.

3.9.2 The Firm's Responsibility Towards Its Primary Stakeholders

The firm is normally bound to its primary stakeholders through contracts and, prima facie, the firm's first obligation is to honour the promises that it has made in these contracts. However, in order to assure distributive justice in its dealings with its primary stakeholders, the firm has to do more than simply fulfill its contracts. In assessing whether a contract delivers distributive justice, many factors should be taken into account, notably:

(i) Neither party to the contract should have been acting under duress when the contract terms were negotiated. A party may be assumed to be acting under duress, when he has no real alternative, for example the traveller in the desert who is dying of thirst (see Chapter 2, Section 2.3).
(ii) Neither party was induced to agree the contract through the other party's false or misleading statements.
(iii) The market price may not be a just price. This will often be the case, where the market is imperfect; for example there are few buyers or sellers.
(iv) Conditions may have changed since the contract was negotiated, which make the original contract terms no longer appropriate.

The firm (that is, the management) should seek justice both in the negotiation of contracts with its primary stakeholders and in their subsequent implementation. However, its responsibility is not limited to fulfilling its contracts; it has a wider responsibility to seek justice in its dealings with its primary stakeholders. In deciding on the extent and nature of this responsibility in respect of particular stakeholders, the firm should follow certain general principles:

(i) The firm has a greater responsibility towards individual stakeholders with whom it has a long-lasting relationship. These stakeholders have demonstrated the greatest commitment to the firm. They have the strongest claim to be treated as permanent members of the nexus of relationships that makes up the firm.

(ii) The firm has a greater responsibility towards individual stakeholders who depend on the firm. The degree of responsibility is a function of the strength of the dependence. There are three dimensions to the concept of dependence:

   • The proportion of the stakeholder's business that is made with the firm. For example where, for a particular supplier, his sales to the firm make up 80% of his total sales, he is highly dependent on the firm's business; if they are only 1%, he is not dependent. A similar test can be applied to shareholders: if the dividend from the firm makes up 90% of a widow's income, she is highly dependent on the firm.

   • The alternatives available to the stakeholder. If the supplier can easily find an alternative customer for his goods, he is less dependent on the firm's business than if there are no suitable alternatives.

   • The nature of the firm's services. A shopkeeper has a greater responsibility towards a customer for whom his shop is her only source of food than towards one who buys only newspapers.

(iii) The firm has to give particular consideration to questions of justice in its dealings with stakeholders, when the market fails to send the correct signals. This may occur when there is a lack of competition. Where the firm is the sole supplier or customer of a stakeholder, then the price (and other conditions) on which a sale is made is not a market price and the firm has to give specific consideration as to the justice of the transaction. Where the firm is the principal employer in a region, people may have no real alternative to working for the firm and, in such a situation, it cannot be assumed that the firm's employees have not contracted with the firm under duress. The unequal bargaining power of the parties to the employment contract (the firm and its employees) casts doubt on the justice of the contract's terms. On the other hand, where the firm is acting in a market, where there are many buyers and sellers, who do not collude, it can often assume that the market price is just. Its responsibility is largely limited to ensuring that its contracts are negotiated in a just manner, for example not under duress and not involving false or misleading statements. In that event, the firm's responsibility may be limited to fulfilling its contracts.

(iv) Justice concerns relations between people and not the relations between amorphous bodies such as 'the corporation' and 'the workforce'. Hence, in deciding how to treat a particular category of stakeholder, the firm (that is, the managers) must always keep in mind that it is dealing with human beings. This may pose a problem for a large firm with thousands of stakeholders. However, it is a practical problem and not a theoretical problem. The principle to be followed in dealing with stakeholders is clear: never treat a fellow human being solely as a means.

The application of these general principles to the firm's relations with the principal categories of primary stakeholder may be analyzed as follows:

(a)   Providers of Capital

All firms need capital in order to operate and, if a firm fails to secure the cooperation of the providers of capital, it will not prosper and may not survive. In capitalist societies, the firm may obtain the capital funds that it needs in a variety of ways, such as shares, loans, bank overdrafts, and trade credit. In all cases, there is a contract between the firm and the capital provider, and, in negotiating the terms of the contract, the firm is bound by the elementary principles of justice. It should not cause the counterparty to enter into a contract that is contrary to its interests, through, for example, exercising duress or making false or misleading statements. In the case of loans to larger firms, there is generally a reasonably competitive market, and the question of distributive justice may be, more or less, settled by the terms of the contract, which generally specifies in detail the benefits to which the lender is entitled, for example the amount of annual interest payments and the date at which the loan is to be redeemed and on what terms. The firm's responsibility is limited to fulfilling the terms of the contract. This is not the case with shares; the amount of the annual dividend has to be decided afresh each year and the level at which it is fixed influences the welfare not only of the shareholders but also of other primary stakeholders, for the more that is distributed to shareholders, the less that is available for the others.

In Britain and the USA, most large firms are corporations and, according to the law, the corporation should be managed exclusively for the benefit of the shareholders (who are the legal owners). As already mentioned, this is not the position with the stakeholder theory of the firm and with the theory of distributive justice that is based on it. These are moral theories, which do not have their basis in law.

(b) Employees

In many firms, the employees are the most important stakeholder in that the survival and success of the firm depends more on the employees than on any other stakeholder group. Compared with shareholders, employees will often have a stronger relationship with the firm, in at least four respects:

  (i) Longer lasting. The relationship between particular employees and the firm can stretch over decades, whereas many shareholders hold their shares for relatively short periods. This applies especially to shareholders in publicly quoted companies.
 (ii) Closer. Employees interact with the management (which represents the firm) on a daily basis. Shareholders have contact with the management once a year at the annual meeting and, in fact, most shareholders do not even bother to attend.
(iii) Greater commitment. Most employees are more closely bound to the firm than is the case with shareholders. Many would experience difficulty in finding another job if they were to leave the firm, whereas shareholders can easily sever their connection with the firm by selling their shares on the stock exchange.
 (iv) Greater mutual dependence: It is frequently the case that a firm's continued success depends much more upon the skill and effort of particular employees, than upon the loyalty of particular shareholders. Also employees are generally more dependent on the firm for their continued welfare than are shareholders. The difference in the degree of dependence may by very great: the employee who is wholly dependent on the firm because there are no other sources of employment in his region may be compared with the shareholder who avoids being dependent on any single firm by holding shares in a number of firms.

For all these reasons the obligations of the firm to employees (and vice versa) will generally be stronger than its obligations to shareholders.

For the assessment of justice, not all employees are equal. Within the category of employees, one can set out a hierarchy, with at the top the employees to which the firm owes the greatest responsibility. These are the employees on whom the firm is most dependent for its continued success and survival and/or who are most dependent on the firm for their continued welfare. They are likely to be those who have been longest with the firm. Thus the lower levels of the hierarchy may consist of employees on short-term contracts and lastly employees seconded from other firms.

(c) Suppliers

A similar hierarchy may be established for suppliers, with, at the top, a supplier who has a long-term relationship with the firm for the provision of an essential input to the firm's production process. The firm may depend on the supplier for this input, as there are no suitable alternatives. Similarly the supplier may be highly dependent on the firm's business for his continued prosperity; for example he may have invested in specialized facilities to meet the firm's demand—facilities that may have no other use. Such a supplier has a greater claim on the firm that one from whom the firm occasionally buy goods at market prices. Given the temporary nature of such a relationship, the firm's responsibility for justice is largely fulfilled by ensuring that the contract is negotiated in a just manner.

(d) Customers

With customers, the firm has the greatest responsibility towards those who are dependent on the firm for their continued welfare or even survival. The firm would be such a customer for the supplier mentioned in the previous section. A customer with a similar claim on the firm would be a consumer who relied on the firm for essential goods, such as an old person who depends on the village shop for her groceries. These customers have a stronger claim than one who occasionally buys goods from the firm at the market price.

3.9.3 The Firm's Responsibility Towards Its Secondary Stakeholders

Evan and Freeman (1993, 79) hold that '[t]he corporation and its management are responsible for the effects of their actions on others'. In principle this implies that the firm should never harm others. However, in practice, this is impossible. For example, the only way in which a firm could reduce its impact on global warming to zero would be to reduce its emission of polluting gases to zero, which would entail such drastic measures as renouncing almost all forms of transport. Hence the objective must be restated.

One possibility is to follow the philosophical approach of utilitarianism (see Chapter 2, Section 2.5). According to the utilitarian calculus, it is reasonable for the firm to inflict harm on others provided that the overall effect is a net benefit to society—the benefits are greater than the costs. The appropriate costs and benefits are those of society as a whole and not simply the firm's private costs and benefits as reported in its financial statements. Hence the firm should identify those people who are harmed by its actions and evaluate the harm that they have suffered. Clearly this is no easy task but, at least, the firm could attempt to make a reasonable estimate of the magnitudes involved. If this showed that the social costs of the firm's activities exceeded the social benefits, the firm should, in principle, cease operations or seek alternative modes of operation that generate lower social costs. However, if the social benefits exceed the social costs, then it is in society's interest that the firm should continue its operations, notwithstanding that they cause harm to certain people.

However, many people reject the utilitarian calculus because it implies that other people may be harmed in order that the firm may benefit. This objection would lose much of its force, if the firm were to compensate people who were harmed by its activities. There are many practical difficulties with such an approach, such as identifying the people concerned, measuring the degree of harm, and agreeing the level of compensation. However, where it can be implemented, the firm is under a moral obligation to adopt it.

However in most cases, this approach is not possible, because the firm is not able to identify the secondary stakeholders concerned. The firm is obliged to consider categories of people rather than individuals whom it can compensate. It should attempt to measure the harm suffered by categories. The harm may often be expressed in statistical terms, for example that 1% of the inhabitants of a particular region will die next year as a result of the firm's actions. The figure of 1% is subject to uncertainty (there is a probability that it could be as low as 0% or as high as 20%), and it is not possible to identify the individuals who will die. Where the causal connection between the firm's actions and the suffering of others is probable but uncertain, the firm's responsibilities are less clear-cut than where it can identify the individuals concerned. I propose that, in respect of secondary stakeholders who cannot be individually identified, the firm is under a moral obligation:

(i) To measure the harm suffered by these stakeholders; the firm should not use ignorance as an excuse but should actively seek to determine the harm caused to others by its activities.

(ii) To seek to limit such harm (by modifying or ceasing its operations) when its investigations show that the harm is significant.

3.9.4 The Libertarian Challenge

Libertarians, such as Sternberg (1997), deny that the management has any significant obligation towards stakeholders. They argue that the Kantian categorical imperative to treat others with respect means only that the firm's managers should treat as fellow human beings all those with whom they have dealings: employees, customers, and so on (whom they refuse to call 'stakeholders'!). It is sufficient that the managers ensure that these people should not be forced to deal with the firm against their will. Stakeholders are not obliged to deal with the firm and, if they are unhappy with the manager's decisions, they are free to sever their connection with the firm. There is no obligation on the firm to consider distributive justice beyond making sure that its agreements with others are not made under duress. Two other moral principles take precedence over distributive justice:

- That the property rights of the owners should be respected.
- That persons should honour their contracts. The relations between the firm and others should be governed by contract and not by the vague principle of distributive justice.

3.9.5 My Position

These arguments certainly have weight, but I do not consider that they are fatal to the cause of stakeholder theory. The rights of property owners are not absolute. Property is a social construct and it is perfectly in order for society to place restrictions on property owners' rights, as happens all the time in the modern state. For example, in most countries, land-owners are not permitted to erect whatever building they choose on their land. This is a restriction imposed by the law, but most people consider that it is also morally justified. Also the commitments imposed by contracts may not be morally binding. For a contract to be morally binding on the parties, it is necessary that neither party acts under duress and has sufficient information, conditions that are frequently not met in contracts with firms; for example, where a customer or an employee has no other choice, it may reasonably be argued that he is acting under duress. Also the commitments made by a person under contract have to be balanced against other moral considerations; for example a chemical manufacturer is not morally bound to fulfill his contract to supply poison gas to a concentration camp. In my opinion, libertarian philosophy makes sense only in a world that is so different from the current world that it may be dismissed as idealistic.

There is clearly no consensus on the validity of the stakeholder theory. However, I believe that the analysis presented here forms a valid and rational basis for the proposition that the firm has an obligation to pursue distributive justice in its dealings with its stakeholders. The argument in this section may be summarized as follows:

With respect to primary stakeholders:

   (i) The firm is a cooperative venture which unites various groups of people (the firm's primary stakeholders) for mutual benefit.
  (ii) Primary stakeholders deal with the firm in order to enhance their welfare.
 (iii) The firm's activities are directed by the firm's manager.
  (iv) The manager has a moral obligation to consider the welfare of the persons with whom he deals.
   (v) The firm's manager should take decisions that maximize the welfare of the primary stakeholders, balancing competing interests so as to ensure the firm's survival and continued prosperity.

With respect to stakeholders in general (both primary and secondary):

  (vi) A person should not harm another person without justification.
 (vii) The manager, in directing the firm's activities, should take into account its effect on stakeholders and should seek to limit the harm inflicted on them. Where it can identify the people harmed, it should compensate them.

Points (v) and (vii) support the proposition that the firm (that is, the firm's managers) should aim to achieve distributive justice in its dealings with its stakeholders.

3.10 SUMMARY AND CONCLUSIONS

Does the firm have a moral responsibility to strive for distributive justice in its activities? The first two philosophical theories that are considered in this chapter (libertarianism and Rawls's theory of justice as fairness) deny that it does. Both theories have been developed by highly respected philosophers, contain no logical errors, and have substantial support in the academic community. However I consider that, in the present circumstances, they do not form a proper basis for determining the moral responsibilities of the firm. Libertarianism leads to acceptable results only in a society of individuals, each of whom is endowed with equal resources and equal bargaining power. That is not the society in which we live. According to Rawls, the firm is freed from the obligation to seek justice only if the basic structure is just. I do not believe that the basic structure in Britain and the USA (although not extremely unjust) is sufficiently just to assure distributive justice, as evidenced by the glaring injustices in the distribution of income and wealth. In these countries, the state has not intervened with sufficient force to assure distributive justice; it has made few laws that relate to the level of distributive justice produced by firms; very few of the obligations that the state imposes on firms relate to the justice of its activities. Hence, to achieve justice, it is insufficient that firms restrict their actions to obeying the law; they need to do something extra. For these reasons, I consider that libertarianism and Rawls's theory of justice do not provide appropriate guidance for the management of firms. Instead, I endorse the stakeholder theory of the firm, which is based on the social contract theory of the firm and Cohen's theory of the personal responsibility of the individual. I consider that it provides the best justification for the thesis that firms should strive for distributional justice and offers the best arguments that may induce firms actually to do so.

Hence I propose that the firm has a responsibility to seek distributive justice in its dealings with its stakeholders and that this objective should have precedence over the earning of profit. This does not imply that firms are the only agents who should seek distributive justice. Most certainly, as argued by Rawls, the state also has a major responsibility and, in many cases, given its authority, powers, and central position, it is better placed to achieve justice in society than the individual firm. The respective roles of the state and of the firm is one of the topics discussed in the next chapter.

4 The Contribution of Financial Reporting to Distributive Justice

The first three chapters have set out a reasoned argument for the principle that the firm's overriding objective should be to achieve distributive justice among its stakeholders. The remainder of the book considers the contribution that financial reporting can and should make towards the achievement of this objective. Hence there is a change of emphasis from broad issues of philosophy and the responsibility of the firm to the narrower issue of financial reporting. This chapter presents an analysis of the role that financial reporting should play in the process by which the firm achieves distributive justice. This book's thesis is that the firm should behave in a way that achieves distributive justice; that the costs and benefits of its activities are distributed in a just and fair manner among its stakeholders. As a first step in assessing what contribution financial reporting can make towards this objective, it is necessary to analyse the factors that govern the behaviour of firms.

4.1 THE FACTORS THAT GOVERN THE FIRM'S BEHAVIOUR

In mixed economies, such as Britain and the USA, the behaviour of firms is governed by the complex interplay of two principal actors: the state and the firms' managers.

4.1.1 The Role of the State

In Chapter 2, it was argued that society should aim to achieve distributive justice among its members. It is natural that society should place the principal responsibility of achieving distributive justice on the state, for a number of reasons:

(i) The state has the authority and the power to impose coercive measures (such a redistributive taxation) on its citizens; it is highly probable that, to achieve justice, such measures will be necessary;

(ii) The state is neutral. In principle it should not favour one group of citizens over another.

(iii) The state is best able to gather the information on the situation of its citizens that is necessary to enact measures in this field. Its central position enables it to gain a comprehensive picture of the overall situation. The knowledge of other actors, such as firms, is essentially partial.

(iv) Citizens are more likely to accept unpleasant measures (such as taxation) if they are aware that all people are being treated alike. Similarly it is possible that all firms in an industry would favour a measure that promoted distributive justice (for example, the banning of certain dangerous processes) but no firm is prepared to be the first to act, because of the competitive disadvantage that it would suffer vis-à-vis other firms. Only the state is able to break such a deadlock by imposing the measure of all firms.

In Britain and the USA, the state plays a leading role in the quest for distributive justice. Its most effective measures are those that bring about a transfer of income from the better-off to the most disadvantaged: measures such as the progressive taxation of higher incomes and transfer payments to the worse-off, in the form of unemployment benefit, sickness benefit, and other income-support measures. Other significant measures are the state provision of education and health services. But, in addition, the state often seeks to influence directly the behaviour of firms towards greater distributive justice. It enacts laws that apply directly to firms. These laws are of three main types:

(i) Those that alter the size and the distribution of the firm's revenue among its primary stakeholders. Examples are the British law that requires firms to pay their employees a specified minimum hourly wage, and price-control regulations that forbid firms to increase prices.

(ii) Those that seek to prevent firms inflicting negative external costs on the rest of the community. Examples are laws that regulate the amount of noxious greenhouse gases that a firm may emit and regulations that restrict night flights.

(iii) Those that seek to protect vulnerable members of society. Examples are laws that forbid the employment of children and regulations that forbid discrimination on grounds of race or gender.

However, in democracies, the state does not seek to dictate to the firm every aspect of its activities. Basically the state does not consider that its function is to direct every action of its citizens; the liberty of citizens (and firms) to act as they will should be circumscribed only for good reasons. The state limits its interventions to the more pressing problems; for example, when the level of poverty among lowly paid workers becomes a scandal (as evidenced by the degree of concern expressed by citizens) it may enact a law on a minimum wage, or when the amount of pollution emanating from firms begins to cause noticeable damage to the environment, it may pass a law that prohibits or constrains certain activities, such as the use of coal-fired heating in London. In a very wide area, the law does not constrain the firm's actions. Hence in general in democracies, firms are given considerable freedom of action. This means that considerable discretion is given to managers in deciding how to run their firms.

4.1.2 The Role of the Firm's Manager and Other Stakeholders

In the previous chapter it was argued that the firm's manager is morally responsible for ensuring that the firm achieves distributive justice among its stakeholders. But the manager is under an additional moral obligation: to obey the law. In an unjust state, such as Nazi Germany, there may be occasions when the individual citizen may morally break the law. However this is not permissible in a just state. Modern democracies, such as Britain and the USA, are not completely just, but the level of injustice is not such that the citizen may morally disobey the state's laws. The proper response of the citizen who considers that a law is unjust is to seek to change the law by political action appropriate to a democracy, such as lobbying and voting.[1]

However, as argued in the previous chapter, the manager's moral responsibility is not limited to obeying the law. Modern capitalist societies allow the managers of firms very considerable freedom of action and, according to the thesis presented in this book, they should use this freedom to ensure that the firm practises justice. It is evident that, within the firm, the manager has the prime responsibility for achieving distributive justice. What is the responsibility of the other stakeholders? Certainly all stakeholders have a moral responsibility to seek justice. For example, a trade union official should not forcefully pursue a claim for higher wages for the firm's employees when he knows that this would lead to other stakeholders, such as customers, suffering a greater injustice. But the manager has a special responsibility that surpasses that of the trade union official. The manager has the responsibility of balancing the conflicting claims of the different stakeholders with the aim of ensuring the firm's survival and continuing prosperity.[2] The manager is at the centre of the nexus of stakeholder relationships that makes up the firm. The other stakeholders are on the periphery. They do not have the information that is needed to assess how best to assure the balance between competing stakeholders that is essential for the firm's survival. Only the manager has the comprehensive information on the situation of the different stakeholders that is needed to make decisions about the distribution of costs and benefits. This is the reason why, of all the stakeholders, the manager has the prime responsibility for achieving justice.

The responsibility of the other stakeholders (employees, customers, suppliers, and capital providers) is essentially subordinate to that of the manager. It comes into play when the firm's manager fails in his responsibility to achieve justice. For example, if the manager fails to achieve a just distribution of the firm's income between its employees and its shareholders (say the employees' wages are too low and the shareholders' dividend too high), then the employees are justified in taking action to redress the injustice. The aim of such action, for example a strike, is to put pressure on the manager to change his decision, so that it better reflects justice. Even secondary stakeholders may take action to influence the firm to act in a more just fashion. For example, citizens, outraged at the damage that the firm inflicts on the environment, may organize a boycott of the firm's products, such as that led by Greenpeace against Shell in the Brent Spar affair.

Since, in reality, the manager often fails to achieve justice, there will generally be a need for the intervention of other stakeholders. In effect, the achievement of distributive justice by the firm will often depend on how successful the manager is in balancing the pressures put on him by the different stakeholder groups so as to achieve the most just result.

4.2 THE ROLE OF FINANCIAL REPORTING

The term 'financial reporting' refers to the statements issued by firms that provide information about their position (for example in a balance sheet) and their activities (for example in an income statement). In the following chapters, it is argued that final reporting can and should make a significant contribution towards the achievement of distributive justice by the firm. The firm's financial statements should be drawn up with the aim of maximizing this contribution, which entails a detailed analysis of their form and content.

4.2.1 The State's Role in Financial Reporting

In both Britain and the USA, the state has enacted laws that oblige firms to prepare financial statements and which regulate their form and content in some detail. One motivation of the state is the promotion of justice, particularly to assure a balance of justice between the firm's creditors and its shareholders. This aspect of the state's regulation of financial reporting is developed further in later chapters. A major theme of these chapters is the degree to which currently the state's regulation of financial reporting promotes distributive justice and whether it should be developed further with a view to achieving greater justice.

4.2.2 The Responsibility of the Firm's Manager for Financial Reporting

Notwithstanding the state's laws, the firm has considerable freedom of action in drawing up its financial statements—for two reasons:

(i) The law does not regulate every detail of the firm's financial statements;
(ii) In general there is no prohibition on the firm's preparing supplementary statements that are in addition to its regulated financial statements and which present information that is more relevant for justice.

The firm's manager has the ultimate responsibility (within the discretion allowed him by the law) for the form and content of the firm's financial statements, but it is common for the manager to delegate the task to an employee, such as the firm's accountant.

Later chapters analyse the way that firms have used their discretion to prepare statements that better promote the cause of justice and discuss how such statements may be further developed.

4.3 THE CONTRIBUTION OF FINANCIAL REPORTING

The next three chapters analyse the contribution that financial reporting can and should make towards the achievement of distributive justice. Each chapter deals with a different function of accounts:

(a) The Reporting Function

Chapter 5 presents an analysis of the reporting function. With this function, the role of the financial statements is limited to reporting what has happened in the past. When the firms' objective is defined as the achievement of distributive justice, then ideally the accounts should report the degree to which this objective has been achieved.

Chapters 6 and 7 present two further alternative functions of the accounts which place more emphasis on the future: the underlying idea is that the financial statements should influence the future actions of the firm. They differ in the degree of this influence.

(b) The Distribution Function

Chapter 6 presents an analysis of the distribution function. With this function, the financial statements determine, either completely or partially, certain future actions of the firm. The term 'distribution function' refers to the fact that certain payments to stakeholders ('distributions') are based on the figures in the accounts. In certain countries, for example Germany, the financial statements perform the distribution function with respect to the firm's tax payment. The amount of the firm's future tax payment is largely determined by the figure that it reports as profit in its income statement. With the distribution function, the financial statements play an active role in shaping the firm's future actions.

(c)   The Information Function

Chapter 7 presents an analysis of the information function. With this function, the financial statements provide information to the firm's stakeholders (including its manager), which they then use in making future decisions. An example of the financial statements performing the information function is when the firm's manager and the trade union official who represents the firm's employees negotiate wage rates and each refer to the past year's income statement to support his case. With the information function, the role of the accounts is essentially passive; the stimulus to action comes from the person who reads the financial statements.

(d)   Comparison of the Three Functions

The final chapter sets out a comparative analysis of the three functions and assesses the contribution that each makes to distributive justice.

5   The Reporting Function

The financial statements play a passive role in the quest for distributive justice, when their function is limited to reporting a firm's actions. With the passive role, it is not considered that the function of the accounts is to influence directly the firm's future actions. Rather their function is to report past and present facts; hence the term, the reporting function. With the reporting function, the accountant is a record keeper or chronicler, akin to a historian, although, like a good historian, she may also interpret the facts that she reports. This chapter analyses the contribution that the accounts play in assisting the firm to achieve distributive justice, when their function is limited to reporting.

5.1 INFORMATION ON DISTRIBUTIONS

For the firm, distributive justice concerns the distribution of the costs and benefits arising from its activity among its stakeholders. Hence an essential function of the financial statements is to report the amount of the costs borne and the benefits enjoyed by each category of stakeholder. Where a stakeholder receives a benefit, there has been a transfer of wealth from the firm to the stakeholder. In this book, such a transfer of benefits is termed a 'distribution'. All of the following are distributions of the firm: a wage paid to an employee; tax paid to the state; a dividend paid to a shareholder. Where the stakeholder incurs a cost, the transfer of wealth is from the stakeholder to the firm and may be considered a negative distribution. In the standard usage of the term, only a dividend is considered to be a distribution. In this book, the term 'distribution' is given the wider meaning of the sharing out of the firm's revenue. With this definition of a distribution, it is not appropriate to define the firm as a nexus of stakeholders, for in that case, the cash that represents an employee's wages would not leave the 'firm' (as defined in this very wide sense). At most there has been a transfer of wealth from one stakeholder to another. To avoid this anomaly, it is necessary to define the 'firm' as the management (as proposed in Chapter 3, Section 3.8.1). In the case of the employee's wage, there is a transfer of wealth from the management (the assets under its control have diminished), and hence (given the narrower definition of 'firm') there has been a transfer of wealth from the firm.

The question of how the accounts may report distributions will now be considered, starting with the firm's standard financial statements.

5.2 THE STANDARD FINANCIAL STATEMENTS

According to the IASB's standards, a firm should prepare a balance sheet, an income statement, and a cash flow statement.[1] None of these standard statements is specifically designed to provide information about the justice of the firm's activities. This is unsurprising given that justice does not figure in the IASB's stated objective of financial reporting (see Chapter 1, Section 1.1). However, these statements do provide some information about the distributions made by the firm, which may be considered to be the absolute minimum information that is needed in order to judge the justice of the firm's activities.

5.2.1 The Income Statement

The IASB's IAS 1 recognizes two alternative formats for the income statement: they differ in the way in which the expenses are classified:

  i. A natural classification in which expenses are classified by the nature of the expense: for example, depreciation, employees' remuneration, consumption of raw materials, fuel, etc.
 ii. A functional classification in which expenses are classified according to their function: for example, cost of sales, administrative expenses, marketing costs, etc.

Table 5.1 illustrates the alternative classifications using the income statement of a hypothetical corporation.

With the functional classification, payments to different stakeholders are often aggregated under one heading, masking the distributions to stakeholders. Thus cost of sales will be presented as a single figure which is made up of a number of different types of expense, including:

 • Wages to workers
 • Consumption of raw materials, which reflect (imperfectly) distributions to suppliers, and
 • Depreciation of machinery, which is not a distribution at all!

With the natural classification of expenses, these costs are reported separately. Hence this format yields the more useful information about

Table 5.1 XYZ Corporation: Income Statements

Natural classification of costs		Functional classification of costs	
Income statement for 2009	€	*Income statement for 2009*	€
Sales	2,460	Sales	2,460
		Less cost of sales	1,444
Less		Gross profit	1,016
Materials	800	Less	
Wages	1,000	Distribution costs	290
Depreciation	125	Administration expenses	191
Other operating costs	150	Other operating costs	150
Interest	10	Interest	10
Total costs	2,085		641
Net profit before tax	375	Net profit before tax	375
Tax on profit	125	Tax on profit	125
Net profit after tax	250	Net profit after tax	250
Dividend	100	Dividend	100
Retained profits	150	Retained profits	150

distributions. However the income statement (even with the natural classification of expenses) is not particularly good at communicating distributions to stakeholders. One reason is that its principal function is to report the profit accruing to shareholders, who are but one category of stakeholder. However, the principal reason is that the figures for income and expense reported in the income statement are calculated using the accruals concept. With accruals, there is a time difference between the reporting of an expense in the income statement and the transfer of wealth (the distribution) to a stakeholder. The reported expense precedes the transfer of wealth when the firm records a provision or a liability; the reported expense comes after the distribution when the firm records a prepayment. Hence a reporting basis other than the accruals concept is called for.

5.2.2 The Cash Flow Statement

Distributions are transfers of wealth from the firm to stakeholders. Hence, the cash flow statement, which aims to report the flows of cash into and out of the firm, may be considered to be a statement of distributions. The IASB's IAS7 prescribes two alternative formats for the cash flow statement: the direct method and the indirect method. The indirect method (which is preferred by most firms because it is easier to implement) does not present the figures for certain important distributions; for example the figure for wages paid is not shown separately and cannot be derived from the disclosed information. Hence the direct method is to be preferred. Table 5.2 presents the cash flow statement of the same hypothetical corporation, using the direct method in the format prescribed by IAS7, with separate subtotals for operating activities, investing activities and financing activities.

The operating activities section of the cash flow statement in Table 5.2 may be compared with the income statement of Table 5.1. There are striking differences between the two tables. Thus, in the income statement, wages are stated to be €1000, compared with €850 in the cash flow statement. The difference represents unpaid wages. The difference with respect to tax is even more remarkable: €125 in Table 5.1 and nil in Table 5.2; this is caused by a provision for deferred tax being set up in 2009 but no tax actually being paid.

It is evident that a firm does not make a distribution to the state when it includes a provision for deferred tax in its accounts. This figure represents a potential distribution, which may never materialize. However, in respect of

Table 5.2   XYZ Corporation: Cash Flow Statement for 2009

Cash flow statement for 2009	€	€	€
Cash flow from operations			
Receipts from customers		2,400	
Payments to suppliers		-900	
Other payments			
Consultancy firm	-60		
Donation to charity	-40		
Compensation	-50	-150	
Wages		-850	
Interest		-10	
Dividend		-100	
			390
Cash flow from investing activities			
Purchase of plant			-250
Cash flow from financing activities			
Issue of bond		100	
Buy back of shares		-200	
			-100
Net cash flow			40

the unpaid wages, it can be argued that the firm made a distribution when it incurred a legal liability to pay the wages; from the employees' viewpoint the firm's obligation represents an asset: their wealth has increased. However, if this line of argument is followed to its logical conclusion, the cash paid by a shareholder for her shares would not represent a (negative) distribution, as there has been no change in her wealth—she has exchanged one asset (cash) for another (shares). Hence distributions are best measured in terms of cash transfers.

5.2.3 The Value-Added Statement

Although the value-added statement does not figure among the IASB's required statements, it is appropriate to consider it in conjunction with the standard statements, because it is derived from a standard statement: the income statement. A very few corporations include such a statement in their full set of accounts, although there is no obligation (either in the law or in the IASB's standards) to do so.

The basic idea behind the value-added statement is that a firm buys goods and services from other firms and converts them into other goods and services using its labour force and its capital. The surplus of the revenue from the sale of these goods and services over the cost of the goods and services acquired from other firms represents the value added by the firm. This surplus is divided between the parties that made it possible (the firm's capital providers and employees), with a share going to the state. That part of the surplus that is not distributed is retained by the firm. The 'firm' is considered to consist principally of the employees and the capital providers.

The principal theoretical problem with this statement is how to treat depreciation. Janice Monti-Belkaoui (1996: 81) refers to two methods:

(i) The gross value-added method. Depreciation is treated as part of the surplus, as being the depreciation provisions that are retained in the firm and not distributed.
(ii) The net value-added method. Depreciation is treated as an expense to be deducted in calculating the surplus. This approach considers that the depreciation expense for the year represents the allocation of a payment to other firms made in previous years. It is essentially of the same nature as the current payments to firms for goods and services.[2]

Most firms that prepare value-added statements adopt the net method, which is also the method that I favour on the grounds that it best represents the relationship between the reporting firm and other firms.

Table 5.3 presents the value-added statement derived from the income statement of Table 5.1. The firm's value added is calculated as €1385, being the difference between the sales to customers of €2460 and the costs that are

Table 5.3   XYZ Corporation: Value-Added Statement for 2009

Value-added statement for 2009	€	€
Sales to customers		2,460
Less transfers to other firms		
Suppliers	800	
Other firms	150	
Depreciation	125	
		1,075
Value added		1,385
Distribution of value added		
Employees	1,000	
Capital providers	110	
State	125	
		1,235
Retained in the firm		150

based on payments to other firms of €1075. In the lower half of the statements, this surplus is divided between employees, capital providers, and the state, the balance of €150 being retained in the firm. Note that the value-added statement does not provide any information that is not already implicit in the income statement (with the natural classification of expenses)—it simply rearranges the figures and calculates certain subtotals.

There is no consensus as to the principal function of the value-added statement. Some consider it to be a statement of performance; they place the emphasis on the first half of the statement: the calculation of the value added. For example, according to Stoloway and Lebas (2000), '[V]alue added is a measure of the economic performance of an economic entity, especially a measure of its contribution to creating a customer-oriented supply. Thus it is a form of "income" measure.' Others consider it to be principally a statement of distributions; they place the emphasis on the second half of the statement. Janice Monti-Belkaoui (1996: 88) writes that 'value added is the increase in wealth generated by the use of the firm's resources before its allocation among shareholders, bondholders, workers and government'.

It can be argued that the principal function of the value-added statement is neither to measure performance nor to report distributions but rather to enable the firm (that is, the management) to signal that it considers employees to be on a par with shareholders, since the statement treats both equally.[3]

5.3 A PROPER STATEMENT OF DISTRIBUTIONS

Of the standard statements, the value-added presents the best information on distributions but it suffers from the following defects.

(i) It is based on the accruals concept, with the consequence that the reported figures do not generally represent transfers of wealth (which is a fundamental characteristic of a distribution).

(ii) It reports distributions to a limited group of primary stakeholders: providers of capital, employees, and the state. Other primary stakeholders are ignored, as is the whole category of secondary stakeholders: the local community and the wider world.

(iii) It covers only distributions relating to the income transactions and excludes those relating to capital transactions.

What is required is a statement that reports all transfers of wealth to all stakeholders. The first fault can be rectified by basing the statement on cash flows rather than accruals. The second fault can be rectified by including cash flows relating to secondary stakeholders. The third fault can be rectified by including cash flows relating to capital transactions. It is essential that such transactions be included in a statement of the overall distributions made to stakeholders. For example, the cash flow statement (Table 5.2) indicates that, during 2009, the firm, in addition to a dividend of €100, paid shareholders €200 to buy back some shares. The total distribution to shareholders made by the firm in 2009 was €300. The fact that some part of the cash payment was labelled 'buy back' and another part 'dividend' is irrelevant for the measurement of distributions. Similarly in 2009, the firm paid an equipment supplier €250 for new plant. There is no essential difference between this payment and the payment of €900 to suppliers of raw materials. Both represent transfers of wealth from the firm to a stakeholder. Therefore a complete statement of distributions should include both current and capital transactions.

Such a statement is presented in Table 5.4, which reports all cash flows between the firm and its stakeholders. Stakeholders are classified into primary stakeholders and secondary stakeholders. Almost all the firm's payments are to primary stakeholders, to persons and firms with whom it has direct dealings. This is reflected in Table 5.4, which reports distributions of €2270 to primary stakeholders and only €90 to secondary stakeholders. Payments to secondary stakeholders are exceptional. Table 5.4 reports two such payments: a donation of €40 to a charity and compensation of €50 to a fisherman who was harmed by the firm's pollution of the local lake.

The information content of this statement could be enhanced by providing a more detailed analysis of certain items. For example, to gain a full understanding of the distributions to employees, it would be necessary to have a detailed breakdown of this expense between different categories of employee (for example, analysed by gender, age, location, and skill level).

Table 5.4   XYZ Corporation: Statement of Cash Distributions 2009

Statement of cash distributions 2009	€	€	€
Receipts from customers			-2,400
Distributions			
Primary stakeholders			
Employees		850	
Suppliers			
Materials	900		
Consultancy firm	60		
Plant	250		
		1,210	
Capital providers			
Shareholders			
Redemption of shares	200		
Dividend	100		
	300		
Bondholders			
Issue of bond	-100		
Interest	10		
	-90		
		210	
The state		0	
Total of primary stakeholders		2,270	
Secondary stakeholders			
Donation to charity	40		
Compensation	50		
		90	
Total distributions			2,360
Retained in the firm (increase in cash)			40

As a report on the justice of the firm's distributions, this statement of distributions, suffers from two substantial defects:

(i)   It gives no indication as to whether the reported distributions to stakeholders are just.

(ii) It does not cover all the costs and benefits that result from the firm's activities,

5.4 THE JUSTICE OF DISTRIBUTIONS TO PRIMARY STAKEHOLDERS

5.4.1 The Problem

The problem of the justice of distributions to primary stakeholders may be analysed with the aid of a highly simplified example. Three men set up a widget-making firm, each contributing €1000 in capital. They buy raw materials on the market at the market price and sell their widgets at the market price. To simplify the exposition, the justice experienced by the suppliers, customers, and the state will be ignored.[4] The relevant primary stakeholders are the three men. If it is further assumed that each devotes the same amount of time to the manufacture of widgets, that each is equally productive, and that there are no significant differences in their personal circumstances, then the just division of the firm's surplus between the three men is one third to each. There is no justification for any other division. The fundamental assumption is equality, and deviations from equality must be justified.

This presumption of equality is challenged when the example is made more complicated. Assume that one of the three men provides the entire capital of €3000 and the other two make the widgets. How should the firm's surplus be divided between them? It hardly seems logical to retain the equal division, for, if five men were involved of which three supplied the capital (€1000 each) and two worked, an equal division among the five would give a smaller amount to the workers than would an equal division among the three, but the work done by the two workers would be the same. What is required is a principle for dividing the firm's surplus between the two categories of stakeholder: capital providers and labour providers. Karl Marx was firmly of the opinion that any reward to capital was unjust as it deprived the workers of some part of the value of their output to which they were entitled. The Marxist labour theory of value provides a simple and straightforward answer to the problem of the division of the surplus: none to the capitalist and all to the workers.[5] Most modern economists and philosophers reject Marx's labour theory of value, but there is no consensus on an alternative theory that explains and justifies the division of income between capital and labour. In the present state of knowledge, the problem seems unsolvable. If further categories of stakeholder are added (the state, customers, and so on), the problem of the just division of income between the different categories becomes even more complex. For example, the proper level of taxation (or, which is roughly the same thing, the proper size of the public sector in the economy) is a most hotly disputed topic on which there is no consensus. The basic problem is that, if the share of one category is increased, that of other categories is reduced. To decide on the justice of the division requires balancing the interests of one category against those of the others, a task on which there is no consensus on the general principles to be followed.

However, the problem of the just division of surplus arises not only between categories but also within categories. Assume that the three men have agreed that the capital provider should receive €300 per year (10% of €3000) and that the remainder is to be divided between the two workers. Further assume that the production of widgets involves two different processes and that each man specializes in one process at which he becomes proficient, thus assuring the higher productivity from the division of labour that so impressed Adam Smith. Moreover the working conditions in one process are very unpleasant, compared with those in the other process. It would seem that justice requires that the man who worked in the unpleasant process should receive a larger share of the firm's surplus compared with his fellow, to compensate him for the arduous nature of his work. Perhaps the two men can agree on the shares, but, if they cannot, are there any general principles that may be used to determine the just and fair division of the surplus? Some economists would argue that each man should be paid the market wage for his job, but this assumes that the wage set by the market is just. But, if it is now assumed that one of the partners is a woman, then this would imply that she should receive a lower share, for it is a fact that, in almost every market economy, women are paid less than men for identical work. Few people would consider that this is just. Difficulties in assessing the relative justice of the treatment of the two workers arise whenever there is any significant difference in their relative circumstances.

The problem of determining the just wage has occupied philosophers for centuries. Dick (1975) listed the factors that various philosophers have argued should be considered in establishing a just wage:

(i) Need: The wage should depend on the needs of the recipient. A single mother with triplets should be paid more than the bachelor. A blind man should be paid more than a sighted man. The ideal that remuneration should be based on need is well expressed in the Marxist slogan 'from each according to his abilities, to each according to his needs'.

(ii) Ability: The wage should depend on the recipient's ability. But, if one man produces more than his fellows, because of factors that are morally irrelevant (such as his superior education provided by his parents), is he morally entitled to a higher wage?

(iii) Effort: The wage should depend on the effort expended by the recipient. If one man puts more effort into his work than his fellow, should he receive a higher reward, even if his output is lower?

(iv) Compensation: If one type of work is inherently less attractive than another, should the worker receive a higher wage?

(v) Contribution: Workers should be paid the value of what they produce. This is essentially the economist's argument—people should be paid their marginal value product.[6]

It is abundantly clear that there is no consensus on the just wage.

So far the problem of justice has been considered largely in terms of how the firm's revenue stream is to be divided between its workers and capital providers. However the justice experienced by customers and suppliers is also strongly affected by the make-up of the firm's revenue stream. For example, a reduction in the selling price of the firm's products may lead to greater justice for customers, but at the expense of a reduction in justice for employees. And there are similar problems when the circumstances of these stakeholders differ; for example how should a firm treat a customer who is expensive to serve because she lives in a remote area but who is dependent on the firm's services, as compared with a customer who is cheaper to serve because she lives in a nearby town? Difficulties in assessing justice always arise when the circumstances of stakeholders are not identical.

The conclusion of this analysis is that, with respect to primary stakeholders, there is no consensus on how to assess the justice of the firm's activities.

5.4.2 The Solution?

How should the accountant evaluate the justice of the firm's treatment of primary stakeholders, given this lack of consensus? There would appear to be three possible courses of action:

  (i) Choose one theory of justice and use it in the evaluation.
 (ii) Provide several different accounts, each based on a different theory of justice.
(iii) Provide information that enables the user of the accounts to assess the justice of the firm's activities according to his (the user's) chosen theory.

Alternative (i) has a number of disadvantages. The accountant is imposing her set of values on the user. For example, a Marxist accountant might report that the dividend paid to shareholders was thoroughly unjust as it deprived the workers of part of the value of their output. Many users of the accounts would reasonably object that they reject Marx's philosophy. Moreover, in concentrating on one theory of justice, the accountant is shutting out the possibility of evaluating the firm's actions according to alternative theories.

Alternative (ii) avoids the problems of alternative (i) but creates new problems: it involves more work but, more seriously, the presentation of multiple accounts is likely to confuse the user.

Alternative (iii) is much more attractive in a pluralist society in which different people hold different conceptions of justice. Furthermore it does not assume that it is possible to evaluate the justice of the firm's activities and present the results in a comprehensible form, which is the implicit assumption of alternatives (i) and (ii). It seems highly probable that, in the present state of man's knowledge, it is not feasible to evaluate objectively the justice of many complex activities. Perhaps justice, like beauty, lies in the eye of the beholder—in practice, if not in principle.

Alternative (iii) is the approach favoured by those firms who have sought to report on the justice of their actions, as becomes clear when current practice is examined later.

5.5 MISSING COSTS AND BENEFITS

5.5.1 The Problem

The second defect of the statement of distributions (Table 5.4) is that it does not cover all of the costs and benefits arising from the firm's activities. The statement covers the firm's private costs but not those connected with its externalities. For many firms the most important externality is pollution. Consider the case of a fisherman who experiences a fall in his income of €50 (derived from the sale of fish that he has caught in a local lake) caused by water pollution emanating from the firm. The €50 is a cost of the firm's operations. It should be taken into account in deciding whether it is society's interest that the firm should continue its activities. But the cost is only borne by the firm (and hence recognized in the firm's accounts) when the firm pays compensation to the fisherman (as is assumed in Tables 5.2 and 5.4). But the payment of compensation to persons harmed by pollution is the exception rather than the rule. In the great majority of cases, the firm pays no compensation and hence the loss suffered by society is not reported in the firm's financial statements.

5.5.2 Possible Solutions

Would it be possible to draw up a statement which covers both the firm's private costs and its external costs—that is, a statement of the firm's social costs, covering the costs borne by all members of society?

Before considering this question, I will first consider whether such a statement would give an indication of the justice experienced by the firm's secondary stakeholders. At first glance, it would seem reasonable to argue that the fisherman's income loss of €50 is a good measure of the injustice that he has suffered as a result of the firm's activities. But there are complications. Assume that there are two fishermen; both suffer a fall in income of €50. One fisherman is rich (he has a large additional income from investments); the other is poor with fishing being his only source of income. The rich man hardly notices his income loss; the poor man is reduced to destitution. The rich man experiences hardly any decline in his utility; the poor man suffers a catastrophic fall. Many people would consider that the injustice suffered by the poor man is greater than that of the rich man.

Jeremy Bentham, the founder of utilitarianism, proposed a 'felicific calculus', by which the utility experienced by an individual would be measured in common units, and the sum of the units of utility for all individuals would represent the utility experienced by society as a whole. To implement Bentham's approach, the monetary amounts (€50 for the rich man and €50 for the poor man) would have to be converted into units of utility (say minus 5 'utils' for the rich man and minus 1000 'utils' for the poor man) in order to give a more accurate picture of the harm that they have suffered.

It is generally agreed by philosophers and economists that, in the present state of knowledge, it is not possible to measure the utility experienced by an individual in common units that enable comparisons between individuals. Therefore there is no alternative to measuring social costs in money terms. Monetary amounts are, in principle, poor measures of justice, but, often, they are the only one available.

But is it practicable to compute the firm's social costs even in money terms? In the example, in order to calculate the loss suffered by the fisherman, the firm must:

(i) Identify the fisherman as a person likely to be adversely affected.
(ii) Quantify the losses that he has suffered.[7]
(iii) Ascertain that the cause of the fall in the fisherman's catch was the pollution of the lake; for example that there was not another cause, such as over-fishing.
(iv) Ascertain that the pollution of the lake was caused by the firm's activities; in practice it is likely that the firm is only one of several sources of pollution.

Whereas, with primary stakeholders, the principal problem is how to divide the firm's revenue stream between them, with secondary stakeholders it is how to assess the impact of the firm's externalities. This will often involve intractable problems of assessing cause and effect. Moreover the number of secondary stakeholders in respect of whom the computation should be made may, in the case of a large multinational, number many millions—perhaps consisting of many different sub-sets, each differently affected by the firm's externalities. In practice, a direct calculation of the firm's social costs seems impossible.

For this reason, with reporting the justice experienced by secondary stakeholders, the conclusion seems to be rather similar to that adopted for primary stakeholders: information should be provided that is relevant to assessing justice. For example, instead of attempting to measure the losses suffered by the fisherman mentioned in the last paragraph, the firm should provide information that the reader of the report can use to assess for herself the likely level of harm. This would include information directly related to the firm's activities (for example the quantities of different chemicals that it has discharged into the local river) and other information that it should endeavour to acquire in view of its relevance (for example an analysis of the quality of the lake water and statistics on fish catches).

However, the reason why a direct evaluation cannot be provided is different for secondary stakeholders than is the case with primary stakeholders. With primary stakeholders, the reason was the lack of consensus on the principles to be adopted for dividing the firm's revenue stream between the various categories of primary stakeholder and also within categories. For secondary stakeholders, there is a general consensus that they have suffered an injustice when they suffer harm caused by the firm's activities. There is no theoretical problem—only the practical problem of identifying the relevant secondary stakeholders and measuring the harm that they have suffered.

5.6 WHAT THE USER NEEDS TO ASSESS JUSTICE

The conclusion of the foregoing analysis is that it is not feasible for the firm to produce a report that presents directly the justice experienced by stakeholders. Instead, it should provide information that enables the user to assess for herself using her own criteria the extent to which the firm has treated its stakeholders justly. The nature and extent of the information that such a report should contain may be analysed with respect to one important category of stakeholder: employees.

The justice experienced by employees is not adequately represented by the wage paid by the firm. In order to judge whether the firm has treated its employees justly (that is, whether the wage paid represents a just return for the employees' services), it is necessary to have information not only on the wage paid but also on a wide range of other matters, including:

(i)   Deferred monetary benefits, for example the promise of a pension.
(ii) Benefits in kind, for example the provision of a company car.
(iii) Working time. The amount of the wage paid is rather meaningless without information on the number of hours worked, the prevalence of shift work, the holiday entitlement, and similar matters.
(iv) Working conditions. Clearly the nature of the physical working conditions is a factor that must be taken into account. Where the working environment is particularly unpleasant, hazardous, or dangerous, the monetary rewards should be higher in compensation. Where the employee suffers injury or damage to her health attributable to the job, this may be a most significant aspect of the costs of the firm's activities that are inflicted on its stakeholders;
(v)   Security of employment. There is a world of difference in the justice experience by employees between those of a firm that has a policy of 'hire and fire', dismissing its workers as soon as it has no more need for them, and those of a firm that offers stable employment to its workforce through good times and bad.

(vi) Respect of employees' autonomy. In Chapter 3 (Section 3.9.1), it is argued that the firm must respect the autonomy of its primary stakeholders, who should participate in decisions that affect their welfare. This is a very wide subject, covering such matters as the procedure for consulting employees, the prevalence of discrimination against women and racial minorities, the denial of the right of employees to associate in trade unions, and how the firm deals with employees' grievances. The common thread that runs through all these matters is whether the firm is treating its employees as free, autonomous human beings.

Some of the preceding factors involve payments by the firm (for example pensions) and may therefore be covered in a comprehensive statement of distributions that forms part of the financial statements. But many more do not involve payments and, moreover, some cannot be expressed adequately in monetary terms—for example how is it possible to put a money value on the autonomy of a firm's employees

All the factors just listed have to be taken into account in assessing the justice of a firm's treatment of an employee. It is combined effect that is relevant. Thus relatively poor treatment under one heading may be compensated by better treatment under another heading. For example, arduous working conditions (which may be an unavoidable feature of the production process) may not constitute injustice, if the worker receives a higher wage or shorter working time in compensation. Similarly a policy of 'hire and fire' is not necessarily unjust; the worker may willingly accept less secure employment (for example a temporary contract) in return for a higher wage. However, information on *all* the factors listed previously is necessary in order to judge the overall justice experienced by an employee.

For a full report covering all the firm's stakeholders, information similar in quantity and complexity of that required for employees should be presented for other categories: customers, suppliers, and the whole group of secondary stakeholders. This suggests that a full report would be extraordinarily long and complex. This question is examined further in the next section, which deals with current practice in the reporting of justice.

5.7 CURRENT PRACTICE IN THE REPORTING OF DISTRIBUTIVE JUSTICE

The analysis so far suggests that any firm, which seeks to report adequately on distributive justice, is faced with a major practical problem—how to communicate all the information that the user needs to assess justice in a report of manageable length. In this section, the present reporting practice of firms is examined with a view to gaining an insight on how this problem may be solved.

5.7.1 Voluntary Reporting

I have been unable to find a single report whose primary function is stated to be the reporting of the justice of a firm's activities. However many firms do issue reports that provide information that is relevant for the assessment of justice—in some cases highly relevant. The common characteristics of these reports are:

(i)   They are voluntary in that generally the firm is under no formal legal obligation to publish.
(ii) They are separate from and in addition to the regular financial statements.
(iii) They supplement the financial statements in that they provide information on matters that are either not covered in the financial statements or covered inadequately.

5.7.2 Why Firms Report Voluntarily

Throughout the world, the financial reporting of firms is closely regulated by the law, with the aim of ensuring that the owners (shareholders) receive the information on the firm's financial position and performance that they need in order to monitor the actions of the managers who run the firm. Hence, in general, the principal information that a firm is legally obliged to publish is that which directly affects the firm's (that is, the shareholders') own wealth and income in monetary terms. Hence typically firms must provide information on wages paid to employees but not on working conditions; they must report the cost of pollution when it affects them directly, for example when they incur costs in clearing up polluted land, but not when it affects some-one else; they report the profit that they gain from their operations, but not the costs and benefits that others experience.

Outside of the conventional financial statements, firms are not legally obliged to provide much information that is relevant for the assessment of justice, for example on social and environmental matters. In most countries, the legal requirements are limited to highly specific matters. For example, British firms are required to report on the employment of disabled people but not on other matters relating to employment, such as health and safety, equal opportunities, and training.[8] In no country is a legal obligation placed on firms to provide an overall report on social, environmental, and economic impact.[9] However, a number of firms do issue such reports; why should they do so, when there is no legal obligation?

Buhmann (2006) points out that the imposition of a legal obligation is but one way by which society influences the behaviour of firms. Law is often the last stage of a long process of which the successive stages are:

(i)   Citizens form the opinion that firms should behave in certain ways.

(ii) Civil society, that is, associations of citizens, such as NGOs (non-governmental organizations—Greenpeace, Oxfam, etc.) and trade unions, campaigns to achieve this end. There are two targets: the firms (to change their behaviour) and the state (to change the law). One tactic is the development and dissemination of recommendations and ethical codes to guide firms' activities.

(iii) International bodies, such as the United Nations, the ILO (International Labour Organization), and the OECD (Organization for Economic Cooperation and Development), respond to civil society's concerns by enacting measures within their area of competence. Examples are the UN's Universal Declaration of Human Rights, the ILO's Conventions on Employment, and the OECD's Guidelines for Multinational Enterprises. In general these acts are not binding on individual firms and are binding on national governments, only in so far as they have been ratified. Hence these acts, in themselves, have no legal authority but often have considerable moral authority, which is enhanced by the national governments being represented on the international bodies.

(iv) Some firms change their behaviour. For example, they adopt ethical codes of conduct, abolish child labour, and reduce pollution. Their motives for doing so are often complex: to improve the firm's image, to deflect criticism from NGOs, and to forestall possible more coercive action by the state. It is not impossible that certain managers take action for ethical reasons. The role of civil society and international organizations in motivating firms to publish information on social and environmental matters is examined further in the next section.

(v) The state enacts a law that requires all firms to act, as it perceives that there is a consensus in society on this matter, made up of civil society and enlightened firms (who may be suffering from the competition of unenlightened firms and thus demand 'a level playing field').

The preceding analysis is highly simplified and omits elements that are important in certain countries, for example the role of semi-private rule-making bodies that are given a degree of official recognition. An example is Britain's Accounting Standards Board; its standards are not law in a formal sense, but are always followed by British companies, because the courts of law consider them to be evidence of what constitutes 'a true and fair view' which is a legal requirement. Also official regulatory bodies that have formal coercive powers often prefer to influence a firm's behaviour through persuasion and publicity. There is not a clear-cut 'black and white' distinction between purely voluntary actions on the one hand and mandated actions forced on the firm under pressure of legal sanctions on the other hand. Bebbington[10] comments: '[L]awyers regard regulation as a continuum with traditional "command and control" type regulation at one end and voluntary regulation through industry codes of conduct or agreements with regulators at the other.'

5.7.3 Firms' Voluntary Reporting: The KPMG Survey

Many firms voluntarily issue reports that supplement their regular financial statements. There is no consensus on the titles of these voluntary reports; typical titles are: 'Report to Society' of Anglo-American (UK), 'Corporate Social Responsibility Report' of Deutsche Bank (Germany) and John Lewis Partnership (UK), 'Corporate Citizenship Report' of Office Depot (USA), 'Corporate Responsibility Report' of the ING Group (Netherlands), Vodaphone (UK), and Sing Tel Optus (Australia), 'Global Citizenship Report' of Hewlett-Packard (USA), 'Corporate Sustainability Report' of Hess (USA), and 'Sustainability Report' of the Co-operative Group (UK) and Royal Dutch Shell (Netherlands). The terms that figure most frequently in the report titles are 'corporate responsibility' and 'sustainability'.

Do these reports contain information that is relevant for justice? Some information about such reports issued by firms in 2007–08 (mid-2007 to mid-2008) is provided by the KPMG International Survey of Corporate Responsibility Reporting.[11] KPMG surveyed over 2400 large companies, including the 250 largest multinationals (based on the Fortune Global 500) and the largest 100 companies in twenty-two industrialized countries (mainly in Europe and North America, but including Japan, Australia, South Africa, and South Korea). Seventy-nine percent of the global companies and 45% of the national companies issued stand-alone reports on 'corporate responsibility' which KPMG defined as 'the ethical, economic, environmental and social impacts and issues that concern the private sector'. Ideally, to appreciate the relevance of these reports for the assessment of justice, it would be necessary to undertake a detailed examination of a large representative sample. However, in this book, I have adopted a less laborious approach and left the full study of these reports to a younger researcher with more time and energy. My approach makes use of the fact that, according to the KPMG survey, 70% of the firms' reports were based on guidelines issued by an NGO (the Global Reporting Initiative). Hence an initial understanding of the relevance of these reports may be gained by an analysis of these guidelines, as presented in the next section.

5.8 THE GRI GUIDELINES

The Global Reporting Initiative is a non-governmental organization, whose objective is to promote sustainability reporting by companies. To this end, it has published detailed guidelines on the form and content of a sustainability report. As an NGO, the GRI does not have the authority to require firms to follow its guidelines, but, as demonstrated by the findings of the

KPMG survey, many companies in fact do so. In 2006, the GRI updated its guidelines and its current set is known as the 'G3 Guidelines'. This section presents a brief summary and analysis of these guidelines.[12] The reader should consult Appendix A for a fuller explanation and analysis.

5.8.1 Reporting Principles

Ten pages of the guidelines are taken up with defining and explaining the principles that the firm should follow in drawing up its sustainability report. Accountants will be familiar with most of these principles: materiality, completeness, balance, comparability, accuracy, timeliness, accuracy, and reliability. There are two principles that reflect the GRI's distinctive approach: sustainability context and stakeholder inclusiveness.

(a) Sustainability Context

The fundamental subject of the firm's report is sustainability. The GRI states that 'the underlying question of sustainability reporting is how an organization contributes, or aims to contribute in the future, to the improvement or deterioration of economic, environmental, and social conditions, developments and trends at the local, regional or global level'.[13] The concept of sustainability is derived from the Bruntland report, which defined the goal of sustainable development as 'to meet the needs of the present without compromising the ability of future generations to meet their own needs'.[14] A central idea is that the present mode of economic development is unsustainable in the long run and that, for mankind to survive and prosper, a radical change is necessary in man's behaviour and in the behaviour of firms. The GRI's chosen method for promoting this change is the diffusion of information. It considers that, if firms and those who deal with firms (such as consumers and governments) are provided with full information of the firms' impact on sustainability, then they will make the right decisions, that is, decisions that lead to sustainable development. Clearly the diffusion of information is not a sufficient condition for sustainable development, but arguably it is a necessary condition.

As is made clear in the preceding quotation, the concept of sustainability has three dimensions: the economic, the environmental, and the social. Of the three, the environment is the most crucial for sustainability. The principal reason why the present mode of economic development is unsustainable is because of its impact on the environment (particularly on climate change) and its using up of the earth's finite natural resources.

The reason that there is an economic dimension to sustainability is that the firm's conventional financial statements are inadequate as a measure of the firm's economic impact on others (for example they ignore externalities) and even of the long-term prospects of the firm itself (that is, the sustainability of the firm rather than of the planet). Therefore it is logical, when the firm prepares a report that supplements its regular financial statements, that this report should cover economic matters.

However, the relationship between sustainability and social conditions and trends is by no means obvious. Some commentators claim that only a society that is based on social justice is sustainable in the long run. This claim is at least contestable and, in my opinion, wholly false. In the past, many societies have survived and prospered for centuries despite incorporating extreme injustice. Examples are the Roman Empire, whose economy was based on slavery, and Feudal Europe with its great inequality between lord and serf. Hence, in my opinion, it is illogical to include a social dimension in the concept of sustainability. However, both the GRI and those who follow its advice do not agree with me! This is made clear in the GRI's definition of sustainability reporting as 'a broad term synonymous with others to describe reporting on economic, environmental and social impacts (e.g. triple bottom line, corporate responsibility reporting, etc.)'.[15]

The inclusion of a social element in sustainability means that the firm's sustainability report provides much information that is relevant for the assessment of justice. In my opinion, the social element of sustainability covers the same ground as social justice and hence distributive justice. The GRI is concerned about 'the continuing burden of poverty and hunger on millions of people'[16] primarily because these people are suffering from injustice—they are receiving an unjust share of the world's wealth. The GRI does not stress this point and, in its guidelines, makes no reference to 'justice'. However, it makes many references to rights, particularly those defined in international agreements. Thus it states that its proposals concerning the information that firms should provide on social performance 'are based on internationally recognised universal standards'[17], such as the United Nations Universal Declaration of Human Rights and the ILO Declaration on Fundamental Principles and Rights at Work. It would seem that the GRI justifies the inclusion of a social element in sustainability on the ground that these declarations demonstrate that there is a world-wide consensus on the importance of these rights. The basis of these rights is justice, and therefore the social element in sustainability is based on social justice and thus distributive justice.

Furthermore, there is a close relationship between the environmental dimension of sustainability and distributive justice. One aim of sustainable development is to check the degradation of the environment, which is a major cause of injustice suffered by secondary stakeholders.

The concepts of sustainability and distributive justice are not identical, but the differences are ones of emphasis and are not fundamental. For example, sustainability, as conceived by the GRI, gives relatively little attention to the division of the firm's revenue stream between its primary stakeholders. For example, the guidelines make no reference to a value-added statement or to a statement of distributions along the lines of Table 5.4. For the GRI, the division of the revenue stream becomes important only when the injustice suffered by certain stakeholders becomes conspicuously obvious, for example when workers in developing countries are paid starvation wages. But, in principle, the GRI accepts that the division of the firm's revenue stream is a factor in sustainability. Hence, for all practical purposes, sustainability and distributive justice may be considered to be congruent subjects. Information that is relevant for assessing sustainability will also be relevant for assessing distributive justice.

(b) Stakeholder Inclusiveness

The guidelines give considerable prominence to the firm's stakeholders, who are defined as 'entities or individuals that can reasonably be expected to be significantly affected by the organization's activities, products and/or services; and whose actions can reasonably be expected to affect the ability of the organization to successfully implement its strategies and achieve its objectives'.[18] This definition is consistent with that presented in Chapter 3 (Section 3.8) but is somewhat wider, as it includes terrorists and competitors.[19]

The guidelines' stakeholder emphasis may be explained by their origins. The GRI states that the guidelines 'are developed using a process that seeks consensus through dialogue between stakeholders from business, the investor community, labour, civil society, accounting, academia and others'.[20]

The guidelines refer to the role of the firm's stakeholders in three areas: the firm's impacts, stakeholder consultation, and the preparation of the sustainability report.

(i) The firm's impacts. According to the GRI, a major element of a sustainability report is the analysis of the impact of the firm's activities on stakeholders. When the GRI refers to reporting on 'the improvement or deterioration of economic, environmental and social conditions',[21] it is essentially referring to the impact on stakeholders. This is clearly true of the economic and social impact; it is also ultimately true of the environmental impact. Mankind is concerned about the impact of the firm's activities on the environment, because of their ultimate impact on people, including future generations, who are considered to be secondary stakeholders.

(ii) Stakeholder consultation. The GRI recommends that the firm 'should identify its stakeholders and explain in the report how it has responded to their reasonable expectations and interests'.[22] There is a basic assumption that the firm should engage with stakeholders in developing its sustainability strategy. Thus the firm should report on 'approaches to stakeholder engagement' and 'key topics and concerns that have been raised through stakeholder engagement, and how the organization has responded to these key topics'.[23] It seems very unlikely that a firm that followed the GRI guidelines would be comfortable with reporting that it refused to engage with stakeholders or that it consistently ignored their concerns. Hence a firm that follows the guidelines would normally subscribe at least to dialogue with stakeholders.

(iii) Preparation of the sustainability report. The firm's sustainability report should be prepared in collaboration with stakeholders. The guidelines state that 'the reasonable expectations and interests of stakeholders are a key reference point for many decisions in the preparation of a report'.[24] The firm's stakeholders are considered to be the report's principal recipients. In order that the report meets stakeholders' information needs, it should manifest the quality of transparency which is defined as 'the complete disclosure of information on the topics and indicators required to reflect impacts and enable stakeholders to make decisions'.[25]

5.8.2 The Report's Content

The guidelines define the contents of the firm's sustainability report in remarkable detail. About half of the guidelines' forty pages are taken up with their specification under two broad headings: context and performance.

(a)   Context

The report should include information on the firm's structure, management, and policies which should enable the reader to assess the extent to which the firm is committed to the goal of sustainable development and how it plans to achieve this goal. There are four sub-headings: strategy and analysis; organizational profile; report parameters; and governance. The guidelines specify over forty different points on which the firm should report. For some points, they ask for quite specific detail; for example, under the sub-heading 'governance', point 4.10 reads 'Processes for evaluating the highest governance body's own performance, particularly with respect to economic, environmental and social performance';[26] and point 4.14 reads 'List of stakeholder groups engaged by the organization'.[27] The information provided under these headings is primarily of a narrative nature, perhaps supplemented by diagrams.

(b)   Performance

This section provides information about the impact of the firm's activities on its stakeholders, analysed under three headings: economic, environmental, and social. Under each heading, the firm should provide a concise analysis of its management approach covering the organization's policies, strategy, and goals, together with an assessment of progress towards achieving its goals. In addition the firm should report its sustainability performance as measured by the GRI's 'performance indicators'.

The performance indicators are probably the guidelines' most interesting element. There are some eighty performance indicators. Some are wholly quantitative; an example is indicator EN16 'Total direct and indirect greenhouse gas emissions by weight'.[28] Some call for a mixture of quantitative and narrative information; for example indicator EC7 'Procedures for local hiring and proportion of senior management hired from the local community at locations of significant operation'.[29] Others have no quantitative content; an example is indicator LA9 'Health and safety topics covered in formal agreements with trade unions'.[30] As these examples demonstrate, most performance indicators are defined in quite specific detail. However there a few that are rather discursive; an example is indicator EC9 'Understanding and describing significant indirect economic impacts, including the extent of impacts'.[31]

In all, the guidelines call for the disclosure of a very substantial amount of information on over 120 different points: some 40 under 'context' and some 80 under 'performance'.

5.8.3 Analysis of Information on Employees

In this section, an analysis is made of the information content of the guidelines' provisions relating to a particular stakeholder category: employees. The aim is to assess whether the information required by the guidelines is sufficient to judge the impact of the firm's activities on employees. The guideline's relevant provisions are summarized in Table 5.5. In all, the firm should provide information on twenty points: one point relating to context and nineteen performance indicators (eleven quantitative and eight descriptive). For some points in Table 5.5, the GRI's text has been edited (indicated by . . .), but the table still gives a good impression of the amount of detail that the GRI demands. In respect of each point, the GRI provides further guidance in the form of a protocol, which is typically a single sheet that deals with such matters as definitions of terms.

The information required by the guidelines may be compared with the information that is needed to assess the justice experienced by employees (as discussed earlier in Section 5.6). Full details of this comparison are given in Appendix A. Its conclusions may be summarized as follows:

(i) A distinction may be drawn between information that is directly relevant for justice (in that it concerns a matter that is good or evil in itself) and information that is indirectly relevant (in that it signals a problem). An example of directly relevant information is that provided under indicator LA7 (rates of injury and death). Injury and death are evils in themselves. It is obvious that employees are experiencing grave injustice if, in the course of their work, they suffer high rates of injury and, a fortiori, death. An example of indirectly relevant information is that provided by indicator LA2 (rate of employment

Table 5.5 The GRI Guidelines' Points Relating to Employees

Context

4.4 Mechanisms for... employees to provide recommendations or direction to the highest governance body.

Include reference to processes regarding... informimg and consulting employees about the working relationships with formal representative bodies, such as... 'work councils'...

Quantitative performance indicators

EC5 Range of ratios of standard entry level wage compared to local minimum wage at significant locations of operation.

LA1 Total workforce by employment type, employment contract, and region

LA2 Total number and rate of employment turnover by age group, gender and region

LA4 Percentage of employees covered by collective bargaining agreements

LA5 Minimum notice period(s) regarding operational changes...

LA6 Percentage of total workforce represented in formal joint management-worker health and safety committees...

LA7 Rates of injury, occupational diseases, lost days, absenteeism and work-related fatalities by region.

LA10 Average hours of training per year per employee by employee category

LA12 Percentage of employees receiving regular performance and career development reviews

LA13 Composition of governance bodies and breakdown of employees... according to gender, age group, minority group...

LA14 Ratio of basic salary of men to women by employee category.

Descriptive performance indicators

LA3 Benefits provided to full-time employees that are not provided to temporary or part-time employees...

LA8 Education, training... programs to assist workforce members, their families... regarding serious diseases

LA9 Health and safety topics covered in formal agreements with trade unions

LA11 Programs... for life-long learning that support the continued employability of employees...

HR4 Total number of incidents of discrimination and action taken

HR5 Operations identified in which the right to exercise freedom of association and collective bargaining may be at significant risk, and actions taken to support these rights.

HR6 Operations identified as having significant risk for incidents of child labour and measures taken to contribute to the elimination of child labour.

HR7 Operations identified as having significant risk for incidents of forced or compulsory labour and measures taken to contribute to the elimination of forced or compulsory labour.

Source: GRI G3 Guidelines, © Global Reporting Initiative, page 27 for EC points, page 31 for LA points and page 33 for HR points

turnover). A high rate of worker turnover is not an evil in itself, but it may signal the existence of injustice; for example workers leave the firm because they feel that they are being treated unjustly.

(ii) Some points are only weakly relevant or hardly relevant at all. An example is LA12 'Percentage of employees receiving regular performance and career development reviews'.

(iii) Many of the guidelines' points are highly specific and ask for very narrowly defined information. An example is LA3 which requires that employee benefits need be disclosed only if they are different for part-time employees.

(iv) In some cases the GRI seems to be asking for a great deal of information about a rather minor matter. An example is LA8 for which the full text reads, 'Education, training, counseling, prevention, and risk control programs in place to assist workforce members, their families, or community members regarding serious diseases.'[32] The protocol for LA8 specifies the information to be reported in even greater detail. It asks for a 4×3 table that analyses the firm's programmes along two dimensions: nature of program (education/training, counseling, prevention/risk control, treatment) and recipients (workers, workers' families, and community members). With such a plethora of information, there is a distinct danger of the reader not being able to see the wood for the trees.

(v) Notwithstanding the considerable amount of information demanded, the guidelines do not cover all the information that the reader needs in order to assess the justice experienced by the firm's employees. Examples of matters that are not covered are working time, physical working conditions, and benefits in kind.[33]

The overall conclusion with respect to the firm's impact on employees is that the guidelines ask for a great deal of information, which is a curious hotchpotch of wide-ranging highly aggregated information (such as that required by indicator LA1 on employment statistics) and highly specific detailed information on a very limited topic, such as that demanded by indicator LA8, quoted previously in (iv) . But they neglect much other information of greater relevance. Hence it is concluded that the information provided by the guidelines is not sufficient to enable the reader to assess the justice (the social element of sustainability) of the firm's impact on its employees.

5.8.4 OVERALL ASSESSMENT OF THE GUIDELINES

After having read all forty pages of the guidelines and twenty pages of protocols, I am left with two rather inconsistent and contradictory impressions:

- The amount of information that the firm should provide is enormous—on well over a hundred different points

- It is by no means certain that the reader, after having absorbed all this information, would have a clear idea of the impact of the firm's activities on sustainable development and distributive justice. Perhaps the assessment of sustainability and justice is such a multi-faceted subject that it is virtually impossible to communicate to the reader all the information that she needs for a full understanding.

Which of these impressions is correct (or both or neither) is best established by the detailed analysis of an actual sustainability report that has been prepared in accordance with the guidelines. This is done in the next section, which presents an analysis of the sustainability report of the British Co-operative Group. This organization was chosen because of the excellent reputation of its sustainability reporting, as evidenced by the awards won by its reports. The Group's report for 2007/8 (analysed in the next section) was judged the runner-up in the ACCA's competition for the best sustainability report[34] and was judged by Corporate Register[35] to be the best report in the 'Openness and honesty' category.

5.9 THE SUSTAINABILITY REPORT OF THE CO-OPERATIVE GROUP

This section presents an analysis of the sustainability report of the British Co-operative Group. The aim of this analysis is to gain an insight into the practical problems of applying the GRI guidelines.

5.9.1 The Co-operative Group

The Co-operative Group (hereafter referred to as the Co-op) is a large commercial business with the legal form of an Industrial and Provident Society established under British law. The principal difference between the Co-op and a limited company is that, in the Co-op, the members, who elect the directors and receive dividends as their share of the firm's profits, are not the shareholders but the registered customers. Essentially the Co-op is managed for the benefit of its customers. The Co-op is organized in two groups: the Trading Group (food supermarkets, pharmacies, and travel agents) and the Finance Group (banking and insurance). Its business is largely confined to the United Kingdom. Its only foreign activities relate to its supply chain.

5.9.2 The Co-op's Sustainability Report

Each year since 2003, the Co-op has issued a printed sustainability report. This chapter presents an analysis of the report for the year 2007.[36] The full analysis is presented in Appendix B. Only a summary of this analysis and the principal conclusions are presented in this chapter.

The Co-op's sustainability report for 2007 is a massive document of 135 pages that contain well over 100,000 words. Table 5.6 presents an idea of the document's size and of the topics covered. There are five principal sections: an Introduction, a final section, and three sections that deal with the elements of the 'triple bottom line', entitled 'Social responsibility', 'Ecological responsibility', and 'Delivering value'.

(a) The Introduction

Full information on the contents of this section is given in Appendix B. Of particular interest is the statement on the Co-op's approach to reporting, which 'aims to provide a warts and all account of the Co-op's economic, social and environmental performance'.[37] It states that the Co-op engaged with stakeholders in designating the issues that are covered in the report and identified six classes of stakeholder, 'upon whom its continued success is, to varying degrees, dependent', being:

- Members: that is, registered customers, of whom 1.7 million are 'economically active' (who made purchases in the year) and 278,000 are 'democratically active' (such as voting in board elections).
- Customers: these are some 20 million customers, most of whom are not registered members and therefore do not have the right to receive dividends or to vote.
- Employees: numbering over 81,000.
- The co-operative movement: that is, other co-operative societies in Britain and abroad.
- Suppliers.
- Wider society: this 'encompasses the communities within which the Co-op trades, local governments and national governments, NGOs, industry organizations, multi-stakeholder groups, charities and external expert organizations'.

The Co-op's definition of 'stakeholder' is consistent with that presented in Chapter 3, on the assumption that bodies such as NGOs, charities, and external expert organizations are considered to represent secondary stakeholders.

(b) Social Responsibility

This is the largest section, with fifty-two pages. As demonstrated in Table 5.6, it covers a wide variety of topics, including human rights, animal welfare, and ethical finance.

Table 5.6   The Co-op Sustainability Report 2007/8

Number of pages per topic	
Introduction	
Chief executives' overviews	2
Sustainable development policy	1
Approach to reporting	1
Sustainable management	6
Sub-total	10
Social responsibility	
Approach to social responsibility	2
International development and human rights	13
Animal welfare	7
Diet and health	6
Ethical finance	8
Social inclusion	5
Diversity	6
Community investment	5
Sub-total	52
Ecological sustainability	
Approach to ecological sustainability	2
Climate change	13
Waste and packaging	7
Biodiversity	7
PBT chemicals	5
Sub-total	34
Delivering value	
Approach to delivering value	2
Modern co-operation	8
Economic impact	4
Employees	8
Customers	5
Public policy	5
Sub-total	32
Assurance and commentary	
Performance commentary	3

continued

Table 5.6   continued

Auditor's assurance statement	2
Reporting according to the GRI guidelines	2
Sub-total	7
Total number of pages	**135**

(c)   Ecological Responsibility

This is the second-longest section. The titles of its four sub-sections are given in Table 5.6. The longest sub-section, 'climate change', is considered further in Section 5.9.4 (d) .

(d)   Delivering Value

This section deals with the economic element of the triple bottom line. The sub-sections on employees and customers (the two most important stake-holder groups) are analysed later.

(e)   Final Section: Assurance and Commentary

This is a very short section, which however contains one of the most important elements of the Co-op's sustainability report—the statement of assurance. The reason why this statement is so important is discussed later.

5.9.3 The Co-op's Reporting on Employees

The Co-op's reporting on the impact of its activities on its employees is analysed in considerable detail in Appendix B under three aspects:

(a)   Compliance with the GRI Guidelines

The Co-op's report was scrutinized to check whether it contained all the information required by the GRI guidelines (as set out earlier in Section 5.8.3). It was concluded that the report contained most of the required information. For certain items, the Co-op stated that it did not currently report but would consider doing so in the future, thus displaying a positive attitude. It seems to be the GRI's policy that a firm is not obliged to report on a topic on which it does not collect data.

However, on two points, the Co-op stated that it did not report because the point was not material. For example, it gave this reason for not reporting on management-worker committees. In my opinion, the role that management-worker committees play in the governance of an organization is an important factor in assessing whether the firm respects the autonomy of its employees. Hence the information is material even if it is negative, for example that such committees do not play a material role. The GRI developed its guidelines in collaboration with the representatives of stakeholder groups. The Co-op in assessing that this information is not material is giving priority to its judgement over that of stakeholders. On point EC5 (ratio of the entry wage to the legal minimum wage), the Co-op answered 'not applicable', which seems to be wrong, as the UK's minimum wage law certainly applies to the Co-op's workers.

(b)   Additional Information

The Co-op's report gives some information on employees that is in addition to that required by the guidelines. Of particular interest are the results of surveys of employee opinion. Employees in the Trading Group were asked whether they agreed with the statement 'My pay is equal to or better than it would be for, similar jobs in other companies'; 40% answered 'disagree', rather more than those who answered 'agree'. They were also asked about benefits; to the question, 'The benefits I receive (pensions, holidays, etc.) are fair for the work I do', 65% answered 'agree'. These answers are clearly subjective, but, equally clearly they represent valid evidence of the employees' perception of the justice that they experience, which, for the complete picture, should be supplemented by more objective evidence, for example the ratio of the wage paid to the legal minimum wage (on which the Co-op does not report, in breach of the GRI guidelines).

(c)   Evaluation of the Co-op's Reporting on Employees

Does the Co-op provide sufficient information to enable the reader to judge the justice of the Group's treatment of its employees? The Co-op provides a reasonable proportion of the information prescribed by the GRI guidelines. However, as demonstrated by the earlier analysis in Section 5.8.3, this information is by no means sufficient for the assessment of justice; hence, even if the Co-op were to have complied fully with the guidelines, there would still be gaps. The Co-op has provided much information in addition to that required by the Guidelines. Much of this is certainly relevant for the assessment of justice. However, notwithstanding this additional information, there are still a number of important areas on which virtually no information is given, notably working time and physical working conditions.

However, even if information were to be provided on these missing matters, it is doubtful whether the reader would be able to assess the justice experienced by the Co-op's employees. The reason is that the assessment of justice is a highly complex matter. As argued previously in Section 5.6, this involves consideration of all the factors that bear on justice, balancing short-comings in one area against better treatment in others. Furthermore each employee's experience of justice is different. Clearly one cannot provide detailed information on each of the Co-op's 81,000 employees. A possible solution might be to divide the workforce into different categories such that all employees in a particular category experience roughly similar levels of justice. However this solution does not seem to solve the problem of complexity. For example, within the Co-op organization, one could divide employees according to their physical working conditions with separate categories for shop assistants, office workers, cleaners, drivers, farmers, bakery workers, and so on. Probably at least ten categories would be necessary. When account is taken of the necessity to draw up similar categories for all the other factors listed in Section 5.6, the number of different categories becomes unmanageable.

These comments should not be taken to imply that the information provided by the Co-op cannot be improved. That it is possible for a firm to provide much better information on employees (in terms both of quantity and of relevance) is demonstrated by the bilan social of French companies, which is the subject of Appendix C.

5.9.4 The Co-op's Reporting on Other Stakeholders

This section examines the reporting of the firm's impact on stakeholders other than employees.

(a)   Capital Providers

Share capital plays a very minor role in the financing of the Co-op: only £67.9 million compared to accumulated reserves of £3,831.3 million.[38] The members are not principally capital providers but customers. The extent to which the Co-op's sustainability reporting meets their information needs is considered under the next heading.

(b)   Customers

The printed report includes a five-page section entitled 'Customers'. There are three principal topics:

 (i) The Co-op's reputation with consumers in general: According to a survey of 4000 consumers carried out by a market research organization, the corporate reputation of the Co-op was slightly above the average for companies with a similar range of activities.
 (ii) Customer satisfaction. Some five hundred customers are surveyed each month to determine the level of customer satisfaction. Only 33%

of customers in the food business were 'very satisfied'; the percentages in other sectors (pharmacy, travel, and banking) were about double.

(iii) Complaints. Statistics are given for the number of complaints. The number seems enormous: in 2007, 175,000 in the food sector, up from 145,000 in the previous year. It is not obvious how to interpret this figure. It may represent improved efficiency on the part of the complaints department in advertising its services.

Presumably a customer who felt that she was not being treated justly would not declare that she was very satisfied, and therefore the index of customer satisfaction has some limited relevance for assessing the justice of the Co-op's impact on this stakeholder group. However it seems likely that the management's motive in collecting the data on customers mentioned earlier was not to assess justice but rather to help it run the business more efficiently.

(c)   Suppliers

Relations with suppliers are covered in several sections of the report, but there is no specific section devoted entirely to this topic. Of particular interest is the section entitled 'International development and human rights' which concerns the Co-op's efforts to ensure that its suppliers in foreign countries respect human rights. It contains a detailed table that lists the issues on which it engaged its suppliers in 2007. The list gives a good indication of the Co-op's concept of justice (and injustice); there are nine issues: 'exploitation of labour', 'freedom of association', 'a safe and hygienic working environment', 'child labour', 'living wages to be paid', 'working hours are not excessive', 'no discrimination', 'regular employment', and 'no harsh or inhuman treatment'. These issues are certainly central to the justice experienced by the employees of suppliers.

(d)   Other Secondary Stakeholders

The report contains a thirteen-page section on 'Climate change', which provides a very substantial amount of information on a number of topics. There is a plethora of statistics of which the most interesting are:

(i) In 2007, the Co-op's overall energy consumption was 9% less than in the previous year, indicating that the Co-op is on track to meeting its target of reducing overall energy consumption by 25% by 2012 (compared with 2006).

(ii) Ninety-nine percent of the electricity used by the Co-op comes from renewable sources: wind and hydro.

(iii) The Co-op generates much of the energy that it uses from its own renewable sources, principally wind turbines located on its farms. Its

target is to generate 15% of its energy requirements in this way by
2012.

(iv) Greenhouse gas emissions were 49% lower in 2007 compared with
2003. In part this reduction was achieved by phasing out old-fashioned refrigeration equipment.

In summary, this section of the report provides a good overview of the
impact of the Co-op's activities on climate change. Its principal deficiencies are that it does not deal systematically with the impact of firms in
its supply chain (other than its own production facilities). The impact of
other aspects of the Co-op's operations is not covered: for example, the
Group includes a chain of travel agencies, which surely contribute massively to global warming in recommending to their clients package holidays in far-flung places!

Another aspect of the Co-op's impact on secondary stakeholders is
dealt with in the section entitled 'Community investment', which deals
principally with cash payments to projects that serve the community,
totalling £8.3 million. The projects cover a bewildering range of objects:
examples are solar panels for schools, the integration of refugees, help
for the mentally ill, and support for a local theatre. Brief descriptions are
given of some half-dozen projects. The report provides a useful breakdown of this expenditure: 64% is classified as 'community investment'
(long-term strategic involvement in community partnerships to address
social issues) and 31% as 'commercial initiatives in the community'
(community activities that directly support the company and promote
its brand). This addresses the sceptical reader's concern that the firm
engages with local communities only for selfish commercial reasons.
This is clearly a factor in the 31% but presumably not for the 64%. In
addition to cash payments, there is an estimate of the value of employee
time spent on community projects (£1.5 million).

An example of 'community investment' is the grant of £4480 to a group
in Stockport 'that provides complementary therapies to adults who are
experiencing mental, physical or emotional ill-health'.[39] It would seem that
the motivation behind that grant was a sense of responsibility towards society and not to advance the Co-op's business. The people who benefitted
from this grant were certainly secondary stakeholders of the Co-op, in that
they were affected by the firm's activities—positively and not negatively, as
is more commonly the case.

5.9.5 COMMENTARY ON THE CO-OP'S REPORT

This analysis of the Co-op's Sustainability Report brings out very clearly a
number of important issues concerning the reporting of justice.

(a) Quantity of Information

The Co-op uses 135 pages and well over 100,000 words to report on its impact on sustainability. As demonstrated by Table 5.6, the report covers over twenty different topics. These data illustrate the complexity of the information that is relevant for the assessment of sustainability and justice. The Co-op tackles this problem by the simple expedient of providing a great quantity of information. However, notwithstanding this effort (which is certainly praiseworthy) there are still many topics that are covered inadequately (or not at all) in the Co-op report. An example is the balance of justice between employees, customers, and suppliers, which depends crucially on the level of the prices charged to customers and paid to suppliers.

In issuing such a long and wide-ranging report, the Co-op is using a 'scatter-gun' approach. It reports on a large number of different topics, in the hope that, among these topics, the reader will find the information that she needs. This is certainly one way in which a firm can provide the reader with (some of) the information that she needs to judge the sustainability and justice of the firm's activities. Yet, as indicated in the analysis of the information on employees presented previously in Section 5.9.3, the Co-op has by no means supplied all the information that the reader needs for a full assessment.

(b) Types of Information

In reporting on sustainability, the Co-op makes imaginative use of different types of information:

(i) Survey data. The Co-op made much use of survey data in two areas (employees and customers) as previously analysed in detail in Sections 5.9.3 and 5.9.4 (b). This is probably the most effective way of discovering other people's perception of the justice that they experience.

(ii) Quantitative data: Often statistics are the easiest way to communicate information. The Co-op makes good use of statistics in its review of its impact on climate change—see Section 5.9.4 (d). The statement that in 2007 greenhouse gas emissions were 49% lower compared with 2003 conveys, in one line, information that is of greater import and easier to appreciate than many paragraphs on how this was achieved (for example by replacing out-dated refrigeration equipment). The most convincing statistics are those relating to physical quantities that may be scientifically measured. Such statistics are presented in the report's sections on waste, biodiversity, and persistent, bio-accumulative, and toxic (PBT) chemicals. However, they are not available for most of the report's topics.

Data involving monetary values can be equally objective and relevant. Examples are the number of employees in each of five salary bands and the breakdown of the £8.3m donated to community projects.

(iii) Narrative. However most of the Co-op's report is taken up with narrative. Quantitative data simply does not exist on many topics and, where it does, it needs to be backed up by narrative. An example is the Co-op's support of community projects mentioned in the previous paragraph. In order that the reader gains a fuller understanding of the impact of this expenditure, she needs more information on the actual projects. The report supplies this with descriptions of some half-a-dozen projects. The descriptions are very short (generally less than a hundred words) so they do little more than give a flavour of the project's character; and they cover only a tiny proportion of the total number of projects supported (over two thousand). But, in the space available in a 135-page report, this is best that can be done, and they certainly add to the reader's understanding of the impact of this aspect of the Co-op's activities.

(c) Assurance

In accordance with the GRI guidelines, the Co-op's report includes a statement of assurance. This statement has a very clear and very important function: it adds credibility to the report. It should be noted that the report is prepared by the Co-op's employees under the supervision of the Co-op's managers. They both choose the topics on which to report and decide what to report and (perhaps more importantly) what not to report on each topic. The skeptical reader may worry that the Co-op, in choosing topics, reports only on those which reflect favourably on the organization whilst suppressing 'bad news'. Furthermore, how is the reader to be sure that the information provided on a topic has not been 'massaged' or even falsified? The function of the assurance statement is to reassure the reader on these points—that the report gives a complete and correct picture (or, to put it in the words beloved of accountants, the report gives a true and fair view) of the Co-op's impact on sustainability and justice.

The function of the assurance statement on the sustainability report is essentially the same as that of the auditor's report on the financial statements. They both should convert documents over which the sceptical reader has doubts (principally because they were prepared by the firm itself) into one whose information may be relied upon. However, in my opinion, the assurance statement attached to the sustainability report does not add the same degree of credibility to that report as the auditor's report does to the financial statements—for two reasons:

(i) The organization that provided the sustainability report's assurance statement (csrnetwork) does not have the same reputation for competence and integrity as does the accounting firm that audited the financial statements (KPMG Audit Plc). There is not the slightest evidence that csrnetwork is incompetent or dishonest. However it was founded only in 1999 and, according to its web-site,[40] has been providing assurance services only since 2003. This should be compared with the over one hundred years of audit experience of the accounting firms that merged to make up KMPG. It takes decades of error free work for a firm to build up the reputation that ensures that its signature on a document transforms it from a worthless piece of paper into one that the reader can trust. Csrnetwork has not been in the business long enough to build up such a reputation.

(ii) The size of csrnetwork's fee seems too low for the amount of work that would be necessary to verify all the information in the Co-op's report so as to provide adequate assurance. Csrnetwork's fee of £66,000 should be compared with KPMG's fee of £1,390,000 for the audit of the financial statements,[41] which is over twenty times higher—despite the fact that sustainability report contains more information on a greater variety of topics compared with the financial statements.

5.9.6 Evaluation of the Co-op's Report

My overall conclusion is that, with its sustainability report, the Co-op has made a creditable and praiseworthy effort to provide relevant and useful information in a very new field in which it has still a great deal to learn on how to report most effectively. However, the analysis both of the GRI guidelines and of the Co-op's report has confirmed my initial suspicion that justice is such a complicated and multi-faceted subject that to provide the reader with all the information that she needs for its assessment requires a report of extraordinary length and complexity.

5.10 THE REPORTING FUNCTION: SUMMARY AND CONCLUSIONS

The financial statements perform the reporting function when their task is limited to reporting past facts. At present, the conventional financial statements do not report adequately distributions to stakeholders. To remedy this deficiency, it is suggested that the firm should issue a full statement of distributions (following the model in Table 5.4). However such a statement is considered to be inadequate for three reasons:

(i) It does not cover the aspects of justice that are not expressed in terms of money, such as the working conditions of employees.

(ii)   It does not cover the firm's external costs, such as the harm inflicted on others by pollution emanating from the firm.
(iii) It does not include an evaluation of the justice of the firm's activities.

It is argued that it is not feasible to remedy these defects by reforming the financial statements, for example by reporting social costs or by denominating them in 'utils'. Fuller information on the justice of the firm's activities should be provided by special reports which supplement the conventional financial statements.

The current practice of firms with respect to such special reports is examined, with particular attention to sustainability reports prepared in accordance with the GRI guidelines. An analysis of these guidelines and of a report based on them (of the Co-operative Group) shows that the reporting of justice is an extremely complex subject. There is no consensus on the topics that should be covered in such a report; the Co-op report covered over twenty topics in 135 pages, but even with this extended coverage, it could be argued that not all important matters were included. Justice may be such a complex and multi-faceted subject that to deal with it adequately requires a report of inordinate length and detail. The strong impression left by this limited examination of current practice is that firms have not yet found a satisfactory method of reporting on justice.

What should be the future role of accountants in the reporting the justice of the firm's activities? One can conceive of three rather different roles:

(i)   The accountant would limit her responsibility to the conventional financial statements, as presently conceived, with one simple addition: a full statement of distributions modelled on Table 5.4.
(ii)   The accountant would co-operate with experts in other fields (such specialists on climate change) in preparing a comprehensive report that covered all aspects of justice. This is essentially the approach being taken by the firms whose special reports are the subjects of the KPMG survey mentioned in Section 5.7.3. The accountant could take the lead in co-ordinating the work of the other experts or could limit her contribution to the financial aspects of justice, which lie within her core competencies.
(iii) The accountancy profession would seek to develop ways in which justice may be measured in quantitative terms—for example to prepare statements expressed in social costs or denominated in 'utils'—an approach that was rejected in this chapter as being too difficult.

Personally I am rather pessimistic. I feel that justice is such a profound and multi-faceted subject that to treat it adequately requires a report of quite extraordinary length and complexity. Both the accountancy profession and business firms have still a long way to go before they develop a practical and effective way of reporting justice.

APPENDIX A: GRI SUSTAINABILITY REPORTS

A.1 The Global Reporting Initiative and Sustainability

The Global Reporting Initiative (GRI) is an independent NGO (non-governmental organization). It was formed in 1997 by CERES (an American NGO) in close association with the United Nations Environmental Programme (UNEP); thus initially it was a partnership of the two elements that, according to the analysis presented in chapter 5, section 5.7.2, have been most influential in moulding firms' reporting behaviour: NGOs and international organizations. However the GRI became a fully independent body in 2002.

Its objective is to promote sustainable development. It follows the Bruntland Report in defining the goal of sustainable development as to 'meet the needs of the present without compromising the ability of future generations to meet their own needs'[1]. A central idea is that the present mode of economic development is unsustainable in the long run and that a radical change is necessary in mankind's behaviour and particularly in the behavior of firms.

The principal method by which the GRI seeks to achieve its aim of sustainable development is the diffusion of information. It believes that, if the managers of firms and those who deal with firms (such as consumers and governments) are provided with information about the firm's impact on sustainability, then they will make the right decisions, that is decisions that are more likely to lead to sustainable development. It is perhaps optimistic to assume that good information is a sufficient condition for sustainable development, but there is a good case for arguing that it is a necessary condition. This is the GRI's justification for its efforts to get firms to publish a sustainability report.

A.2. The GRI Guidelines

The GRI has issued guidelines on the form and content of a firm's sustainability report. The latest version of these guidelines, known as the GRI G3 Guidelines, was issued in 2006[2]. According to the guidelines, 'a sustainability report ... should provide a balanced and reasonable representation of the sustainability performance of the reporting organization'.[3]

The guidelines cover some forty pages, consisting of two parts: Part 1: Reporting principles and Part 2: Standard disclosures.

A.2.1. Reporting Principles

Most of these principles are familiar to accountants: materiality, completeness, balance, comparability, clarity, accuracy, timeliness and reliability.

However there are two that are specific to the GRI's distinctive approach: Sustainability context and stakeholder inclusiveness.

1. Sustainability context: The fundamental subject of the report is sustainability. The firm's report should present the organization's performance in the wider context of sustainability—'how the organization contributes or aims to contribute to the improvement or deterioration of economic, environmental and social trends at the local, regional or global level[4]'.
2. Stakeholder inclusiveness: The GRI states that the guidelines were developed in collaboration with representatives of stakeholder groups. Hence it is not surprising that there is a strong emphasis on the role and importance of stakeholders. According to the guidelines, the firm should take into account the interests and expectations of stakeholders, both in developing its sustainability strategy and in reporting on it. Stakeholders are defined as 'entities or individuals that can reasonably be expected to be significantly affected by the organization's activities, products, and/or services; and whose actions can be reasonably be expected to affect the ability of the organization to successfully implement its strategies and achieve its objectives.'[5] This is a wider definition of stakeholder than that presented in chapter 3, section 3.8[6], and, in the case of a multinational company with widespread operations may be construed as embracing millions of people. The GRI considers that one of the main purposes of a sustainability report is to provide information to stakeholders and it urges firms to respect the principle of transparency which it defines as 'the complete disclosure of information on the topics and indicators required to reflect [economic, environmental and social] impacts and enable stakeholders to make decisions'[7]. It states that, in its report, a firm should identify its stakeholders and explain how it has responded to their reasonable expectations and interests. In principle, according to the GRI guidelines, the sustainability report should be prepared by the firm in consultation with stakeholders.

A.2.2. Standard Disclosures

Part 2 of the guidelines defines the content of the sustainability report. What the firm should report is specified under two broad headings: context and performance.

(a) Context:

This section provides information about the firm's structure, management and policies, which hopefully enables the reader to assess the extent to which the firm is committed to the goal of sustainable development and to learn how the firm seeks to achieve this goal. There are four principal sub-headings:

(i) Strategy and analysis: The firm should provide two narrative sections, the first on the firm's impacts on sustainability with particular reference to how it plans to address any problems and the second on the impact on financial stakeholders.

(ii) Organizational profile: A brief description of the firm, covering such matters as its legal form, its ownership structure, its operational structure, its principal assets, revenues and costs.

(iii) Report parameters: In addition to such formal matters as the period covered by the report and the entities included, this also covers assurance: the extent to which an external body has provided assurance as to the report's accuracy and relevance.

(iv) Governance: This covers principally how the firm is governed and, in particular, how the firm's management interacts with stakeholders. The report should clarify the processes in place for consulting stakeholders, concerning both the firm's general policies and, more narrowly, the preparation of the sustainability report. In principle the stakeholders should collaborate with the firm in preparing the report.

The guidelines define in considerable detail what should be reported under each heading. In total, the firm should provide information on 42 different points.

(b) Performance

This section provides information about the impact of the firm's activities on its stakeholders, analysed under three headings: economic, environmental and social. Under each heading, the firm should provide a concise analysis of its management approach covering the organization's policies, strategy and goals, together with an assessment of progress towards achieving its goals. In addition the firm should report its sustainability performance as measured by the GRI's 'performance indicators', which are defined in considerable detail in the GRI's guidelines and associated protocols.

(i) Economic performance: This covers the information that the firm should provide on its economic performance, which covers 'the organization's impact on the economic conditions of its stakeholders and on economic systems at local, national and global levels'[8]. It should provide information on nine performance indicators. The first covers the distribution of the firm's income; it reads: 'Direct economic value generated and distributed, including revenues, operating costs, employee compensation, donations and other community investments, retained earnings, and payments to capital providers and governments.'[9] This is the guidelines' sole reference to distributions. Other performance indicators ask for a surprising degree of detail. For example, indicator EC7 reads: 'Procedures for local hiring and proportion of senior management hired from the local community at locations of significant operation'. Others are rather more discursive; for example indicator EC9: 'Understanding and describing significant indirect economic benefits, including the extent of impacts'.

(ii) Environmental performance: This covers the impact of the firm's activities on the environment, covering the 'organization's impacts on living and non-living natural systems, including ecosystems, land, air and water'. Information should be provided on no less than 30 performance indicators. Many are quite detailed, for example indicator EN16 'Total direct and indirect greenhouse gas emissions by weight'[10], indicator EN23 'Total number and volume of significant spills' and point EN28 'Monetary value of significant fines and total number of non-monetary sanctions for non-compliance with environmental laws and regulations'.

(iii) Social performance: According to the guidelines, 'the social dimension of sustainability concerns the impacts an organization has on the social systems within which it operates'[11]. The firm should provide information under four sub-headings: labour practices, human rights, society and product responsibility. Two of these sub-headings relate to specific primary stakeholders (employees and customers), one (society) to secondary stakeholders in general and one (human rights) applies to all stakeholders.

- Labour practices: This section of the guidelines is analysed in detail in the next section.
- Human rights: The firm should report on 'the extent to which human rights are considered in investment and supplier/contractor selection practices'[12] and also with respect to its labour force. There are nine performance indicators, covering such matters as information on violations of the rights of indigenous peoples.
- Society: There are eight performance indicators, which 'focus attention on the impacts organizations have on the communities in which they operate.'[13] There are eight performance indicators, covering such matters as corruption and contributions to political parties.
- Product responsibility: This covers 'the aspects of a reporting organization's products and services that directly affect customers'[14]. There are nine performance indicators covering such matters as health and safety impacts of products and amount of fines for non-compliance with laws concerning the provision and use of products.

Overall the guidelines specify 79 performance indicators on which the firm should provide report. Together with the 42 points defined under 'context', the firm has to provide information on no less than 121 different points. To gain a clearer insight into the degree of detail set out in the guidelines and into their relevance for justice, the next section analyses the guidelines' treatment of one specific topic: the firm's impact on its employees.

A.3 The Impact on Employees

According to the GRI, the firm should report on the impact of its activities on its stakeholders. A very important group of stakeholders are the employees. In this section, the guidelines' provisions relating to reporting the impact on employees are analysed in detail with a view to gaining an insight as to whether they cover all important matters in a comprehensive manner.

The guidelines deal with the relations between the firm and its employees principally under the sub-heading 'labour practices'; however some of the information specified under the sub-headings 'economic performance' and 'human rights' is also relevant. The preamble to the section on 'labour practices' refers specifically to 'internationally recognized universal standards' embodied in various declarations of the United Nations and associated bodies, notably[15]:

- The United Nations Universal Declaration of Human Rights;
- The United Nations Convention: International Covenant on Civil and Political Rights;
- The United Nations Convention: International Covenant on Economic, Social and Cultural Rights;
- The ILO Declaration on Fundamental Principles and Rights at Work;
- The ILO Tripartite Declaration concerning multinational enterprises and social policy;
- The OECD's Guidelines for Multinational Enterprises.

These references offer a clue as to the GRI's reasons for including a social dimension in its concept of sustainability. These declarations are evidence that there is a world-wide consensus on the rights of employees and provide a justification for the GRI's efforts to induce firms to report on how well they have respected these rights.

Table 5.5 sets out the guidelines' text that specifies the information that the firm should provide of its impact on its employees. In some cases the GRI's text has been edited (indicated by . . .). However, the text as presented, still gives a good impression of the nature and quantity of the information that the GRI demands. There are twenty points, being one under 'context' and nineteen performance indicators, of which fourteen relate to 'labour practices' (prefix LA), one to 'economic performance' (prefix EC) and four to 'human rights' (prefix HR). Eight of the performance indicators are largely descriptive and the remaining eleven primarily or wholly quantitative.

(a) Quantitative Performance Indicators

The text of the eleven quantitative performance indicators is presented in table 5.5. They may be analysed into five groups:

(i) Employment statistics: EC5, LA1 and LA2. These performance indicators provide information that is certainly highly relevant for the assessment of social justice. The reader's doubts about the justice of the firm's treatment of its employees would be greater the lower the ratio of the entry level wage to the legal minimum wage (EC5), the higher the proportion of workers on temporary contracts (LA1) and the higher the employment turnover (LA2). These statistics are in no sense a definite measure of justice or injustice; their relevance is that they may signal a problem that needs further investigation.

(ii) Employee relations: LA4, LA5 and LA6. These performance indicators were probably included in the GRI guidelines in response to the demands of organizations representing employees, such as trade unions. The information that they provide gives a good indication of whether the company is serious about treating its employees as human beings whose interests should be respected.

(iii) Health and safety: LA7. This information seems absolutely essential for an assessment of social justice. There is a strong presumption that a firm is not treating its employees justly when they suffer high rates of disease, injuries and death. Unlike certain other statistics presented here (for example LA5 on collective agreements), those on disease and injuries refer to something that is definitely an evil. The reader is certain that a higher level of injuries represents a greater injustice than a lower level. However the reader needs a point of reference to decide the level of the injustice.

(iv) Training: LA10 and LA12: These cover matters whose impact on justice seems to be slight.

(v) Discrimination. LA13 and LA14. For the reader who considers that discrimination by gender, age or race is a grave social evil, these points provide highly relevant information on the firm's actions (as opposed to rhetoric) in this matter.

Some performance indicators call for very specific information. Thus the full text of LA6 reads: 'Percentage of total workforce represented in formal joint management-worker health and safety committees that help monitor and advise on occupational health and safety programs.'[16]

This analysis suggests that the GRI's eleven quantitative performance indicators vary significantly in their relevance for social justice: some are strongly and directly relevant (LA7 on rates of injury and disease); some are strongly relevant but indirectly as they may signal a problem (LA2 on turnover) and some are only weakly relevant.

(b) Descriptive Performance Indicators

The text of the eight descriptive performance indicators is also presented in table 5.5

(i) Labour practices: The wording of all four labour performance indicators is highly specific. For example, LA8 reads: 'Education, training, counseling, prevention, and risk-control programs in place to assist workforce members, their families, or community members regarding serious diseases'.

One has the impression that the GRI is asking firms to provide a great deal of information on four rather minor points, whose relevance for the assessment of justice is marginal Furthermore, within the four chosen topics, only certain information has to be given; thus employee benefits are covered only if they are different for full-time workers, and education programs are described only in so far as they cover serious diseases.

(ii) Human rights. In contrast to the position with labour practices, the four human rights performance indicators deal with matters that are absolutely central to justice: discrimination, freedom of association, child labour and forced labour.

(c) Protocols

For each of the nineteen performance indicators listed in table 5.5, the GRI provides further guidance in the form of a 'protocol'. This is typically a single sheet which gives information on such matters as definitions. For example, the protocol for LA3 defines 'benefits' as including life insurance, health care, disability/invalidity coverage, maternity/paternity leave, retirement provision and stock ownership. In-kind benefits such as provision of sports or child day care facilities, free meals and similar general employee welfare programmes are excluded. The principal value of these protocols would seem to be that they assure a degree of consistency in the information reported by different firms.

(d) Evaluation of Coverage

Do the GRI performance indicators provide for adequate coverage of employment matters? In order to assess their adequacy, it is necessary to establish the total information that one would need for the assessment of the justice of a firm's actions in relation to its employees. This has been done in Chapter 5 (section 5.6.3), which concludes that, in order to evaluate the justice experienced by employees, it would be necessary to have information on the following points:

- Monetary rewards
- Benefits in kind
- Working time
- Working conditions
- Security of employment
- Respect of the autonomy of the employee

On almost all the points in the above list, the GRI Guidelines require the firm to provide some information. The exceptions are benefits in kind and working time. However, in every case, the information demanded is incomplete. For example, there is no analysis of remuneration by employee category, and information on other benefits is required only when they are different for full-time and part-time employees. In some cases, the GRI asks for information that may signal the existence of a problem, rather than describe the actual problem. An example is the rate of employee turnover (point LA2); if this is abnormally high, there is a suspicion that the firm is not treating its employees fairly. The information required by the GRI guidelines on employment is in no way sufficient for the assessment of sustainability and justice; it is a hotch-potch of wide-ranging, highly aggregated information (such as that required by LA1 on employment statistics) and highly specific information on a very limited topic, of which LA8 (which is quoted in full in a previous paragraph) is a good example. The protocol for LA8 specifies the information to be reported in even greater detail. It asks for a 4x3 table that analyses the firm's programmes along two dimensions: nature of programme (education/training; counseling; prevention/risk control; treatment) and recipients (workers; workers' families; community members). With such a plethora of information, there is a distinct danger of the reader not being able to see the wood for the trees.

A.4 OVERALL EVALUATION OF THE GRI GUIDELINES

The analysis of the guidelines on employment has shown that the information demanded is not sufficient to assess the sustainability of a firm's activities in this field. However, the GRI is confronted with a dilemma: it can ask firms to provide sketchy information on a full range of topics or to provide full information on a narrow range of topics. It would seem that it is, in practice, impossible for a firm to provide full information on a full range of topics.

After reading all forty pages of the GRI's guidelines and twenty pages of protocols, I am left with two rather inconsistent and contradictory impressions:

- The information that the firm should publish is enormous—on well over a hundred different points.
- It is no means certain that the reader, after having absorbed all the information required by the guidelines, would have a clear idea of the impact of the firm's activities on sustainable development and (and even more problematically) on distributive justice. Perhaps the impact of the firm on sustainability is such a multi-faceted subject that it is virtually impossible to communicate to the reader all the information that she might consider necessary for a full understanding.

Which of these impressions is correct (or both or neither) is best established by a detailed analysis of an actual sustainability report that has been drawn up in accordance with the guidelines. Annex B presents an analysis of the sustainability report of the British Co-operative Group. This organization was chosen because of the excellent reputation of its sustainability reporting, as evidenced by the awards won by its reports. The Group's report for 2007/8 (analysed in Annex B) was judged to be the runner-up in the ACCA's competition for the best sustainability report[17]; and was judged by CorporateRegister[18] to be the best report in the 'Openness and honesty' category.

APPENDIX B: ANALYSIS OF THE CO-OP'S SUSTAINABILITY REPORT

B.1 The Co-operative Group

The Co-operative Group (hereafter referred to as 'the Co-op') is a large commercial business organized on co-operative lines. Its legal form is that of an Industrial and Provident Society established under British law; formally it is owned by its 1,700,000 members[1]. It has 81,000 employees, which puts it among the top twenty British companies as measured by size of work-force. It is organized into two sub-groups: the Trading Group whose principal activity is retailing (food super-markets, pharmacies and travel agencies) and the Finance Group which provides financial services (banking and insurance). The Trading Group also has some production facilities: farms and food processing plants. Almost all its business is carried on in Britain; its only foreign activities relate to its supply chain.

The Co-op is controlled and operated for the benefit of its members. However, in a co-operative, the term 'member' does not have the same meaning as with a limited company. In a company, the members are its shareholders but, for the Co-op, the members are its registered customers. Both the Co-op and a limited company report a profit out of which they pay dividends to members. However, at the Co-op, the amount of the dividend is calculated on the basis of the amount of members' purchases, whereas in a limited company, the amount of the dividend paid to a member is based on the number of shares held. The Co-op's balance sheet reports a tiny amount of share capital (£67.9 million) compared to reserves of £3,831.3 million. The Co-op's shareholders are not paid dividends (they are paid a fixed rate of interest) and have no voting rights. The Co-op is controlled by its registered members (customers), who elect the members of the Board of Directors, who in turn appoint the executives who actually manage the firm. The Co-op's two tier structure is not unlike that of a German Aktiengesellschaft.

B.2 The Co-op's Printed Sustainability Report

The Co-op provides information about sustainability both in the form of a printed report and on its web-site: www.co-operative.coop/corporate/sustainability (covered in the next section).

The printed sustainability report for the year 2007, entitled 'The Co-operative Sustainability Report'[2], is a massive document. Table 5.6 presents a list of the reports contents, together with the count of the number of pages given to each subject. There are approximately one thousand words per page; taking into account the space taken up with pictures, diagrams and tables, I estimate that the report contains well over one hundred thousand words. Whether these words convey much useful and relevant information will now be considered.

The report is divided into five principal parts: an Introduction, three specialized sections (covering the three elements of the triple bottom line) entitled, 'Social responsibility', 'Ecological sustainability' and 'Delivering value', plus a final section 'Assurance and commentary'. .

(a) Introduction

This consists of ten pages covering the following topics:

(i)   Statements of the joint chief executives on the Co-op's policy for sustainability. Such a statement is a specific requirement of the GRI guidelines.

(ii) A statement on the approach to reporting, which 'aims to provide a warts and all account of the Co-op's economic, social and environmental performance'[3]. It states that the Co-op engaged with stakeholders in designating the issues that are covered in the report and identified six classes of stakeholder, 'upon whom its continued success is, to varying degrees, dependent', being:

- Members: that is registered customers, of whom 1.7 million are 'economically active' (who made purchases in the year) and 278,000 are 'democratically active' (such as voting in board elections).
- Customers: these are some 20 million customers, most of whom are not registered members and therefore do not have the right to receive dividends or to vote.
- Employees: numbering over 81,000
- The co-operative movement: that is other co-operative societies in Britain and abroad.
- Suppliers
- Wider society: this 'encompasses the communities within which the Co-op trades, local governments and national governments, NGOs, industry organizations, multi-stakeholder groups, charities and external expert organizations.'

The Co-op's definition of 'stakeholder' is consistent with that presented in chapter 3, on the assumption that bodies such as NGOs, charities and external expert organizations are considered to represent secondary stakeholders.

(iii) Six pages entitled 'Sustainability management': This refers to a 'balanced scorecard', a concept not unlike the triple bottom line, which measures the group's success under three headings: Commercial success, Social goals and Competitive advantage. One of the elements of commercial success is 'Growing profit', which confirms that, at least in this respect, the Co-op is not all that different from a commercial company. There is a reference to the 'Values and Principles Committee', a senior committee of the Group Board, which has endorsed the Co-op's social goals strategy, which refers specifically to sustainable development. According to this strategy, 'no business can lead in every aspect of sustainable development and . . . issues need to be prioritized and resources focused'. Hence the environment is singled out as a primary issue, with other important areas being international development, community involvement, tackling crime and food ethics. Of particular interest is the attention given to reporting; there is reference to 'the need for the Group to improve the quality of its sustainability accounting, auditing and reporting'.

(b) Social Responsibility

This is the largest section, taking up 52 pages. It covers a wide range of rather diverse issues. There are seven sub-sections:

 (i) International development and human rights. This is largely concerned with ethical issues in the supply chain.
 (ii) Animal welfare. This subject and the next one were given priority following a poll of over 100,000 members on the ethical policy of the Co-op's Food division.
(iii) Diet and health. This concerns principally the composition and labeling of food products sold in the Co-op's supermarkets.
(iv) Ethical finance. The prominence given to this subject reflects the important position of the Co-operative Bank and the Co-operative Insurance within the Co-operative Group. One of the subjects covered is business (for example loans) refused on ethical grounds.
 (v) Social inclusion. This covers the Co-op's actions in relation to the most disadvantaged groups in society, such as the location of shops in deprived areas and offering banking services to prisoners.
(vi) Diversity. This consists largely of an analysis of the composition of the workforce by age, gender, ethnicity and disability
(vii) Community investment. This covers donations to projects working in the community. It also includes an estimate of the hours spent by employees on voluntary work.

(c) Ecological Sustainability

This is the second longest section with 34 pages. It consists of four subsections:

 (i) Climate change: This is covered in detail in section B5 (d) below
 (ii) Waste and packaging. This section reveals that the retail sector is the largest producer of industrial and commercial waste in Britain. The Co-op has set up a waste accounting scheme which provides a reasonably accurate account of waste arising in the majority of the Co-op's businesses. Unfortunately this system reveals that in recent years there has been an increase in the absolute level of waste generated, although there has been a slight decrease in waste per £m of turnover.
(iii) Bio-diversity. This covers largely the Co-op's procurement policy relating to fish, wood and peat, with the aim of preserving bio-diversity.
(iv) Persistent, bio-accumulative and toxic (PBT) chemicals. This concerns the Co-op's actions to limit the presence of these chemicals in the goods it sells.

(d) Delivering Value

This section deals principally with employees and customers. Its title reflects the different approach to business of a co-operative compared to a commercial company. The objective of both is to maximize the welfare of their members; in the case of a company, this implies maximizing profits;

in the case of the Co-op, this implies maximizing the value received by its registered customers, which implies that there is no conflict between providing value for money for customers and earning a profit (from which the customers will also benefit through their dividend). The inclusion of employees in this section reflects the strong tradition in the co-operative movement that employees are partners and not simply factors of production. In this section, there are five sub-sections:

(i)   Modern co-operation. This concerns relations with other co-operative societies, who are considered to be important stakeholders.
(ii) Economic impact. This covers much the same ground as the separate financial statements[4], including analyses of sales by business segment and by region. However it includes a crude value added statement, which is not to be found in the financial statements.
(iii) Employees. This is dealt with in detail in section B.4 below.
(iv) Customers. This is dealt with in detail in section B.5 (b) below
(v)   Public policy. This covers the Co-op's lobbying activities and its political donations. The Group is closely associated with a political party, the Co-operative Party, which it supports financially.

(e) Assurance and Commentary

This consists of a two page commentary by Jonathan Porritt, a well-known figure in the ecological movement in Britain and a two page 'Auditor's Assurance Statement' from csrnetwork, an organization that specializes in providing such statements. This assurance statement seems to be vulnerable to two criticisms:

- The fee paid to the auditors (£66,000) seems inadequate to cover the work necessary for a thorough verification of all the information in the report. The fee paid to the Co-operative Group's auditors (KPMG Audit Plc) for the audit of the 2007 annual accounts was £1.39 million, over twenty times higher.
- The assurance statement is full of praise for the Co-op; typical examples are 'the Group's overall carbon performance is impressive', and 'its lobbying on climate change demonstrating strong leadership'. This praise tends to undermine the statement's credibility. The whole issue of credibility is discussed more thoroughly in section B.6 (c) below and in chapter 5 (section 5.9.5).

However, in one important respect, the Co-op's assurance statement is to be commended. It sets out clearly the auditor's opinion: 'Our overall opinion is that the report is a fair and balanced description of the Group's impacts during 2007 and it meets the GRI B+ level'[5]. Also the auditor's statement includes details of the audit work performed, for example, 'review of the processes for gathering and ensuring the accuracy of data', and 'detailed verification of key data and claims made in the report, through meetings with managers in the Social Goals team responsible for gathering data'. These statements add to the reader's confidence that the auditor has performed a workmanlike job.

B.3 The Co-op's Web-site

The Co-op's Sustainability Report is also available on its web-site, but it is not necessary to go to the web-site for the greater part of the information required by the GRI guidelines. This is demonstrated in a table that shows where the information specified under each of GRI's 121 points is to be found[6]: most of the points are covered in the printed report, some in the annual accounts, a few on the web-site and a few are not covered. Hence, with the Co-op, the web-site is not significant source of information on sustainability.

B.4 The Co-op's Reporting on Employees

According to the GRI, the firm should report on the impact of its activities on its stakeholders. This section presents an analysis of the Co-op's reporting of its impact on its employees, a very important stakeholder category. The information in the Co-op's report falls into two categories:

- Information required by the GRI guidelines
- Additional information

(a) Information Required by the GRI Guidelines

The guidelines' information requirements relating to employees are analysed in section A.3 of Annex A, and summarized in table 5.5.

In its report, the Co-op rates the information that it provides under each of the Guidelines' 121 points (not just those relating to employees) using five levels: 'full reporting'; 'partial reporting'; 'don't report, will consider', 'don't report, not material' and 'not applicable'.

I have examined the information that the Co-op provides under each of the GRI's twenty points, (see table 5.5) with a view to assessing the validity of the Co-op's own rating.

(i) 4.4 (Governance mechanisms). The Co-op report gives full information on the mechanisms by which *members* can participate in governance, but virtually no information about the involvement of *employees*. In this area, there seems to be important differences between the Finance Group (Co-op Financial Services (CFS), which employs some 8,000 people) and the Trading Group (which employs some 73,000 people. 63% of CFS employees are members of trade unions, whereas the equivalent figure for the trading group is only 33%. Consultation with employees seems to be more advanced in the Finance Group, which includes a committee that brings together representatives of management and trade unions 'in order that organizational change and integration of the business be managed optimally'. There is virtually no information on consultation mechanisms for the 90% of the Co-op's employees who belong to the Trading Group. The Co-op's rating for the information that it provides under this heading is 'full'. Thus seems correct for CFS employees but not for Trading Group employees.

(ii)   EC5 (Minimum wage): No information is given: Co-op's rating is 'not applicable', which seems wrong.

(iii)   LA1 (Employment statistics): Information is given on employment by business segment, by employment type (full-time versus part-time) and by contract type (permanent versus temporary). There is no breakdown by region, presumably because the Co-op considers that this is not relevant as it operates only in the UK. Co-op's rating is 'partial', which seems to be rather self-depreciatory, as virtually full information is provided.

(iv)   LA2 (Turnover): Information is given on employee turnover, analysed by gender but not by age. Co-op rating is 'partial', which seems to be correct.

(v)   LA4 (Collective bargaining): Full information is given: 33% of employees in the retail sector and 63% in the banking sector are members of trade unions. Co-op's rating is 'full', which is correct.

(vi)   LA5 (Notice period): No information given. Co-op's rating = 'don't report, will consider'.

(vii)   LA6 (Management-worker committees): The information is given only for the banking sector. Co-op's rating = 'not material'. This judgment seems questionable. Presumably the GRI, in asking firms to provide this information, considered that it was important for assessing the firm's sustainability performance. The GRI consulted widely with stakeholder representatives in developing its guidelines. The Co-op in deciding that the information is not material is placing its judgment before that of stakeholders. Possibly the Co-op's rating indicates that it considers that management-worker committees are not a materially important element in the Group's governance structure. If this is the case, the Co-op has misunderstood the question, which concerns the extent to which such committees exist. If the answer is that there are none, then this should be stated.

(viii)   LA7 (Statistics of injuries etc.): Detailed figures are given for accidents, fatalities and absenteeism. Comparative figures are given, which indicate that the retail sector's performance is worse than the national average: 530 reportable accidents per 100,000 employees compared with 429 in the retail sector as a whole. Co-op's rating is 'partial', which seems correct, as no information is given on occupational diseases.

 (ix) LA10 (Training): The information is given for the retail sector: an average of one day per year. It is not given for the banking sector; instead the training expenditure per employee is offered as a proxy. Co-op's rating is 'full', which is materially correct.

  (x) LA12 (Employee reviews): On this point, it is stated (on the web-site): 'employees do receive regular performance and career development reviews . . . Data is not collected centrally and it is not considered relevant to collate data at this level'. Co-op's rating is 'don't report, will consider'.

 (xi) LA13 (Governance): Very full information is given of the proportion of women and minorities in the workforce, in management and on the board of directors. This reveals that, in the retail sector, women make up 64% of the work-force, but only 53% of managers and a derisory 9% of the board ; minorities make up 7% of the work-force and 8% of managers, but there are none on the board. The Co-op management is unable to control the composition of the board, which is elected by the members.[7] The breakdown of employees by gender is given, but not by age group or minority group. Co-op's rating is 'partial', which seems correct, as there is no analysis of the work-force by age-group or minority group.

(xii) LA14 (Salaries): The proportion of the workforce in each of five salary bands is given, but not analysed by gender. The Co-op comments: 'Men and women can receive the same low/high range of pay within each band. As there are such diverse job roles within the Co-operative, it is not meaningful to compare the basic salary for men and women' This rather opaque comment refers obliquely to one of the major difficulties in measuring the discrimination suffered by women in wage levels. Often firm pay the same rates for men and women within grades, but women are disproportionately represented in the lower paid grades. Co-op's rating is 'don't report, will consider'.

The information that the Co-op provides on the four narrative points relating to labour practices (see table 5.5) may be summarized as follows:

  (i) LA3 (Employee benefits): On this point, the printed report is clear: 'All part-time employees are entitled to the same benefits as their full-time equivalents'. Co-op's rating is 'full'.

 (ii) LA8 (Diseases): There is a reference to a 24-hour help-line which employees may use if they have personal problems and need advice on financial, family and legal matters. Only about 1% of employees availed themselves of this service in 2007. Co-op's rating is 'full'. This assessment seems correct. The Co-op reports fully on the only programme that it has in this field, even though it is of only minor significance.

(iii) LA9 (Agreements with unions): There is a reference to the 'Well Being Forum' where union representatives discuss with management, matters relating to workers' well-being, such as diversity, health and safety. Co-op's rating is 'not material'. This judgment seems questionable for the same reasons as given for LA6 in sub-paragraph (vii) above.

(iv) LA11 (Training): According to the employee survey, 70% of employees agree with the statement: 'At work I am able to learn and develop as a person'. Co-op's rating is 'don't report, will consider'.

In respect of the four points relating to human rights of workers (see table 5.5), the report refers to the 13-page section entitled 'International development and human rights', which deals only with human rights in the Co-op's supply chain and not with the human rights of its own employees. There are references to the actions that the Co-op took in 2007 to monitor labour conditions at its suppliers and to bring about improvements. A detailed table in this section reports on these actions, which cover all four areas mentioned in the guidelines: discrimination, freedom of association, child labour and forced labour. For example, under the heading 'freedom of association', the Co-op reports that it undertook 18 'improvement actions' in 2007; of these, 11 were completed, 5 are due for completion in 2008, one is overdue and one supplier was de-listed. The Co-op's rates the information that it provides under these headings as 'full' except for discrimination' which is 'partial'. These ratings seem correct.

In summary, the Co-op provides full information on seven performance indicators and partial information on a further five. On four indicators, it did not report for 2007 but it is considering whether to report in the future. The GRI's policy seems to be that it does not insist that firms report on matter on which they do not keep records. That leaves three points on which I disagree with the Co-op's rating. The Co-op judges indicators LA6 and LA9 to be not material. I consider that this judgment is wrong for the reasons given in sub-paragraph (vii) above. Finally the Co-op states that, with reference to indicator EC5, that the minimum wage is 'not applicable'. This explanation is incomprehensible, as the statutory minimum wage certainly applies to the Co-op's employees in Britain.

My assessment is that the Co-op supplies a reasonably high proportion of the information set out in the GRI's Guidelines. Of the seven performance indicators for which it does not provide information, the Co-op expresses a willingness to consider doing so in the future in respect of four. That leaves three points where the Co-op provides no information for reasons that I consider to be wrong.

(b) *Additional Information*

The printed report includes an 8 page section entitled 'Employees'. This includes much information on matters that are not covered in the GRI guidelines. These include an analysis of the proportion of staff in each of five salary bands, which shows that 75% of the Trading Group staff are paid less than £15,000 a year. The proportion in the Finance Group is much lower: 29%. There is a similar contrast between the two sides of the Co-op's business in the statistics on the proportion of staff who are members of the pension scheme: 18% for the Trading Group and 67% for the Finance Group.

Of particular interest is the use made by the Co-op of employee surveys. Each year the Co-op carries out a questionnaire survey of all its employees, In 2007, the response rate was over 70% which is highly satisfactory given that the response rate for the first survey in 2003 was only 19% and that the response rate has improved in each subsequent year. Employees are asked for their opinion on a number of matters, including pay, benefits and opportunities for learning. Clearly the answers are subjective, but they do provide an indication of how this group feels that it is being treated by the firm, that is its appreciation of the justice that it experiences.

One can conceive of two ways in which a firm's management may respond to the information yielded by surveys. Consider the employees' response to the question: 'How do you rate your total pay, in comparison to pay for doing the same job in other similar companies'; 46% of employees in the banking sector answered 'poor/very poor'. The management may interpret this response as an indication that the firm is treating its employees unjustly and resolves to increase salaries for moral reasons. However, is justice best measured by the perception of the person involved (who may be excessively selfish or sensitive) or by objective measures (for example the firm's salaries compared with the amount necessary to support a decent standard of living)? But it seems clear that the justice of the firm's activities towards stakeholders cannot be measured solely in terms of quantitative data and that the stakeholders' perception of the justice that they experience is highly relevant for the overall picture; but that it needs to be supplemented by other data.

An alternative approach that the management might take to the response is to treat it as an indication that its salaries are uncompetitive and that it is in danger of losing its better staff to competitors. It therefore resolves to increase salaries for purely business reasons. This is essentially the 'business case' for sustainability—that it helps to improve the bottom line, that is the single bottom line (reported profit) and not the triple bottom line.

(c) Evaluation of the Co-op's Reporting on Employees.

Does the Co-op provide sufficient information to enable the reader to judge the justice of the Group's treatment of its employees? The Co-op provides a reasonable proportion of the information prescribed by the GRI guidelines. However, as demonstrated by the analysis in section A.3 of Annex A, this information is by no means sufficient for the assessment of justice; hence, even if the Co-op were to have complied fully with the guidelines, there would still be gaps. The Co-op has provided much information in addition to that required by the guidelines. Much of this is certainly relevant for the assessment of justice. Of particular interest is the use made of employee surveys; the survey results tell the reader much about the employees' subjective appreciation of the justice that they experience from the Co-op. However, notwithstanding this additional information, there are still a number of important areas on which virtually no information is given, notably working time and physical working conditions.

However, even if information were to be provided on these missing matters, it is doubtful whether the reader would be able to assess the justice experienced by the Co-op's employees. The reason is that the assessment of justice is a highly complex matter. As argued in section in Chapter 5 (section 5.6) above, this involves consideration of all the factors that bear on justice, balancing short-comings in one area against better treatment in others. Furthermore each employee's experience of justice is different. Clearly one cannot provide detailed information for each of the Co-op's 81,000 employees. A possible solution might be to divide the work-force into different categories with all employees in a particular category experiencing similar levels of justice. However this solution seems to run up against the problem of complexity. For example, within the Co-op organization, one could divide employees according to their physical working conditions with separate categories for shop assistants, office-workers, cleaners, drivers, farmers, bakery workers and so on. Probably at least ten categories would be necessary. When account is taken of the necessity to draw up similar categories for all the other factors listed in chapter 5, the number of different categories becomes unmanageable.

These comments should not be taken to imply that the information provided by the Co-op cannot be improved. That it is possible for a firm to provide much better information on employees (both in terms of quantity and of relevance) is demonstrated by the bilan social of French companies, which is the subject of Annex C.

B.5 The Co-op's Reporting on Other Stakeholders

This section examines the reporting of the firm's impact on stakeholders other than employees.

(a) Capital Providers

The members of the Co-op are its registered customers; they are divided between individual members (consumers) and corporate members (other co-operative societies which buy goods and services from the Co-op). Members are required to buy shares in the Co-op. However the minimum investment is trivial (£1 for an individual member and £5 for a corporate member); moreover (unlike shares in a limited company) the shares are redeemable at a fixed nominal value and are paid a fixed low rate of interest. Share capital plays a very minor role in the financing of the Co-op: only £67.9 million compared to accumulated reserves of £3,831.3 million.[8] Therefore the members are not principally capital providers but customers. The extent to which the Co-op's sustainability reporting meets their information needs is considered next under the heading of customers.

(b) Customers

The printed report includes a five-page section entitled 'Customers'. There are three principal topics:

(i) The Co-op's reputation with consumers in general: According to a survey of 4,000 consumers carried out by a market research organization, the corporate reputation of the Co-op was slightly above the average for companies with a similar range of activities.

(ii) Customer satisfaction. Some 500 customers are surveyed each month to determine the level of customer satisfaction. Only 33% of customers in the food business were 'very satisfied'; the percentages in other sectors (pharmacy, travel and banking) were about double.

(iii) Complaints. Statistics are given for the number of complaints. The number seems enormous: in 2007, 175,000 in the food sector, up from 145,000 in the previous year. It is not obvious how to interpret this figure. It may represent improved efficiency on the part of the complaints department in advertising its services.

Presumably a customer who felt that she was not being treated justly would not declare that she was very satisfied and therefore the index of customer satisfaction has some limited relevance for assessing the justice of the Co-op's impact on this stakeholder group. However it seems likely that the management's motive in collecting the data on customers mentioned above was not to assess justice but rather to help it run the business more efficiently.

(c) Suppliers

Relations with suppliers are covered in several sections of the report, but there is no specific section devoted entirely to this topic. Much of the section entitled 'International development and human rights' concerns the Co-op's efforts to ensure that its suppliers in foreign countries respect human rights. The Co-op is a member of the Ethical Trading Initiative, an alliance of companies that work together to improve working conditions in supply chains and which has developed a code of conduct based on the ILO conventions. The report contains a detailed table that lists the issues on which it engaged with its suppliers in 2007. The list gives a good indication of the Co-op's concept of justice (and injustice); there are nine issues: 'exploitation of labour', 'freedom of association', 'a safe and hygienic working environment', 'child labour', 'living wages to be paid', 'working hours are not excessive', 'no discrimination', 'regular employment' and 'no harsh or inhuman treatment'. These issues certainly are central to the justice experienced by the employees of suppliers.

In the section on 'Animal welfare', the Co-op reports on its programme to restrict its purchases of eggs and chickens to suppliers who maintained high standards of animal welfare. In the section 'PBT chemicals' it reports on its programme to persuade its suppliers to eliminate dangerous chemicals from their products.

In respect of secondary stakeholders, two aspects of the impact of the Co-op's activities are given particular prominence in its report: climate change and community investment.

(d) Climate Change

The report contains a thirteen page section on 'Climate change', which provides a very substantial amount of information on a number of topics. There is a plethora of statistics of which the most interesting are:

   (i) In 2007, the Co-op's overall energy consumption was 9% less than in the previous year, indicating that the Co-op is on track to meeting its target of reducing overall energy consumption by 25% by 2012 (compared with 2006).
  (ii) 99% of the electricity used by the Co-op comes from renewable sources: wind and hydro.
 (iii) The Co-op generates much of the energy that it uses from its own renewable sources, principally wind turbines located on its farms. Its target is to generate 15% of its energy requirements in this way by 2012.
 (iv) Greenhouse gas emissions were 49% lower in 2007 compared with 2003. In part this reduction was achieved by phasing out old-fashioned refrigeration equipment.

These statistics relate to the Co-op's own operations: its shops, offices and own production facilities, such as its farms. They do not relate to the operations in its supply chain. However there are three references to suppliers which cast light on the difficulties in assessing the sustainability of supplier operations:

   (i) Biofuels; The Co-op decided not to use bio-fuels in its fleet of lorries 'in recognition of the adverse environmental impacts that certain bio-fuel feedstocks can lead to'.

(ii) Food miles: The Co-op is against labeling its food products with information on the distance travelled between the producer and the shop. It gives two reasons: Firstly, in many cases, the more distant product is less energy intensive. For example, New Zealand lamb sold in Britain has a lower CO_2 impact than British lamb, which is fed on concentrates during the winter. Secondly, many farmers in Africa are dependent on sales to the British market. This is an interesting example of a conflict between the social and the ecological aspects of sustainability. The report comments: 'The Co-operative Group has committed to reduce carbon but never at the expense of the world's poorest'.

(iii) Carbon foot-printing. The Co-op calculated the carbon foot-print of the strawberries sold in its shops from two sources: from its own farm in Scotland and from a supplier in Spain. The results were very revealing: 850g CO_2e[9] embodied in a 400g punnet of Scottish strawberries and 600g of CO_2e in the same quantity of Spanish strawberries. The amount of CO_2e created in cultivating the strawberries and getting them to the shop seems extraordinary—greater than the weight of the strawberries!

In summary, this section of the report provides a good overview of the impact of the Co-op's activities on climate change. Its principal deficiencies are that it does not deal systematically with the impact of firms in its supply chain (other than its own production facilities). The impact of other aspects of the Co-op's operations is not covered: for example, the Group includes a chain of travel agencies, which surely contribute massively to global warming in recommending to their clients package holidays in far-flung places!

(e) Community Investment

The report contains a short five-page section entitled 'Community investment', which deals principally with cash payments to projects that serve the community, totalling £8.3 million. The projects cover a bewildering range of objects: examples are solar panels for schools, the integration of refugees, help for the mentally ill and support for a local theatre. Brief descriptions are given of some dozen projects. The report provides a useful breakdown of this expenditure: 64% is classified as 'community investment' (long-term strategic involvement in community partnerships to address social issues) and 31% as 'commercial initiatives in the community' (community activities that directly support the company and promote its brand). This addresses the skeptical reader's concern that the firm only engages with local communities for selfish commercial reasons. This is clearly a factor in the 31% but presumably not for the 64%. In addition to cash payments, there is an estimate of the value of employee time spent on community projects (£1.5 million).

The Co-op's supports a wide range of projects in the community, some of which seem to have very little connection with its business. For example, it made a grant of £4,480 to a group in Stockport 'that provides complementary therapies to adults who are experiencing mental, physical or emotional ill-health'.[10] It would seem that the motivation behind that grant was a sense of responsibility towards society and not to advance the Co-op's business. The people who benefitted from this grant were certainly secondary stakeholders of the Co-op, in that they were affected by the firm's activities—positively and not negatively, as is more commonly the case.

B.6 Review of the Co-op's reporting

The Co-op's Sustainability Report brings out very clearly a number of important issues concerning the reporting of justice.

(a) Quantity of Information

The Co-op uses well over 100,000 words on 135 pages to report on its impact on sustainability. As demonstrated by table 5.6, the report covers over twenty different topics. These data illustrate the complexity of the information that is relevant for the assessment of sustainability and justice. The Co-op tackled this problem by the simple expedient of providing a greater quantity of information. However, notwithstanding this effort (which is certainly praiseworthy) there are still many topics that are covered inadequately (or not at all) in the Co-op report. An example is the balance of justice between employees, customers and suppliers, which depends crucially on the level of the prices charged to customers and paid to suppliers.

My conclusion is that, in issuing such a report, that covers a very wide range of topics, the Co-op is demonstrating one way in which a firm can provide the reader with (some of) the information that she needs to judge the sustainability and justice of the firm's activities.

Yet, as indicated in the analysis of the information on employees presented in section B.4 above, the Co-op has by no means supplied all the information that a reader needs for a full assessment.

(b) Types of Information

In reporting on sustainability, the Co-op makes imaginative use of various types of information:

   (i) Survey data. The Co-op made much use of survey data in two areas (employees and customers) as analysed in detail in sections B.4 and B.5 (b) above. This is probably the most effective way of discovering other people's perception of the justice that they experience.

(ii) Quantitative data: Often statistics are the easiest way to communicate information. The Co-op makes good use of statistics in its review of its impact on climate change (see section B.5 (d) above). The statement that in 2007 greenhouse gas emissions were 49% lower compared with 2003 conveys, in one line, information that is of greater import and easier to appreciate than many paragraphs on how this was achieved (for example by replacing out-dated refrigeration equipment). The most convincing statistics are those relating to physical quantities that may be scientifically measured. Such statistics are presented in the report's sections on waste, biodiversity and PBT chemicals. However, they are not available for most of the report's topics. Data involving monetary values can be just as objective. Examples are the number of employees in each of five salary bands and the breakdown of the £8.3m donated to community projects.

(iii) Narrative. However most of the Co-op's report is taken up with narrative. Quantitative data simply does not exist on many topics and, where it does, it needs to be backed up by narrative. An example is the Co-op's support of community projects mentioned in the previous paragraph. In order that the reader gains a fuller understanding of the impact of this expenditure, she needs more information on the actual projects. The report supplies this with descriptions of some half-a-dozen projects. The descriptions are very short (generally less than a hundred words) so they do little more than give a flavour of the project's character; and they cover only a tiny proportion of the total number of projects supported (over 2,000). But, in the space available in a 135 page report, this is best that can be done and they certainly add to the reader's understanding of the impact of this aspect of the Co-op's activities.

(c) Assurance

In accordance with the GRI guidelines, the Co-op's report includes a statement of assurance. This statement has a very clear and very important function: it adds credibility to the report. It should be noted that the report is prepared by the Co-op's employees under the supervision of the Co-op's managers. They both choose the topics on which to report and decide what to report and (perhaps more importantly) what not to report on each topic. The skeptical reader may worry that the Co-op, in choosing topics, only reports on those which reflect favourably on the organization whilst suppressing 'bad news'. Furthermore, how is the reader to be sure that the information provided on a topic has not been 'massaged' or even falsified. The function of the assurance statement is to reassure the reader on these points—that the report gives a complete and correct picture (or, to put it in the words beloved of accountants, the report gives a true and fair view) of the Co-op's impact on sustainability and justice.

The function of the assurance statement on the sustainability report is essentially the same as that of the auditor's report on the financial statements. They both should convert documents over which the skeptical reader has doubts (principally because they were prepared by the firm itself) into one whose information may be relied upon. However, in my opinion, the assurance statement attached to the sustainability report does not add the same degree of credibility to that report as the auditor's report does to the financial statements—for two reasons:

   (i) The organization that provided the sustainability report's assurance statement (csrnetwork) does not have the same reputation for competence and integrity as does the accounting firm that audited the financial statements (KPMG Audit Plc). There is not the slightest evidence that csrnetwork is incompetent or dishonest. However it was founded only in 1999 and, according to its web-site[11], has been providing assurance services only since 2003. This should be compared with the over one hundred years of audit experience of the accounting firms that merged to make up KMPG. It takes decades of error free work for a firm to build up the reputation that ensures that its signature on a document transforms it from a worthless piece of paper into one that the reader can trust. Csrnetwork has not been in the business long enough to build up such a reputation.

  (ii) The size of csrnetwork's fee seems too low for the amount of work that would be necessary to verify all the information in the Co-op's report so as to provide adequate assurance. Csrnetwork's fee of £66,000 should be compared with KPMG's fee of £1,390,000 for the audit of the financial statements[12], which is over twenty times higher—despite the fact that sustainability report contains more information on a greater variety of topics compared with the financial statements.

My overall conclusion is that, with its sustainability report, the Co-op has made a creditable and praiseworthy effort to provide relevant and useful information in a very new field in which it (and its assurance provider) have still a great deal to learn on how to report most effectively.

APPENDIX C: THE FRENCH LAW ON SOCIAL AND ENVIRONMENTAL ACCOUNTING

There are two principal legal obligations placed on French firms in the field of social and environmental accounting.

C.1 The 'Bilan Social'

The 'bilan social' refers to a special report that French firms with over 300 workers are required by law to prepare for the benefit of their employees. English speakers are often misled by the term: the 'bilan' is not a balance sheet but rather a comprehensive report and 'social' refers not to society as a whole, but to the firm's workforce. The law defines the contents of the report in considerable detail. A very wide range of topics is covered in seven sections:

1. Statistics of numbers employed;
2. Employee remuneration;
3. Health and safety;
4. Work conditions;
5. Training;
6. Industrial relations;
7. Other, including fringe benefits.

The amount of detail that has to be given under each heading is considerable. The 'bilan social' of EDF consists of 70 pages packed with statistical tables. The statistics of numbers employed occupy no less than 28 pages, and includes breakdowns by type of employment contract, gender, age, nationality, salary grade and seniority. There are detailed statistics on joiners and leavers (analysed by retirements, lay-offs, end of contract and death) and of absenteeism (analysed by illness, accident, maternity leave and special leave).

Section 4 is of particular interest, as it covers a very diverse field which is almost completely ignored in the GRI Guidelines. The 'bilan social' of the French railways (SNCF) includes the following information under this heading:

1. The average number of hours worked per employee per year: 1,562.
2. The number of employees on flexi-time: 5,116.
3. The numbers of employees who are not required to work on Sunday: 77,103.
4. The number of employees who, at their place of work, are regularly submitted to a noise level exceeding 85 decibels: 28,062.
5. The number of employees who changed jobs within the firm: 12,971.

The information on working time enables the reader to evaluate the fairness of the wages paid (given with the employment statistics under heading 1). However, since there is no breakdown by gender etc., only a very general evaluation can be made. The information on noisy work places (point 4) is an interesting example of how work conditions may be measured objectively. However noise is only one aspect of the working environment and it is clear that the information in the 'bilan social' fails to capture more than a tiny fraction of the multitude of factors that influence the quality of working conditions.

C.2 Les Nouvelles Régulations Économiques (NRE)

Under article 116 of the law on 'Les nouvelles régulations économiques' (NRE), French companies listed on the stock exchange are required to include in their annual report a statement of 'the manner in which they take account of the environmental and social consequences of their activities'. A government decree[1] has defined the content of this statement in some detail. The most important characteristics of the NRE statement may be summarized as follows:

1. The statement differs fundamentally from the 'bilan social' in that it is contained in the annual report which is addressed to shareholders, whereas the bilan social is addressed to employees.
2. Only listed companies are obliged to make such a report. Thus the situation in France is not dissimilar to that in Britain, where, under the rules of the London Stock Exchange, listed companies are obliged to include in their annual report a statement of significant business risks, including environmental, social and reputational risks.
3. The word 'social' is interpreted almost exclusively as referring to the firm's work force. Hence much of the 'social' information required by the decree reproduces that of the bilan social.
4. Therefore the principal impact of the decree is to require the firm to provide much information on environmental matters, including:

   (i)   Consumption of water, raw materials and energy;
   (ii)   Pollution of air, water and soil;
   (iii) Impact on bio-diversity;
   (iv)   Measures to assure compliance with regulations;
   (v)   Costs of environment protection measures;
   (vi)   The firm's management structures relating to the environment (in training staff and reducing risks);
   (vii) Amounts of fines and other penalties for environmental infringements.

A study[2] of the social information provided in the 2007 NRE reports of the firms in the CAC 40 came to the following conclusions:

(i)   On the quantity of information, the firms, on average, provided only about 90% of the information required by law. Quantity is defined as compliance with the letter of the law.;
(ii) On the quality of information, the study's authors evaluate the quality at 50%. Quality is defined as compliance with the spirit of the law.

The most interesting parts of the report are the authors' reasons for judging quality to be so low. They write: 'Firms aim to charm their world rather than communicate a complicated or gloomy situation'; 'Rarely do firms comment on bad outcomes'; 'Firms skim over themes that are bad for their image'. The authors have detected a tendency for firms to invent new statistical measures that serve only to present the firm's activities in a favourable light. They refer to 'a growing *professionnalisation* which produces much information which is useless on certain subjects and ignores others'. All these problems are connected with the fact that there is no consensus on what a social report should contain and the reports are prepared by the firms themselves. The report's conclusions confirm those of Chapter 5 that a major problem with social and environmental reporting is how to assure objectivity through effective outside verification.

6   The Distribution Function

The financial statements play an active role when the distribution of the firm's income is determined by the figures in the financial statements. When this is the case, the financial statements are said to perform the distribution function. This may happen when the state, through its laws and regulations, requires that certain distributions of the firm should be determined wholly or partially on the basis of the figures reported in the accounts. This is commonly the case with two important distributions to stakeholders: tax and dividends. This chapter starts with an analysis of the distribution function in Germany, where it is particularly important.

6.1 THE DISTRIBUTION FUNCTION IN GERMANY

In this section, the current[1] position regarding financial reporting in Germany is described. In May 2009, a new law was promulgated which will apply to the accounts of German companies from 1 January 2010. Hence some parts of the following analysis will not apply in their full force to financial reporting in 2010 and following years. Although the full impact of the new law will not become apparent immediately, it is expected to be significant. Nevertheless the following analysis of the situation in 2009 is valuable, as it demonstrates the operation of the distribution function in a real as opposed to a theoretical situation.

6.1.1 The Position in 2009

In 2009, the principal function of the financial statements of German corporations is not the provision of information for investors (which, according to the IASB should be their principal function) but rather the determination of distributions: the financial statements perform the profit distribution function (die Gewinnverteilungsfunktion), which is imposed on the corporation by the state through its laws and regulations. Two important payments out of a corporation's profits are determined in part on the basis of the figures in the financial statements: tax to the state and dividends to shareholders. The financial statements involved are those of the legal entity (the corporation)—the so-called individual accounts—and not those of the group (the consolidated accounts). Because of their profit distribution function, the individual accounts play a much more important role in the German economy than is the case in many other countries, such as the USA, where they are generally disregarded.

In Germany, the financial statements, as drawn up in accordance with the law, form the basis on which a corporation's profit is distributed among those entitled to a share: that is, not only the corporation's shareholders, but certain other persons and bodies associated with the corporation: certain stakeholders. This function may be illustrated with the rules relating to the distribution of the profit of a stock corporation (Aktiengesellschaft).[2] These rules apply to the legal entity, the corporation, and its accounts (the 'individual' accounts)—and not to the group and the consolidated accounts, which are not relevant for distributions. Distributions are made by the corporation and not by the group, which is not a legal entity and has not the capacity to make contracts. The detailed rules for the distribution of profit are set out in the Stock Corporation Act (Aktiengesetz).[3] The following exposition of these rules is based on the analysis made by Dieter Ordelheide (1994):

(i) The general rule is that the management board (Vorstand) prepares the accounts and passes them to the supervisory board (Aufsichtsrat) for approval.[4] Each year, the corporation is obliged by law (as a first claim on the profits) to transfer 5% of its profits (as reported in its financial statements) to a legal reserve, until the balance of this reserve reaches 10% of the share capital. The aim of this rule is to improve the protection of creditors, that is, to increase the probability that they will be repaid the amounts owing to them, even if, in a liquidation, the corporation's assets were to realize less than their book value.

(ii) The management (the management board and the supervisory board) decide on the amount of profit to be retained; they may at their discretion retain up to half (but not more than half) of the profits (after the transfer to the legal reserve) for the financing of the corporation.[5] The supervisory board consists of representatives of shareholders and employees.[6] In the supervisory boards of many corporations, the shareholder members include representatives of banks and other major creditors. The management board consists of full-time executives. Since employees are represented on the supervisory board, it is common for the interests of this group to be taken into account in deciding how much to retain. In general the employees prefer that profits should not be distributed as dividends but instead be retained, as this strengthens the corporation's economic position and increases the security of employment. The banks and other creditors who are often represented on the supervisory board (as representatives of the shareholders) also favour retention over distribution. The management board has very similar interests. For all these reasons, it is common for German corporations to retain a high proportion of their profits.

(iii) The shareholders (at the shareholders' meeting) decide on the distribution of the remaining profit between dividends and retained earnings. They have the right to decide to distribute the entire balance of profit as dividends, subject to the overriding condition that this would not endanger the corporation's solvency.

The role of the financial statements in determining distributions to stakeholders is further enhanced by the rules relating to taxation. The state is an important stakeholder, and its interests have to be considered in dividing the corporation's surplus among its stakeholders. Hence Germany, in common with most other countries, levies a tax on a firm's profits. In Germany the amount of the tax payable by a corporation is calculated on the basis of the financial statements.[7] This is known as the authoritativeness principle (die Massgeblichkeitsprinzip)—the accounts (as drawn up in accordance with the law) form the authoritative basis of the tax computation.[8]

The authoritativeness principle is not absolute. The commercial accounts and the tax computation are not identical, because the tax law prescribes that certain adjustments should be made to the figures in the commercial accounts in calculating the taxable profit. The principal adjustments relate to payments to members of the supervisory board, which are properly a deduction from profit in the commercial accounts but not in the tax computation.

In theory, the financial statements determine the tax computation. In practice, the reverse is often the case—the tax rules determine the financial statements; this is known as the reverse authoritativeness principle (umgekehrte Massgeblichkeit). There are two reasons why this occurs: firstly, where the laws relating to financial reporting allows some discretion, corporations tend to choose those options which minimize tax; secondly, where the tax laws offer an option (such as accelerated depreciation) that reduces the tax bill, the corporation may avail itself of this option only if it is reported in the financial statements.[9] The combined result of the authoritativeness principle and the reverse authoritativeness principle is that a corporation's financial statements and its tax computation, although not identical, tell the same story—that the corporation has earned a certain profit of which a certain proportion goes to the state.

Hence the position in Germany concerning the financial statements of stock corporations may be summarized as follows:

(i) The law lays down the rules that govern the form and content of the financial statements.

(ii) The amount of tax payable by the corporation is calculated on the basis of the profit reported in these financial statements.

(iii) From the profits after tax, 5% must be transferred to a legal reserve for the protection of creditors (until the balance on the reserve equals 10% of the share capital).

(iv) From the remaining profits, the management (which includes representatives of shareholders and employees) decide how much to retain in the business (up to a maximum of 50%).

(v) From the remaining profits, the shareholders decide how much to distribute as dividend.

There are some elements of flexibility in the system. In certain areas, the law allows some choice in the rules to be followed for the preparation of the financial statements; and, at steps iv and v, the parties involved have some discretion as to the amounts retained and distributed. However the overall effect is that the financial statements have a strong influence (in some cases a determining influence) on the distribution of the corporation's profit among its stakeholders. In the case of tax, the accounts determine the amount of the distribution; in the case of dividends, the accounts determine the maximum amount that may be distributed. This is the justification for the term, the distribution function.

In determining distributions, the interests of all principal stakeholders are taken into account: the state, creditors, employees,[10] and shareholders. German law recognizes that companies have a responsibility to stakeholders in general and not solely to shareholders. Dieter Ordelheide (1994) commented:

> German law has not yet come round to the view that the interests of shareholders are paramount. As the regulations on worker participation indicate, it relies more on a stakeholder perspective, which entails balancing the interests of shareholders, creditors and employees.

Despite the pressures from multinational companies and from the IASB to adopt the precepts of 'shareholder value', German law still retains this stakeholder perspective.

6.1.2 The Future of German Financial Reporting

In May 2009, the law on financial reporting was amended by the Accounting Modernization Act, which applies to the financial statements of German companies from 1 January 2010. The principal changes are:

(i) The connection between the financial statements and the tax computation is greatly weakened. The calculation of the tax payable by a corporation will in future be based on a tax computation that is separate from the financial statements. The principle that a particular tax concession (such as accelerated depreciation) may be claimed only if the corporation reports it in its financial statements (umgekehrte Massgeblichkeit) is completely abandoned. The principle that the financial reporting is the basis of the tax computation (die Massgeblichkeitsprinzip) still applies, but many experts consider that its retention in the future will become increasingly difficult or even impossible. It seems very likely that, in this field, Germany will become more like Britain (see next section).

(ii) The profit distribution function is retained but somewhat weakened. The amount that may be distributed as dividend is, as before, to be calculated on the basis of the financial statements. However, a number of the adjustments must be made to the surplus of assets over liabilities and equity that may be distributed. These adjustments concern principally internally generated intangible assets and tax assets.

With both tax and dividends, the amounts that may be distributed are still based on what is reported in the financial statements, but after adjustments which, especially in the case of tax, may be considerable.

6.2 THE DISTRIBUTION FUNCTION IN OTHER COUNTRIES

In almost all other countries, the financial statements play a significant role in determining the same two major distributions of profit: tax and dividends.

6.2.1 Tax

Text books often draw a distinction between countries (such as Germany, France, and Italy) where the accounts are said to be 'tax-driven' (that is, the tax laws have a substantial influence on the form and content of the financial statements) and other countries (such as the USA and Britain) where this is not the case. In my opinion, this distinction is false. In all major countries, the amount of tax that an enterprise pays on its income is based on the figures that it reports in its financial statements; differences between countries in this matter relate only the extent to which they are permitted to adjust the reported figures in calculating taxable income. In certain countries, substantial adjustments are permitted; in other countries far fewer or even none. However, in all countries, the starting point for the tax computation is the profit figure reported in the accounts, and any deviation from this figure has to be justified. Hence, since enterprises commonly seek to minimize tax payments, in all countries the financial statements are 'tax-driven'; the only differences are ones of degree.

There are two considerable social advantages in basing the tax payment on the figures reported in the accounts:

i. It leads to greater justice in balancing the conflicting interests of shareholders and of society as a whole. The shareholders derive benefit from the enterprise in the form of dividends; society's benefit is in the form of tax receipts. It is both logical and fair that dividends and tax should be based on the same profit figure. This was essentially the reasoning of American legislators when the US Congress stipulated that a corporation that valued its inventory using LIFO ('last in, first out') for tax purposes must report the same value in its accounts. If society is to suffer the burden of lower tax receipts, then shareholders should also receive lower dividends. Enterprises should not be permitted to use the extra cash arising from applying LIFO in paying higher dividends. I feel that most people would consider that the American legislators' reasoning was sound; it certainly met with widespread popular approval.

ii. It avoids the situation where an enterprise reports high profits but pays little or no tax[11] which occurs when the difference between the reported profit and the taxable profit becomes significant. This can lead to a loss of confidence by the general public in the equity of the taxation system—for example private persons, noticing that enterprises paid little or no tax on their profits, would seek to achieve a similarly lower tax burden by illegitimate means. In Japan, there is a general principle (known as the definite settlement of accounts) that (with certain exceptions) a corporation's accounts should agree with its tax computation. Sakurai (2001: 1724–5) points out that this rule has many advantages: it helps to resolve the conflict between the enterprise and the tax authorities, leads to cost savings for both the enterprise and the tax authorities, and avoids the public criticism of companies who pay little tax despite reporting high profits. Sakurai comments: 'The principle of the definite settlement of accounts prevents the occurrence of such criticism and the resultant political costs, through consistency between the taxable income assessment and the income determination in the financial statements.'

My position is that it is of major importance that the firm's financial contribution towards the functioning of the state should be calculated in a just and efficient manner and that the financial statements should play a crucial role in achieving this end. The confidence of the general public that the firm has paid its fair share of taxes is enhanced if this is evident from its published accounts. I contend that, if one were to ask a random sample of the population in most countries what was the most important function of a corporation's financial statements, the most common answer would be the computation of tax. This is certainly true of Britain, at least on the evidence of a small and very unscientific survey (of a very unrepresentative sample) that I undertook during a recent visit to that country. Of course it would be desirable to have this assertion confirmed by a proper survey, but I am not aware of any such survey. The standard reaction of accountants is that the general public is ignorant and mistaken. I find such an attitude arrogant and thoroughly undemocratic. Financial reporting is a social activity that fulfills a social need. Accountants must take account of what the general public expects of them. I am not suggesting that accountants should determine their principles with reference to an opinion poll; but, I consider that a situation where accounting practice is so out of step with public opinion is thoroughly unsatisfactory.

Personally I am convinced of the benefits to society of basing the amount of tax paid by a firm on the figures reported in its accounts. Certainly any difference between the reported profit and the taxable profit is undesirable and should be reduced to the minimum.

6.2.2 Dividends

When, in the nineteenth century, the USA and many European countries imposed a legal obligation on corporations to draw up financial statements, the principal reason was to indicate the maximum amount that a corporation might legally distribute to shareholders as dividends. In many countries, the only financial statement that corporations were obliged to prepare was a balance sheet.

The principal reason for the requirement to present a balance sheet was to check that the corporation had maintained its capital. The need for the corporation to maintain its capital stemmed from the limited liability of its shareholders. A person who was owed money by the corporation could not sue the shareholders for the repayment of his debt; he could sue only the corporation. The only resources that were available for the repayment of this debt were the corporation's assets. In order to protect their position, creditors sought to ensure that the corporation's assets were not dissipated through making unwarranted payments to shareholders. Governments agreed with them and therefore made it illegal for a corporation to pay a dividend that would reduce its net assets below a certain minimum amount—normally set at the amount raised by the corporation through the issue of shares, that is, the corporation's share capital. In effect, the corporation's share capital represented a reserve fund available for the repayment of creditors which could not be drawn upon for the payment of dividends. A corporation was allowed to pay a dividend only to the extent of the increase of its net assets over its share capital, that is, to the extent of its profits, profits being defined as increase in net assets.

The principle that a corporation may legally pay a dividend only out of profits is still as relevant today as it was in the nineteenth century. In all countries, the amount of dividend payable is based on the figures in the financial statements, notably the balance sheet in respect of accumulated past profits and the income statement in respect of the current profits. It is true that, in many countries, it is necessary to adjust the reported figures.

For example, in France and many other European countries, reserves arising from the revaluation of fixed assets may not be distributed and, in Britain, following a series of court cases analysed by French (1977), the depreciation of fixed assets may be disregarded. However, this does not alter the fact that the financial statements form the basis of the calculation of the maximum dividend that may legally be paid.

This analysis makes clear that in all countries the financial statements play a significant role in determining the amount of tax and dividends—two of the most important distributions made by a firm.

6.3 THE REGULATION OF UTILITIES

The firm's financial statements also play a role in determining the distributions of public utilities in Britain and the USA. In these countries, the supply of certain essential goods and services, such as electricity, water, and telecommunications, is provided by private firms. These firms enjoy a natural monopoly, since it is uneconomic for a competing firm to build up an alternative distribution network. To prevent these firms from exploiting their monopoly position, the prices that they charge consumers are subject to control by a state regulatory authority. Examples of such bodies are the UK's Oftel and the USA's Federal Communications Commission, which both have the authority to determine the prices charged by telecommunication companies. One of the major functions of the state regulator is to assure justice between the utility's stakeholders, notably between its shareholders and its customers. Baldwin and Cave (1999) analyse the situation as follows:

> [T]he price control regime must strike a balance between the interests of customers—protecting them from monopolistic exploitation—and the interests of investors, who, when they have sunk considerable sums of money into irrecoverable investment, will be concerned lest the regulator should impose a level of charges that makes it impossible for them to recover their investment.

In very general terms, there are two methods of fixing prices: cost-plus and price cap. The cost-plus method bases the prices that the utility may charge for the coming period on its costs for the past period, adjusted for forecast changes in these costs. In the USA, the prices are fixed at a level that should enable the utility to earn a reasonable rate of return on its capital. With the price cap method, the prices for the coming period are determined by a formula that specifies how changes from the current level of prices are calculated. The typical formula is: future price = current price + rate of inflation of input prices − rate of increase in productivity. With the cost-plus method, the firm's financial statements clearly play a decisive role in determining the prices charged to customers and hence in the justice that they experience. Hence, in a certain sense, they perform the distribution function.

However, a recent development in regulatory practice has enhanced the distribution function of the utility's financial statements. With the price cap method, there is a danger that the given formula allows the utility to charge unreasonably high prices, leading to excessively large profits. This can occur either because the regulator makes a mistake or because of unforeseen events. To avoid this danger, certain regulators have instituted profit sharing. The basic idea is that, if the utility's profits in a period are excessive, some part of the excess over a reasonable profit is shared with the customers. The customers benefit by a reduction in future charges. A typical example of profit sharing is that used by the USA Federal Communications Commission for local telephone companies. It sets the reasonable level of profit as a return of 11.25% on equity. If the utility's actual return for the period exceeds this figure, the utility is allowed to retain a certain proportion of the excess: 100% of the excess up to a return of 12.25%, half of the excess between 12.25% and 16.25%, and none of the excess over 16.25%. The past period's financial statements determine the distribution of the surplus between shareholders and customers; the future period's financial statements demonstrate that the customers have in fact received their share of the surplus through lower charges.

Since the financial statements play a decisive role in determining the returns to shareholders and the price paid by consumers, it is evident that their form and content (and in particular the recognition and valuation rules applied) cannot be left to the discretion of the utility's management. These should be decided by the state, on behalf of society as a whole.

6.4 THE FIRM'S USE OF THE DISTRIBUTION FUNCTION

The analysis so far has been of the distribution function imposed on the firm by the state. However, the firm (that is the management) may impose the distribution function on itself. It may commit itself, by contract, to base certain distributions on the basis of the figures reported in the financial statements. Examples are:

(i) Employee bonuses. An employee may be entitled to a bonus that is calculated as a certain percentage of reported profit.
(ii) Variable rate securities. The firm may issue securities (either debt or preference shares) for which the rate of return is determined by the reported profit.
(iii) Debt covenants. The contract that governs a loan issued by the firm may restrict its right to make distributions; for example the firm may be prohibited from paying dividends or bonuses to management if reported profits fall below a specified figure.

In all these cases, the firm's distributions are to a certain extent governed by the figures reported in its financial statements.

But often it is not in the manager's interest that he restrict his future freedom of action by assigning an active role to the financial statements. He prefers to assign to the accounts a passive role and thereby retain the power to manage the firm as he wills. The state has a much stronger motivation to govern the firm's behaviour through its financial statements, as it does in the regulation of public utilities.

6.5 THE IASB'S NEGLECT OF THE DISTRIBUTION FUNCTION

This analysis of the distribution function brings out very clearly the fact that financial statements perform several diverse functions. In recent decades, accountants around the world (and particularly in the 'Anglo-Saxon' countries, such as the USA and Britain) have come to believe that the principal function of financial reporting is to provide information for the capital market. In fact the International Accounting Standards Board (IASB) considers that this is the *sole* function of accounts. In its recent exposure draft of a revised conceptual framework for financial reporting (FASB, 2008) the IASB asserts: 'The objective of general purpose financial reporting is to provide financial information about the reporting entity that is useful to present and potential equity investors, lenders, and other creditors in making decisions in their capacity as capital providers.'

It is noteworthy that the IASB refers to *the* objective and not *an* objective. For the IASB, all other functions of financial reporting are secondary; at best they may be accomplished as a by-product of providing information for the capital market, as is clear from the sentence that follows the preceding quote: 'Information that is decision useful to capital providers *may* also be useful to other users of financial reporting who are not capital providers' (emphasis added).

I disagree fundamentally with the IASB's approach. I believe that accountants prepare financial statements with many diverse objectives in mind. One may identify no less than seven distinct functions of financial reporting.[12]

> The distribution function: the regulation of distributions, notably:
> Tax
> Dividends
> The stewardship function: the control of management
> The information function: the provision of information to
> Capital providers
> Employees
> The state
> The general public

I believe that most accountants would agree with me on this point and would concede that certain other functions, in addition to the provision of information to capital providers, are important.

As to the distribution function, the IASB seems to ignore it. There is no mention of either taxation or dividends in its proposed revised conceptual framework. However there is a mention in the IASB's current (unrevised) conceptual framework but it is simply to dismiss it, for it asserts: 'Special purpose financial reports, for example, prospectuses and computations for taxation purposes, are outside the scope of this Framework.'

The IASB's denial of the distribution function is well illustrated by its proposals relating to the regulation of utilities (the subject of Section 6.3). In July 2009, it issued the exposure draft of a proposed standard on rate-regulated activities. However, the IASB's proposals do not deal with the distribution function (how the form and contents of the utility's financial statements should be defined so that they provide the basis for distributions to capital providers and customers) but with the reporting function (how the regulator's decisions impact the wealth and income of capital providers). The Exposure Draft is concerned solely with the recognition and measurement of regulatory assets and liabilities, which it defines as cash flows arising from the regulator's decisions. The Exposure Draft does not concern itself with the basis of the regulator's decisions, which it takes as exogenous—that is, as having no connection with the financial statements. It fails to recognize that frequently the regulator's decisions as to prices are based on the accounts and that, for this reason, the accounts play a pivotal role in determining the justice experienced by capital providers and customers.

In my view, the IASB's attitude is completely wrong; the determining of distribution is a most important function of accounts and should be recognized as such.

6.6 THE DISTRIBUTION FUNCTION AND DISTRIBUTIVE JUSTICE

What contribution does the distribution function, as currently practised, make towards the achievement of distributive justice? In my opinion its contribution is very limited for a number of reasons:

(i) In general, it applies to only two items in the accounts (albeit very important ones), tax and dividends.

(ii) Even, with respect to these two items, the amounts distributed are not determined fully by the accounts. With tax, the amounts that are reported in the accounts are adjusted in preparing the tax computation, very substantially in certain countries, for example Britain and the USA. With dividends, the rules that are set by the state specify only the upper limit of the amount that may be distributed. For a firm that has been in business for some time and has accumulated profits, this limit may not impose a very severe restraint.

(iii) The state, in drawing up the tax and dividend laws, is not primarily concerned with the achievement of distributive justice. Certainly with tax, some of the tax revenue collected from the firm may be paid out to needy people in the form of social benefits and thus improve the level of justice in society. But the state has many other aims in taxing firms: for example, to manage the economy and to raise funds for government expenditure on such matters as defence that contribute little to justice. In setting the rules governing dividends, the state is primarily concerned about protecting creditors; it does not concern itself with the justice of the dividend.

On the other hand, with respect to public utilities, the financial statements play an important role in the achievement of justice between customers and shareholders. However, even with the state's regulation of public utilities, justice is often not the overriding objective. There is frequently a conflict between justice and efficiency. For many economists, efficiency is equated with the ratio of output to costs; an increase in output and/or a reduction in costs represent greater efficiency. The state regulator may be prepared to permit a higher return to shareholders in the expectation that this would lead to an improvement in efficiency; this would occur if the reductions in other costs were greater than the increase in dividends. Those academic economists who write on regulatory matters generally give more weight to efficiency than to justice. For example, John Kay, in assessing that the privatization of Britain's utilities in the 1980s and '90s had been a success, based his judgement on the improvement in efficiency resulting from reduction in manning levels.[13] However, this development hardly represented an improvement in justice for the workers who were laid off. I am not stating that these workers suffered an injustice; my point is that increased efficiency and the promotion of social justice have little in common. In the UK, such improvements in efficiency have led to the profits of certain regulated utilities (and bonuses to higher management) reaching levels that the general public considered to be excessive and not manifesting social justice.

Finally there is the case (covered in Section 6.4) where the firm voluntarily accepts that certain distributions are determined by the financial statements. Here distributive justice is clearly an objective. One reason for paying employees a bonus based on profit is that it rewards them for the contribution that they have made to the firm's success.

The question of whether the distribution function can be developed further will now be considered.

6.7 A POSSIBLE EXTENSION OF THE DISTRIBUTION FUNCTION?

This section discusses whether it is possible to further develop the distribution function so that it covers a greater proportion of the firm's distributions than is currently the case. This could be achieved either by the firm acting voluntarily or through the state's laws.

6.7.1 Voluntary Adoption by the Firm

The firm could agree with certain stakeholders that their compensation would be wholly or partially determined by the figures in the financial statements. Could present practice be expanded to cover more firms and more stakeholders? Currently the voluntary adoption by the firm of the distribution function is largely restricted to the payment of bonuses to employees. Only in firms run on co-operative lines has the distribution function been materially developed; commonly part of the co-operative's profit as measured in its financial statements is paid out as 'dividends' to suppliers and customers at the end of each year.[14] However, the co-operative movement occupies only a small niche in the economies of most countries. In a society that respects private property and freedom of contract, a firm and its stakeholders can decide for themselves how the rewards and risks of their common economic activity are to be shared between them. There is nothing to stop them agreeing on a contract whereby part of the stakeholder's return is based on the financial statements. The fact that the distribution function of accounts is largely confined to the co-operative movement suggests that, in general, stakeholders do not want their returns to be determined by the firm's performance, presumably because they are not prepared to take the risk of suffering a poor return if the firm does badly. This analysis suggests that, in Britain and the USA, the voluntary adoption of the distribution function by the firm has probably reached its natural limits.

6.7.2 Forced Adoption by the State

Hence, for the distribution function to be extended to cover a greater part of the firm's distributions, action by the state is necessary. This could occur if society concluded that the distribution of the costs and benefits resulting from the operation of market forces was unjust and decided to impose a particular distribution pattern on firms. The state would enact a law whereby the distributions to stakeholders were determined by the financial statements, with the aim of assuring distributive justice. I shall use the term 'the just distribution function' when the financial statements are specifically designed to achieve justice. No doubt there are, in theory, very many ways in which such a system could be instituted. The following is just one possible approach.

  i. The state enacts a law that determines the form and content of the financial statements.

ii. The financial statements have the status of a legal document which determines the rights of certain stakeholders.

iii. Each period, the firm draw up a statement that reports the value added by the firm—the surplus of the firm's revenue from sales over payments to other firms. Table 5.3 in Chapter 5 is an example of such a value-added statement.

iv. The surplus is divided between the firm's stakeholders in the following proportions: the state (tax) 40%; employees 30%; shareholders 20%; retained in the firm 10%.

It is possible to envisage more complex schemes in which other stakeholders (such as customers and suppliers) share in the surplus.

There are two obvious problems associated with basing the distribution of benefits to stakeholders on the figures in the financial statements: the negative impact on output and the difficulty of measuring the surplus and of determining each stakeholder's proper share.

(a) Impact on Output

The rationale for the just distribution function is that the distribution of benefits assured by the free play of market forces may be unjust. Hence, on occasions, the just distribution function will lead to rewards to stakeholders that are different from those that would arise in a free market—often very different. This may have negative repercussions in two areas:

i. Incentives: Certain stakeholders (those who would receive less when their reward is determined by the just distribution function) may contribute fewer resources and less effort to the firm's operations, leading to lower output. They have less incentive to contribute to the firm's success when their rewards are less.

ii. Efficiency: The final prices of the goods and services that are provided by stakeholders (after taking into account their share of the surplus) would differ from the prices that would be set in a free market. It is often claimed that output is maximized when prices are determined by market forces. Although this thesis cannot be proved and is therefore controversial[15] it is certainly arguable that the interference with the operations of the market that is implicit in the just distribution function would lead to a fall in output. Interfering with the market process leads to lower efficiency.

These considerations certainly cast serious doubts on the practicality of the just distribution function. However, in my opinion, they are not fatal, for two reasons:

i.   The extent of the fall in output that would result from the implementation of the just distribution function is essentially an empirical matter.
It may possibly be so small that it may be ignored.
ii. As already explained in Chapter 1, I consider that the major problem faced by the world is not production but distribution. Hence it is
quite reasonable to accept a small reduction in production in order to
achieve a great improvement in the justice of distributions.

(b)   The Calculation of the Shares

How should the firm's surplus and the percentage share of each category of
stakeholder be calculated? For example presumably the employees' percentage should be higher in a labour intensive firm than in a capital intensive
firm, but how is the exact figure to be calculated? And how are the legitimate demands for justice of different categories of stakeholder to be recon-
ciled? It would seem that the percentage share would have to be calculated
by a philosopher-accountant who was blessed with infinite wisdom, perfect
knowledge, and great integrity. Since it might prove difficult to find such a
paragon, it would seem that the development of the distribution function
to cover distributive justice for stakeholders, although of great theoretical
interest, might prove to be impractical.

However present-day practise offers some guidance: for example the
total annual remuneration of many higher level employees in the financial services industry consists of a salary fixed by contract and a year-end
bonus. Presumably the contracted salary is less than the market wage (as
the employee in agreeing the salary takes into consideration the expected
value of the bonus), and the level of the bonus varies with the level of the
firm's profits. I do not suggest that the bonuses paid to people such as mer-
chant-bankers are a good example of distributive justice. My point is that
a scheme involving a basic wage that is less than the market rate (perhaps
based on an index of Rawls's primary goods) complemented by a share of
the firm's surplus seems to be feasible.

Such an arrangement deals neatly with a further problem with the distribution function: according to standard economic theory, if all stakeholders
were paid the market price for their contributions (including normal profit
for the entrepreneur), then there would be no surplus (on average) to distribute. Hence the initial payment to (at least some) stakeholders must be
less than the market price.

This analysis suggests that it would be unrealistic to base the entire
reward of a stakeholder group on the accounts, but that it would be feasible to use the accounts (as regulated by the state) to determine part of
the return—perhaps to correct manifest injustices arising from the interplay of market forces. Britain and the USA have mixed economies. Much
of the activity of firms is determined by the market, but society expects

the state to intervene when the operations of the market do not result in justice. This is already the case with public utilities. Perhaps the just distribution function could be added to the arsenal of measures that the state employs to regulate the economy. The state could impose the just distribution function to regulate part of the distributions of specified firms. For example, the concept of profit-sharing, as already applied to public utilities, could be extended to selected private firms, say those in a quasi-monopoly situation. This would arguably lead to an increase in justice, with little loss in efficiency. Clearly such an extension of the distribution function merits consideration.

6.8 THE DISTRIBUTION FUNCTION: SUMMARY AND CONCLUSIONS

There is no dispute that, in all countries, the firm's financial statements play an important role in determining the amount of two important distributions to stakeholders: tax to the state and dividends to shareholders. Furthermore, for regulated public utilities, distributions to customers (in addition to tax and dividends) are often determined by the firm's accounts. Hence, the financial statements, to a limited degree, already perform the distribution function. Furthermore, firms often voluntarily bind themselves to make certain distributions dependent on the figures in the financial statements: for example bonuses to managers and the return on variable rate securities. The IASB's failure to recognize this salient fact was criticized. It was concluded that the distribution function of the financial statements, as presently practised, made only a slight contribution to the achievement of distributive justice. It is largely limited to two distributions (tax and dividends), and, even with respect to these, the principal motivation of the state's regulation is not to achieve justice. Only with respect to the regulation of public utilities is the achievement of justice (between capital providers and customers) a major consideration.

Potentially, in principle, the distribution function could be a very effective instrument in promoting justice, because it acts directly and immediately on the amounts received by stakeholders. Hence, it is arguable that its present very limited application is to be regretted and that it should be expanded to cover more firms and more stakeholder categories. It seems unlikely that this would come about through the voluntary actions of firms. In Britain and the USA, firms have freedom of contract and can agree with their stakeholders to base distributions on the accounts. Only a relatively small number of firms have decided to do this. This suggests that state intervention would be necessary to achieve any significant increase in the application of the distribution function.

In theory it is certainly possible that the state could decree that distributions to stakeholders should be based on the figures in the financial statements. Even in Britain and the USA, it is accepted that state intervention may, on occasions, be necessary to assure justice. This already happens with public utilities, where the state regulator determines the price charged to customers on the figures in the accounts. A limited extension of this principle to cover certain distributions of certain firms (say those in quasi-monopoly positions) seems feasible. But the imposition of the distribution function by the state brings certain disadvantages: the interference with the workings of the market may lead to a fall in output caused by a reduction in incentives and the misallocation of resources. However lower output may be acceptable if it is offset by greater justice. A more serious difficulty is how to determine what is to be distributed and how much each stakeholder's share should be. It is argued that, for the distribution function to achieve justice, these would have to be calculated by an accountant blessed with infinite wisdom, perfect knowledge, and great integrity. Since such a paragon does not (at present) exist, it is clear that any application of the distribution function is likely to lead to imperfect justice, which, however, may be an improvement over the previous situation. Perhaps, in the future, the discipline of accountancy may make such progress that the accountant will be able to calculate the perfectly just shares of the different stakeholders, and in this way the accountant would become the dispenser of justice—that is an intriguing thought!

7 The Information Function

This chapter considers a third function of accounts: the information function. The financial statements perform the information function when their role is to provide information that aids decision-making. The IASB and FASB endorse the information function when they define the objective of financial reporting as 'to provide financial information about the reporting entity that is useful to present and potential . . . capital providers'. In order to adopt distributive justice as the objective of financial reporting, it is simply necessary to change the nature of the decision to be taken, from investment decisions to decisions relating to the just distribution of the entity's wealth and income. When this objective is adopted the accounts may be said to perform the just information function.

There is a significant difference between the reporting function that is the subject of chapter 5 and the just information function. The reporting function is essentially backward-looking. It reports what happened in the past. The just information function is forward-looking. Its rules are specifically designed to provide the information that is necessary for the achievement of distributive justice in the future. Its objective is to improve future decision-making. It is not principally concerned with the justice of the firm's past activities.

There is also a significant difference between the distribution function and the just information function in the way that each influences the level of distributive justice. With the distribution function, the impact is direct: the figures that are reported in the financial statements largely determine the distribution of the firm's wealth. The accountant (the person who determines the content of the financial statements) has a direct and substantive impact on the distribution of income. With the just information function, the impact is indirect; the distribution of wealth is determined by the decisions that are taken by the persons to whom the information is supplied. With the distribution function, the financial statements play an active role; with the just information function, they play a more passive role—the important decisions are taken elsewhere. Hence, when financial reporting is assigned the just information function, its contribution to the achievement of distributive justice is less central. Even if financial reporting were to perform the suggested information function with complete efficiency (in that the financial statements provided all the information that is needed in order to achieve distributive justice), this is no guarantee that distributive justice would in fact be achieved, for it is also necessary that the recipients of the information take the right decisions. When it performs the just information function, financial reporting is often a necessary but never a sufficient condition for distributive justice.

With the just information function the objective of financial reporting becomes: to provide financial information about the firm that is useful in making decisions about the just and fair distribution of the firm's costs and benefits among its stakeholders.

As explained in Chapter 3, the firm's manager is an important stakeholder, and his decisions have a major impact on distributive justice. But generally there is another stakeholder who is the counterparty of the manager's decision. In Chapter 3, it was argued that, for the purposes of applying stakeholder theory, the firm should be equated with its manager. This concept is followed in this chapter; all references to the firm should be construed as referring to its manager. When the firm deals with a stakeholder, both parties need information in order to reach a decision. A principal source of this information is financial reporting. This chapter analyses the principles that should govern the firm's financial reporting in order that the decisions of stakeholders are to reflect distributive justice.

7.1 THE PHILOSOPHICAL BASIS OF THE PRINCIPLES OF FINANCIAL REPORTING

To develop these principles, I make use of the analytical technique employed by Rawls (1971/1999) in formulating his theory of distributive justice: the veil of ignorance.[1] The basic idea is that the principles that should be followed by the firm in reporting to stakeholders should be decided by a group of persons behind a veil of ignorance—the persons know that they will be stakeholders in a firm but they do not know in which category of stakeholder they will find themselves: as shareholder, employee, manager, or any of the other categories of stakeholders listed in Chapter 3. Hence they are obliged to give serious consideration to the interests of *all* stakeholders. They would consider the interests both of the user of the financial statements and of the preparers, since the firm's managers are also stakeholders. The persons are rational and are concerned to promote and protect their particular interests as individuals. In the original position, all persons have equal bargaining power; this reflects the fundamental principle that all stakeholders are persons of equal moral worth.

In my opinion, the stakeholders in the original position would agree on the following general principles:

a. Truthfulness. The information provided by the firm should be truthful.

b. Objectivity. The information provided by the firm should be objective.

c. Equality. In the preparation of the financial statements, equal consideration should be given to the interests of all stakeholders.

d. Just exchanges. Stakeholders should be provided with information that will enable them to make a contract with the firm that represents a just exchange.

e. Prevention of harm. The information provided by the firm should not lead to a stakeholder suffering harm.

These general principles should govern the provision of all types of information provided to stakeholders by the firm, not only financial information. In the following detailed analysis of these principles, I do not generally make a distinction between financial and non-financial information—for two reasons:

i. Virtually all non-financial information has a financial impact; for example information on the amount of pollution created by the firm helps stakeholders to estimate the firm's future costs relating to such matters as the installation of pollution control equipment.

ii. For historical reasons, the financial statements have become the principal means of communication between the firm and its stakeholders; accountants have been happy to include non-financial information (such as the number of employees) in the notes to the accounts. Hence it is natural that accountants should continue to play a leading role in providing non-financial information to stakeholders, for example by coordinating the work of other experts.

7.2 TRUTHFULNESS

It seems self-evident that no potential stakeholder behind the veil of ignorance would accept being provided with false information. This is the justification for the principle that the information provided by the firm to stakeholders should be true. However this principle is less straightforward than it might seem for three reasons: misleading information, valuation methods, and the philosophical concept of truth.

7.2.1 Misleading Information

It is comparatively rare for financial reports to contain information that is demonstrably false. For example, in the recent scandal involving Enron, the American energy company, there is no evidence that any information presented in the company's financial statements was actually untrue.[2] A rare recent example of a firm making of an untrue statement is provided by Parmalat, the Italian dairy concern, which reported a bank balance of €3.5 billion that did not exist. More commonly the financial statements give a false picture of the firm's situation in ways that do not actually involve making false statements. There are at least three ways in which this may be achieved:

    i. True information may be presented in a misleading manner.
    ii. The firm's transactions may be structured in a way that, when reported (truthfully) in accordance with GAAP, they misrepresent the firm's profitability. This is essentially what happened at Enron, which made much use of special purpose entities.
    iii. Important information may be omitted from the financial statements (this subject is dealt with later in Section 7.5).

Some philosophers draw a distinction between lying and deception. To lie is defined as to make a false statement that the author knows to be false and to deceive as 'to intentionally cause another person to have a false belief'.[3] However, in terms of the morality of the action, the distinction is insignificant. A person who seeks to make another person believe what is false is acting wrongly, and it is irrelevant whether or not, in the process, he actually makes a false statement.

The most famous example of misleading accounts is provided by the 1926 Profit and Loss Account of the Royal Mail Steamship Company, which was the subject of famous court case in which a partner of a leading British accounting firm was accused of fraud.[4] In 1926 the company in fact made a trading loss of £331,000. But, the management, not wishing to report such a negative picture, transferred £750,000 from a secret reserve, which converted the loss into a profit. Neither the secret reserve nor the transfer was reported in the accounts, which simply reported the profit of £419,000. The auditor insisted that the words 'including adjustment of taxation reserves' be added, and this action saved him from being found guilty of fraud, since he argued in his defence that these words were understood by knowledgeable people as indicating that the accounts had been manipulated. However the general public was shocked that the accounting profession should connive at the issue of such misleading accounts, and, shortly afterwards, the law and accounting practice were reformed to outlaw secret reserves.

A more recent example of deception is provided by the statement made by Bank of America (in connection with its proposed take-over of Merrill Lynch) that Merrill Lynch would not pay year-end bonuses without the prior approval of Bank of America. In fact, at the time of the statement, Bank of America had already given its approval. The SEC charged Bank of America with fraud. It is noteworthy that the judge who dealt with the case described Bank of America's statement as 'materially false and misleading'; he did not describe it as 'true but misleading'.

7.2.2 Valuation Methods

In respect of most items that are reported in the financial statements, there can be reasonable differences of opinion as to their value. This is clearly the case with real property or with a debt owed by a customer in financial difficulties. For example a firm reports in its balance sheet the asset 'Land' valued at €100. In fact the land is valued at its historical cost, and its current market value is £1,000,000. The financial statements cannot be criticized as being untrue. Even such a straightforward asset as a bank balance can cause problems, for to value this asset at the amount reported in the bank's statement is to assume that the probability of the bank becoming insolvent is zero, which is surely wrong.

7.2.3 Philosophical Concepts of Truth

The philosophical concept of truth is not straightforward. A widely held theory is that a statement is true if there is correspondence between the statement and external reality. This makes the application of the principle of truth to financial reporting highly problematic. Many figures reported in financial statements relate to things that do not exist in the 'real world'; an example is deferred income, which is essentially a construction of the accountant. Even the IASB admits this, stating that 'deferred charges and credits do not exist in the real world outside financial reporting'[5]—that is they exist only in the minds of the accountant and of the reader who shares the accountant's thought processes. The accountant's figures for profit and net worth (which include elements of such charges and credits) are subject to the same defect. Hence they cannot be considered as 'true' according to philosophical principles that relate truth to external reality. Alexander and Archer (2003) argue that an alternative concept of truth (the coherence concept) and of reality (internal reality) should be applied to financial reporting. This view is not universally accepted which indicates that the application of the principle of truth to financial reporting remains controversial and problematic.

The conclusion is that the principle of truth does not get us very far and that it needs to be supplemented by other principles.

7.3 OBJECTIVITY

The general principle that the information supplied by the firm should be objective is accepted by most accountants, practitioners, and academics alike. The philosophical theory of objectivity contrasts a person's perceptions and beliefs with the real world outside that person. The statement that the height of the Eiffel Tower is 320 metres is objective, as it can be verified by measuring the object in question; the statement that Bloggs believes that the height of the Eiffel Tower is 320 metres is not objective (it is subjective) as it cannot be independently verified; it refers to an internal state of Bloggs's mind.[6] Since, as argued in the previous section, many figures in the accounts refers to things that do not exist in the 'real world' outside the minds of accountants, this concept of objectivity cannot be applied to financial reporting.

Hence accountants have had to develop an alternative theory of objectivity, based on the relationship between stakeholders and the information provided by the firm. Information is held to be objective if it is free from bias with respect to stakeholders—that it is not manipulated or presented in a way that benefits certain stakeholders and not others. I believe that persons behind the veil of ignorance would agree on this principle.

Although the basic concept of objectivity refers to the characteristics of information, the most practical way to achieve the desired result is by giving attention to how the information is prepared. Objectivity will be assured (or at least fostered) if the information is prepared in a certain way. Hence the definition proposed by Ijiri (1983) refers to the preparer: '[O]bjectivity means the independence of the information content from the preparer of the information, that is, similar or identical information is produced regardless of who prepares it.'

A characteristic of information that is closely related to objectivity is verifiability, which Ijiri (1983) defines as follows: '[V]erifiability means that the information can be verified at a later point in time, that is, that there are sufficient trails to enable anyone to reconstruct the information, should that become necessary.' Verifiability is related to objectivity in that information that is verifiable is more likely to be objective, for two reasons: Firstly, the preparer will be more inclined to make sure that the information is not subjective, if he is aware that it will later be checked by a second person. The need to assure verifiability greatly circumscribes the preparer's discretion. Secondly, if a second person agrees with the preparer's treatment of the information, this is evidence of the quality of objectivity formulated by Ijiri—'the same information is produced irrespective of who produced it'. I am inclined to hold that verifiability is a necessary condition for objectivity, because a verification procedure that is always available is for a second person to attempt to reproduce the information. If this proves impossible, the information cannot be proved to be objective.

The need to assure that information provided to stakeholders is objective has major implications for the way in which that information is produced. These are considered in detail later in Section 7.11.

7.4 ALL STAKEHOLDERS ARE TO BE GIVEN EQUAL CONSIDERATION

The firm should give equal consideration to the welfare of all stakeholders. This principle follows naturally from the principle that all persons are of equal moral worth. The equality principle demands that, in drawing up and disseminating the financial statements, the firm (that is, the management) should give equal consideration to all stakeholders. But this does not imply that all stakeholders should receive the same information. The question of different information for different categories of stakeholder is considered later in Section 7.8.

Sternberg (1994) claims that the firm's management is accountable only to the firm's owners and is under no obligation to render accounts to any other stakeholder, unless required under a specific contract. This view of accountability is reflected in the company law of many countries, which states that the financial statements are addressed exclusively to shareholders. In my opinion, this is fundamentally unjust as shareholders are thus placed in a privileged position in relation to other stakeholders. Hence I agree with Ijiri (1983), who argues that an accountability relationship may exist between a firm and the whole range of stakeholders: shareholders, creditors, government, labour unions, consumers, and the public in general. The justification for this general obligation to present accounts is that without the information contained therein stakeholders cannot be assured of distributive justice.

7.5 JUST EXCHANGE

As already explained in Chapter 3, the relationship between the firm and its primary stakeholders is essentially one of mutually beneficial exchange. Throughout the ages philosophers have reflected on the nature of exchanges. The first philosopher to develop a comprehensive theory of exchange was Aristotle. Aristotle posited that no man is self-sufficient. He has wants that he is unable to satisfy with his own efforts and, in order to satisfy these wants, he has to seek the aid of other men. If he finds another man who is able to meet his wants and, if he is able to reciprocate by meeting that man's wants, then an exchange occurs. Such an exchange is fundamentally good, because it satisfies human needs. However, for Aristotle, the more important effect of exchange was that it created a community. He writes: 'It is proportional requital that holds the state together . . . if this is impossible, no exchange takes place; and it is exchange that holds them [citizens] together.'[7] Only in a community can a man exercise all the virtues of which man is capable. Daryl Koehn (1992) paraphrases Aristotle's position as follows:

> Exchange has the unique feature of binding people into a community in and through which all of the virtues come to be in a humanly complete form. Without exchange, we would not look upon nor share in any of those virtues which our community sees fit to extol as excellences . . . Exchange is itself an excellence or virtue because it is the

active completion of the potential of human desire to become one with other human desire through a common act.

Aristotle held that man was a political animal. Only in the company of other men, that is, in society (the polis), could a man achieve his highest stature; only there could he exercise and display the highest human virtues, such as courage, generosity, and love. However the polis depended for its very existence on the labour of countless men and women, who were able to collaborate by exchanges that were generally mediated through money. Aristotle was no doubt fully aware that he was able to lead a life of philosophical investigation only because, in the polis, he could obtain the necessities of life by offering in exchange his own labour (in the form of teaching and advice). The highest form of human life, that of the philosopher, is possible only in a community built on exchange.

Aristotle held that the supreme value of exchanges was that they made possible the existence of the state. The relevance of this idea to the subject of this book is that exchanges make possible the existence of the firm; the firm is fundamentally good (although of a lower order than the state) because it meets men's needs. However, for the outcome of an exchange to be good, it must be just: the costs and benefits of the exchange must be divided justly between the parties. There are generally considered to be two major conditions necessary for an exchange to be just:

i. Neither party is forced to undertake the exchange.
ii. Both parties should have information that is sufficient to enable them to judge whether the proposed exchange is in their interest.

The principle of no-coercion raises very considerable problems in application, notably the extent to which the fact that the bargaining positions of the parties are unequal renders an exchange unfair. Fortunately such problems are not in the domain of financial reporting, which is more concerned with the second problem relating to sufficient information. The judgement as to whether information is sufficient has to be made from the viewpoint of the parties to the exchange. If either party to an exchange can subsequently claim truthfully that she would not have gone through with the exchange if she had been provided with information that the other party had available, then the exchange was not just. Neither party to an exchange should withhold information in her possession that is relevant to the other party's decision to go through with the exchange, either because the relevance of the information may be reasonably inferred or because she is aware of a particular interest of the other party. The withholding of relevant information makes the exchange unjust.

Such information should relate to matters that existed at the time of the exchange; for example a person who bought a house which shortly after the purchase was destroyed by fire, would no doubt claim that she would not have gone through with the purchase if she had known that this would happen. However she can claim to have been misled only if relevant facts that were known to the other party and which existed at the time of the exchange were withheld from her; for example that the house was constructed of unusually inflammable materials.

This principle would seem to imply that firms should include vast quantities of information in its financial statements so as to ensure that, subsequently, no stakeholder may reasonably claim that the firm withheld relevant information. This raises two issues:

i. The cost to the firm of providing this information may be excessive. This matter is considered later in Section 7.10.
ii. More data may mean less information. The user may be unable to find the information that she needs in the vast amount of data supplied by the firm. For example, how should one judge the situation if the house purchaser in the previous example had been supplied with a 2000-page report in which the fact that the house was constructed of inflammable materials was mentioned in a one-line footnote on page 1723? A recent example in the field of financial reporting is provided by the financial statements of Northern Rock, the British bank that collapsed in August 2007. As reported by Towers (2008), its last annual report before its collapse covered 105 pages, but only three items (which were not given any prominence) were in any way relevant in predicting its collapse. Clearly if one party deliberately seeks to hide relevant information in a mass of irrelevant information, such behaviour is unjust, but there is no evidence that this was the motivation of Northern Rock's management.

I am sure that stakeholders behind the veil of ignorance would agree on the principle that forbids the withholding of relevant information. Clearly such a principle conflicts with the legal rule of 'caveat emptor' (let the buyer beware), which I suspect was developed by judges as a simple rule of thumb for deciding difficult cases and not as a manifestation of justice. Readers may feel that it is unreasonable to expect the parties to an exchange to volunteer information that is to their disadvantage. It may be human to behave in this way, but it most certainly is not just.

7.6 PREVENTION OF HARM

It is a fundamental principle that one person should not, without sufficient justification, harm another person. It is rare for a stakeholder to suffer harm as a direct result of information contained in a firm's financial statements and, when this happens, it will generally be the case that the firm has violated some other principle. For example the loss suffered by a person who invested in Parmalat on the strength of that firm's financial statements can be attributed to the firm's breach of the principle of truth. Of greater significance for financial reporting is the derived principle that, when a person's activities harm another person (or has the potential to harm), the first person has a duty to provide information that will enable the second person to limit the extent of the harm (or avoid it altogether).

Hence when a particular stakeholder's welfare is affected by a firm's actions, the stakeholder rationally should take some action to defend her position. There are several possible types of action:

i. She could cease to be a stakeholder by severing her relationship with the firm, as when, for example, a shareholder sells her shares.

ii. She could intervene directly with the firm's management. Perhaps such intervention initially would consist of the presentation of rational arguments, but ultimately it may consist of more forceful acts such as strikes by employees or boycotts by customers. If the management proves unresponsive, she may decide to appeal directly to the public by organizing a publicity campaign, such as that of Greenpeace directed against the Shell Oil Company.

iii. She could lobby the government to take action with regard to the firm, either by enforcing existing laws (where the information in the financial statements indicated that laws have been broken) or by creating new laws.[8]. Where the stakeholder is the government, the financial statements provide the information that may trigger government action.

The stakeholder requires information in order to decide when she needs to take action and what action to take. The implication of this principle is that, when the firm's activities harm other people or have the potential to harm them, the firm is under a moral obligation to provide information on such activities.

I now consider the implications of these general principles.

7.7 GREATER TRANSPARENCY

The preceding analysis suggests that distributive justice requires far greater transparency on the firm's part than is currently practised. The firms' management may be expected to argue that such transparency would have a negative impact on the firm's economic position, for example in the following ways:

i. Employees may use the extra information to force the firm to pay higher wages.

ii. A supplier may refuse to supply goods on credit, when he learns that the firm is in danger of bankruptcy.
iii. A supplier may demand higher prices when it learns how dependent the firm is on his continued supplies.
iv. The government may use the information to punish the firm for breaches of the law—that is, the firm is being compelled to testify against itself.
v. A citizen of a remote foreign country may organize a consumer boycott of the firm's products, when she discovers the extent of the air pollution caused by the firm.
vi. A competing firm may take action that is detrimental to the firm which it would not have taken in the absence of the information provided in the accounts.

An analysis of these examples gives an insight to the extent to which the arguments against greater transparency are justified. In my opinion, in examples i, ii, iv, and v, the greater transparency leads to greater justice among stakeholders. It should be remembered that the shareholders are only one of many stakeholders. When the diffusion of more information leads to a transfer of wealth from one group of stakeholders to another (as happens in example i where employees benefit at the expense of shareholders), this implies that the previous distribution of wealth depended on the relative ignorance of one of the parties, which cannot be justified on grounds either of economic efficiency or of justice.

Example iii is more problematic. In certain circumstances the relationship between the firm and a particular supplier may be assimilated to a two-person game; in such a game one party may gain a relative advantage over the other by withholding relevant information. In Section 7.5, it was argued that such action would be unjust; justice requires that both the firm and the supplier be open. This example brings out very clearly the difference between the stakeholder theory of the firm and the neo-liberal theory. With the stakeholder theory, a supplier who provides materials that are an essential element of the firm's product and are not available from other sources, is part of the nexus of relationships that make up the firm. Both the firm (the management) and the supplier have an interest in the firm's continued existence and have a mutual obligation to provide information that ensures that their relationship is conducted in a just fashion. With the neo-liberal theory, the firm is independent of the supplier and should use every opportunity to increase its own profit at the supplier's expense, short of engaging in 'deception and fraud'.[9] The firm has no obligation to provide information that is to its own disadvantage.

I argue that the supplier and the firm's management would agree on full disclosure behind the 'veil of ignorance' and hence that this is the more just approach.

A different argument for greater transparency is based on the fact that the firm in the real world (that is, not behind the veil of ignorance) acts in various capacities; it is not only a customer of its suppliers but also a supplier to its customers. Since the firm's management would be in favour of its suppliers and customers practising full disclosure, and since the same principles should apply to the financial reporting of all firms, it follows that the management should accept for itself a duty of full disclosure. This argument can be extended to reporting to shareholders (the firm may be a shareholder in another firm) and to secondary stakeholders (the firm may suffer from pollution emanating from another firm).

Finally let us consider example vi, which is probably the most problematic. A competitor is not *per se* a stakeholder; however, given the very wide range of stakeholders, it will very likely gain access to any information that is distributed to stakeholders. Furthermore a competitor may be a stakeholder in another capacity; for example by being affected by pollution emanating from the firm. This example raises two questions:

i. Does the proper functioning of the economic system depend on certain categories of information being kept secret? The answer must be 'yes'. For example, innovation would be stifled if a firm were compelled to publish full details of all research and development work on which it was engaged. Competitors would be able to benefit from the firm's efforts; they would be 'free-riders'—reaping the benefits without sharing in the costs, which cannot be described as just. The firm would not be able to enjoy the full benefits of its efforts and hence would be less motivated to innovate. Hence there is a good argument for firms withholding certain categories of information from stakeholders; the question is which categories? I feel that there should be a presumption of great transparency and that exceptions to this principle should be justified using convincing arguments, such as that presented here in relation to research.
ii. Is it necessary that all stakeholders should be provided with the same information? For example does the inhabitant of a distant country who is adversely affected by pollution created by the firm need information on the firm's cash flow which a shareholder needs to evaluate her investment? Although the answer seems obvious, there are interesting complications which will now be considered.

7.8 THE SAME INFORMATION FOR ALL STAKEHOLDERS?

As a general rule a stakeholder should be provided with information that is relevant to decisions that he may be expected to make in his capacity as stakeholder. Hence for example:

i. A person whose principal relationship with a firm is that he suffers from pollution created by the firm should be provided with data on such matters as the firm's production processes and the levels of emission of noxious substances. He has no need for information on cash flows, number of employees, sales in different countries, and so on.

ii. A customer should be provided with information on the product's composition, on potential health and safety hazards associated with the product, on problems encountered by other customers that are known to the firm, and so on.

iii. Employees (and their representatives) should be provided with a substantial amount of information relating to the firm's present and projected future activities. This would cover not only specifically employment matters (such as number of employees) but also information that would enable employees to judge the firm's viability and profitability, in both the near and the more distant future. The very wide information needs of employees reflect the fact that, generally, their welfare is more closely dependent on the firm's activities than is the case with any other group of stakeholders.[10]

Since different categories of stakeholder require information as input to different decisions, it is logical that these different categories should be provided with different types of information. However a distinction should be drawn between disclosure and measurement:

a. Disclosure

The minimum amount of detailed information that the firm be required to disclose may reasonably vary between different stakeholder categories.

b. Measurement

It should not be permitted that the principles used by the firm to value assets and to calculate profit should vary according to stakeholder category; for example the firm should not report one figure for profit to one group of stakeholders and a different figure to another group: for example profit based on social costs (for stakeholders affected by pollution) and profit based on private costs (for shareholders). There are two reasons for this prohibition:

i. One of the functions of the financial statements is to aid in the division of the firm's wealth and income among its stakeholders. Such a division makes sense only if there is agreement among all stakeholders as to the value of what is being divided.

ii. If the firm were to report different figures for profit to different stakeholders, this would impair the credibility of the financial statements and undermine the trust that stakeholders would have in their reliability.

However the principle of the same measurement principles for all stakeholders runs into problems in respect of taxation. In Chapter 6, Section 6.2.1, I argued that the taxable profit and the profit reported to shareholders should be identical or at least not differ greatly. But most accounting practitioners and theorists do not agree with me; they hold that there should be no requirement that the profit figure that a firm reports in its income statement should be identical with that presented in its return to the tax authorities on which its taxation charge is computed. The reason is that the rules that are used to measure income and expenses for tax purposes are frequently inappropriate for reporting to other parties, particularly shareholders. For example, the tax authorities sometimes allow a firm to treat the entire cost of a fixed asset as a charge against profits in the year of acquisition, in this way providing an incentive for firms to invest. However from the shareholders' viewpoint, this treatment leads to an overstatement of expenses and an understatement of assets.

In my view, the explanation for this conflict is that the tax authorities, in offering a 100% write-off of fixed assets in the year of acquisition, are not seeking an accurate measure of the firm's profits (which would give a reasonable basis for assessing the contribution that the firm should make to the common weal); rather they are pursuing a quite different objective—the promotion of investment. Therefore it is wrong to label as 'profit' the figure on which tax is computed. However this is exactly what the firm is obliged to do in certain countries (notably Germany and Japan) where there is a legal requirement that, if a firm wishes to claim an expense for tax purposes, it must also report it in its income statement. In effect, one stakeholder (the tax authority) insists that the financial statements be drawn up according to its requirements, which make them less useful for the other stakeholders. This is thoroughly unjust because it privileges one stakeholder over all the others. In Chapter 6, Section 6.2.1, I argue that there are very strong social advantages in making the profit on which the firm pays tax identical with its reported profit. However, the achievement of this desirable state of affairs requires the cooperation both of the tax authorities and of those who set the rules of financial reporting.

I have argued that the firm should not report multiple figures for profit and for asset values. However this does not prevent it providing further information, based on different measurement principles, in the notes to the accounts. Thus one solution to the problem relating to taxes is to include information on the tax computation in the notes.

7.9 BALANCE OF THE COSTS AND BENEFITS OF FINANCIAL REPORTING

In Section 7.4, it was argued that equal consideration should be given to the welfare of all stakeholders. The firm's managers are stakeholders and their interests must be considered. This is of particular significance in relation to the costs of financial reporting, which it is in the interest of the firm's managers to minimize.[11] This requires that the benefits of information to the user should be weighed against the costs to the preparer of providing the information. The user may not reasonably demand to be provided with information if the costs to the supplier exceed the benefits to the user. Ijiri (1983) considers that it is essential to maintain fairness between the supplier and the user and that (to quote) 'the objective of accounting is to provide a fair system of information flow between [supplier] and [user]'. He acknowledges that the accountant's task in this situation is difficult and refers to 'the agony of finding a thin line of fairness between the conflicting interests of the two parties'.

It is noteworthy that both Rawls and Ijiri identify the same quality 'fairness' as important, although of course in quite different contexts. In my opinion Ijiri is right in insisting that 'fairness' requires that the interests of the information supplier (the firm's management) should be taken into account in determining the information flow from the firm to stakeholders. The concept of fairness explains why it is reasonable to balance the costs that are incurred by one person against the benefits enjoyed by a quite different person.

7.10 THE CASE FOR HISTORICAL COST

Section 7.3 identified two important characteristics of accounting information as objectivity and verifiability. Ijiri (1983) argues that the objectivity and verifiability of accounting information can often best be assured by using historical cost as the measurement basis. He identifies the following advantages of historical cost:

i. It is more objective than methods based on current market prices because it is based on an actual transaction and not on a hypothetical transaction.
ii. The reporting of historical cost implicitly assures the existence of historical records regarding items in the accounts because otherwise the historical cost cannot be determined. Other valuation methods do not require information on the history of the item that is to be valued—only its present status. The need to retain and use a historical record greatly restricts the freedom of the preparer to value an item subjectively.
iii. Historical cost figures are often derived as the aggregate of a large number of accountants' decisions and hence are less likely to be affected by bias or error in any one decision.

All three advantages can be illustrated by comparing historical cost with the net present value method. The historical cost is based on past transactions;

the net present value is based on future transactions which do not yet exist and may never exist. Secondly, for the historical cost, the past transactions, in the ideal situation, would be evidenced by documents of such integrity that they would persuade a judge in a court of law that the transactions took place for the indicated consideration; by contrast, the documentary back-up for the net present value might, in the ideal case, consist of a mass of documents, but they would provide evidence of little more than the working methods and opinions of the person who made the forecast. Thirdly, in most cases, the historical costs reported in the accounts would be the aggregate of many past payments; the net present value is crucially dependent on a single figure: the discount rate. If the firm changes its estimate of this variable, this changes the value of every asset that is reported at net present value; a change of the discount rate from 10% to 5% would lead to a significant increase in the reported value of all such assets—in some cases doubling their value.

It is not suggested that measurement methods other than historical cost should never be used. Where other methods, such as market value, pass the tests of objectivity and verifiability their use may well increase the usefulness of the financial statements for stakeholders. An example would be an asset, such as listed securities, which can be easily bought or sold at publicly quoted prices

These suggestions are tentative and do not form part of my central thesis. I can understand that a stakeholder whose principal interest lies in measuring the damage to the environment caused by the firm's operations might prefer that the accounts be based on social costs rather than on historical cost. Ideally this matter would be settled by the standard-setting bodies in a way acceptable to all stakeholders if these bodies were reformed to include representatives of all stakeholders, as will be proposed in the next section.

7.11 THE IMPLICATIONS OF OBJECTIVITY

This section considers the implications of the principles that financial reporting should be objective and should give equal consideration to all stakeholders. A most important quality of financial reporting that should enable it to serve effectively the cause of distributive justice is that it should be accepted by all stakeholders. The proper functioning of the economy depends on mutual trust between the various economic actors, and financial reporting can make a major contribution towards creating and maintaining trust. All stakeholders should trust the financial statements and believe that they present in a true, fair, just, and unbiassed way the financial position and performance of the firm.

To achieve this happy state of affairs, there are at least three preconditions:

a.   Publicly Formulated Rules

The rules that the accountant follows in drawing up the financial statements should be set by a body that is not beholden to any stakeholder. These rules would have the status of law, because of the influence that they have on the wealth of many citizens, and, as a law, they should be enacted by society's accepted procedure and should be promulgated publicly. In a democracy, they should be set by the democratically elected legislature or by an agency (for example a standard-setting body) to which the legislature has delegated this responsibility and which in turn follows due process in its procedures. Since ultimate authority rests with the legislature, it is appropriate that it retains the right to supervise the operations of any subsidiary body and to override its decisions as necessary.

In recent years, the standard-setting process has clearly become more just in many countries, as the standard-setting bodies that originally were dominated by the accountancy profession (such as the USA's APB and the UK's ASSC) have been replaced by bodies (the FASB and the ASB) which reflect a wider range of interests and which make a conscious effort to follow due process. The same is true at the international level, where the IASC, which was a creature of the accountancy profession,[12] has been replaced by the IASB, whose governing body (the trustees) is not dominated by accountants. However the representation of stakeholders on the governing bodies of these standard-setting bodies is still very limited; for example they include no representatives of labour or of public interest NGOs.[13]

An alternative way of setting the rules of financial reporting would be through the establishment of an accounting court which would adopt a public utilitarian view in passing judgement on the principles used in accounting. This was proposed by a leading American practitioner some fifty years ago who argued: '[A]n accounting principle to be of utility to consumer, labour, stockholder and management would require support in each pronouncement as to why the principle adopted produces a fair result from the standpoint of each of these segments of society' (Spacek 1969: 35). In one country, the Netherlands, an accounting court was set up in the 1970s, but it has issued comparatively few judgements and it has had only limited influence on the financial reporting of Dutch companies.[14]

It is clear that currently the bodies that set accounting principles are not organized in a way that assures that they take fully into account the interests of all stakeholders . Hence much more needs to be done before the level of justice in the standard-setting process can be considered to be adequate.

b. Independent and Objective Preparers

The person who prepares the financial statements should not act in the interests of any particular stakeholder. The present arrangement is that the financial statements are prepared by the firm's accountant, who is normally employed and controlled by the firm's management, who in turn is required by law to act in the interests of shareholders. This is clearly undesirable from a wider stakeholder viewpoint. Thus according to Stewart (1986) 'the major ethical problem of financial reporting is that management, which has the responsibility for preparing financial reports, cannot impartially report on its own achievements'. To a certain extent, this defect is mitigated by requiring that the firm's financial statements are audited. However the improvement that the practice of auditing brings to the stakeholder's perception of the objectivity of the financial statements is minimal, given that the auditor is appointed by the shareholders, paid by the firm, and often dependent on the goodwill of management for other remunerative jobs. Hence a more radical approach is called for.

One possible solution is to create a corps of accountants, not employed by or paid by any stakeholder, who would prepare and certify the financial statements of firms; the accountants would be employed and remunerated by the state, which would finance their activities out of a levy on the body of stakeholders. These accountants would be similar in certain respects to present-day auditors, in that they would be independent experts. However they would differ in that they would prepare the financial statements and they would not be appointed and paid by the firm. They would serve all stakeholders and, in principle, there should be some saving in resources in information processing by individual stakeholders. It is a moot point whether, in addition to this corps of accountants, there should also be a corps of auditors who would control the accountants. There is always the question of 'quis custodet custodes?',[15] but at some point it would seem expedient to dispense with further layers of control.

Such a corps of accountants would have a similar function to the 'transnational corporations monitoring units' proposed by Bailey et alia (1994: 55), except that their activities would cover both national and international firms. Bailey suggested that the units be 'designed to collect information on transnationals' performance and impact, to prepare accounts and to use them to influence economic policy and attitudes of and towards transnationals', which implies a very wide function for financial reporting, but one that is limited to providing information.

Past experience of delegating accounting to persons outside the firm is not very positive. In the former Soviet Union, the chief accountant of most firms was a government employee, one of whose functions was to report to the central planning authority on the firm's progress in fulfilling the state's plan. The accountant was an important element in the centrally controlled Soviet economic system and therefore bore some responsibility for the spectacular failure of this system to satisfy the expectations of consumers. In Greece until recently the auditing of companies was carried out exclusively by a government body, Soma Orkoton Logiston (SOL).[16] SOL was criticized by many businessmen as being bureaucratic and inefficient, and in 1993 it was replaced by Soma Orkoton Elekton (SOE), a body that was not so closely linked to the government. This experience suggests that, although the present system in Western countries is not fully satisfactory, it is difficult to design an alternative that will give stakeholders greater assurance as to the objectivity of the firm's financial statements.

c. Objective Evidence

The accountant in deciding on the figures to be reported in the financial statements should base her decision on evidence that all stakeholders accept as providing conclusive proof of the accuracy of the figures. The tests that the accountant should apply to the evidence should be similar to those employed by a judge in deciding a civil case in a court of law: objectivity, credibility, lack of bias, support of expert opinion, and so on. It is a moot point whether the evidence should be available for scrutiny by all interested parties, for it is not acceptable that the accountant's decisions as to the contents of the accounts should be based on information that cannot be checked by those whose welfare is affected.

The fundamental reason for this very stringent rule of evidence is that what is reported in the accounts affects the welfare of all stakeholders. For this reason, the firm's financial statements should have the status of a formal legal document which, at least in respect of the more important stakeholders, defines their rights and obligations. This is already the case in certain countries in respect of certain categories of accounts: the court of auditors judges the accounts and issues a decree that certifies their authenticity.

When this approach is applied to financial reporting, the fundamental academic discipline of accounting becomes not economics (as is presently the case throughout much of the world) but law. In my opinion, compared with economics, the discipline of law provides much better insights into how to resolve disputes between people over the division of limited resources, which is one of basic functions of the financial statements when the objective is distributive justice. This is what judges and lawyers have been practising for centuries, whereas the work of most economists is largely theoretical.

7.12 THE JUST INFORMATION FUNCTION: SUMMARY AND CONCLUSIONS

The financial statements perform the information function, when their objective is to provide information that that is useful in making decisions. When the firm's objective is distributive justice, then the information that they provide should be that which is useful and relevant for decisions that lead to the just and fair distribution of the costs and benefits of the firm's activities among its stakeholders. In that case, the financial statements may be said to perform the just information function. With the just information function, there is no guarantee that the firm will achieve distributive justice—that depends on the decisions made by the recipients of the information (the firm's stakeholders, including its manager). Therefore, the just information function is never a sufficient condition for distributive justice; however, it can be argued that it is a necessary condition.

With the just information function, the principles that govern financial reporting should be set in a way that assures equal consideration of the interests of all stakeholders. This would be achieved if these principles were set by stakeholders behind a 'veil of ignorance'. It is argued that stakeholders would agree to the following principles: truth, objectivity, equal consideration for all stakeholders, justice in exchanges, and prevention of harm. The implications of these principles are great transparency, identical measurement rules for all stakeholders (but not identical disclosure), and the balancing of the costs and benefits of financial reporting.

The IASB endorses the information function (albeit to provide information for capital providers and not as a means of furthering justice). Hence most accountants would understand the arguments for the principles set out herein, even if they would not agree with all of them. They would certainly agree with the principles of truth and objectivity; many would accept, in theory, the principles of equal consideration for all stakeholders, justice in exchanges, and prevention of harm, but, in practice might balk at the level of transparency implied by these principles. As concerns the principles that should govern the form and content of accounts, it would seem that the implications of adopting the just information function are not all that revolutionary.

It was argued that the principles of objectivity and equal consideration for all stakeholders have far-reaching implications for the practice of financial reporting. In order to ensure that the financial statements are truly objective, three conditions are necessary:

(i)   The rules that govern the form and content of accounts should be set by bodies that are truly independent of all stakeholders.
(ii) The financial statements should be prepared by persons who are independent of all stakeholders.
(iii) The financial statements should be based on objective evidence equivalent to that required in a court of law.

Most accountants (including the IASB) accept that the function of the financial statements is to provide information that aids decision-making, albeit not in the cause of justice but in the narrower cause of the better functioning of capital markets. Hence they would accept many of the principles expounded in this chapter, such as truth and objectivity. They would probably balk at those principles that are based on giving equal consideration to all stakeholders, such as great transparency, because they give priority to the interests of capital providers over other stakeholders. Whereas most contemporary accountants would appreciate the relevance and validity of the general principles (although they would certainly argue over details), they would almost certainly reject the chapter's proposals concerning the practice of accountancy, which are certainly revolutionary.

8 Concluding Remarks

The last three chapters have presented three apparently radically different concepts of financial reporting. It would not be surprising if this exposition has left the reader thoroughly confused and with many unanswered questions, such as:

- What is the particular contribution to justice of each of the three functions?
- Must the firm prepare three sets of financial statements, one for each function and each different from the other?
- Is one of the three functions more important than the other two?
- What is the author's position on these matters?

In this concluding chapter I seek to answer these questions, with the aim that, by the end of the book, the reader is hopefully less confused and has a clear idea of my position.

8.1 EACH FUNCTION'S CONTRIBUTION TO JUSTICE

What is the contribution that each function makes towards the achievement of justice by the firm? This question will be analysed with the aid of the following example of the role that each function plays in a particular decision of the firm's manager: to pay a bonus to a key employee.

(i) The Reporting Function

The manager, after having studied the firm's conventional income statement for the past year, decides to pay a bonus to a key employee, even though there is no legal obligation to do so.

(ii) The Distribution Function

The manager pays the key employee a bonus of 10% of the profits as reported in the firm's income statement for the past year, in accordance with the terms of the contract between the firm and the employee.

(iii) The information function

The manager and the trade union official who represents the firm's workers meet to negotiate wage rates for the coming year. In the course of the negotiations, each uses arguments that refer (in different ways) to the firm's income statement for the past year.

This example brings out the following differences between the functions.

(a) The Past and the Future

In order for the firm to achieve justice, its actions must be just. Its present decisions must be such that its future actions are just. This does not imply that the firm may ignore the past. For example, the way in which the firm currently treats its stakeholders should depend on what happened in the past; for example, in Chapter 3 (Section 3.8.1), it was argued that the firm should not ignore the thirty years' past service of the long-serving employee. Hence the achievement of justice involves both the past and the future: information on the past and actions to be taken in the future.

The reporting function differs significantly from the other two in that it is primarily concerned with the past. It is true that, even with the reporting function, after someone has reflected on the information contained in the accounts, he may be motivated to adapt his future action, as happens in the preceding example. However, this impact on future action is essentially a by-product of the reporting function; it is not its raison d'être, which is, however, the case with the other two functions. The role of the distribution function is to determine the amount of the bonus to be paid; the bonus certainly relates to last year, but the action of actually paying it lies in the future. The decisions that are taken with the aid of the information function all concern actions to be taken in the future.

However, with all three functions, the content of the financial statements primarily concerns the past. Generally the influence of the future is limited to such matters as estimating the probability that a debt will not be paid.

(b) Influence on Future Decisions

The influence of the reporting function on the firm's future actions is weak and sporadic. It is far stronger for the other two functions. The information function is distinguished from the distribution function by the degree of influence that the financial statements exercise over the firm's decisions. With the distribution function, the influence is strong and direct. With the information function the influence is weaker and always indirect; the future action is not determined by the information in the accounts but rather by the users of the accounts. In effect the distribution function and the information function lie at opposite ends of a broad spectrum, with strong influence over future actions at one end and weak influence at the other. In fact it is never the case that the accounts fully determine a future action of the firm; even when the amount of the bonus is calculated as a proportion of the reported profit, the actual payment of the bonus entails further actions, for example the firm's manager writing a cheque. Hence the distribution in its pure form (where the financial statements determine the firm's future actions) does not exist. However, to take the examples cited previously, there is a vast difference between the two functions in the degree to which, with the distribution function, the income statement influences the firm's bonus payment and, with the information function, it influences the future level of wages.

(c) The Role of the State

In the preceding example, the firm imposed the distribution function on itself, through the contract that it made with its employee. However, it is more common for the distribution function to be imposed on the firm by the state. There is a relationship (albeit a rather weak one) between, on the one hand, the state and the distribution function, and, on the other hand, the firms' manager and the information function. Often the state finds that it is in its interest to impose the distribution function on the firm, thus obliging it to act in a certain way. But it is rarely in the manager's interest that he should restrict his future freedom of action by assigning an active role to the financial statements. He prefers to assign to the accounts a passive role and thereby retain the power to manage the firm as he wills. However, as demonstrated in Chapter 6, there are occasions when the manager does accept that the accounts play an active role. The state has a much stronger motivation to govern the firm's behaviour through its financial statements; clearly this is feasible only when the state through its regulations controls their form and content.

(d) Influence on Justice: The Distribution Function and the Information Function

Where the state imposes the distribution function on the firm, it is effectively obliging the firm to act justly, or at least in accordance with the state's concept of justice. For example, if the state decrees that justice demands that the firm contributes 40% of last year's profits to the common weal (in the form of tax), then the firm has to obey (or suffer the consequences of breaking the law). The firm is forced to be just.

The position is very different with the information function. Whether or not the firm achieves justice depends essentially on the decisions taken by the stakeholders who use the information provided by the accounts. To take the example of the manager and the trade union official, there is no certainty that the wage rate that they negotiate will be just; one would expect that a host of factors would influence their final decision, including their personal morality and the pressures of other stakeholders (the share-holders in the case of the manager and the workers in the case of the trade union official). The information contained in the financial statements is but one input to their decision. The most that can be expected is that the financial statements provide all the information that is necessary for the stakeholders to achieve justice. Such information may be a necessary condition for justice, but never a sufficient condition.

(e) Influence on Justice: The Reporting Function

The influence of the reporting function on justice differs significantly from that of the other two. The nature of this influence may be assessed by imag-ining what would happen if the firm never reported on the justice of its past actions. The firm's manager would never know whether he made the right decisions in the past—decisions that resulted in justice. The same would apply to other stakeholders; all need information on the outcome of their decisions. The provision of such information is the principal role of the reporting func-tion. The reporting function's role in achieving justice is essential but also sec-ondary to that of the other two functions. Essentially the reporting function provides information that is input to the other functions.

8.2 DOES THE FIRM HAVE TO PREPARE MULTIPLE FINANCIAL STATEMENTS?

Can a single set of financial statements fulfill all three functions or must the firm prepare separate different statements for each function?

8.2.1 The Distribution Function

This question will be considered in relation to the distribution function. In theory, in an ideal world, the state would impose a distribution function on the firm that would result in its income being calculated and distrib-uted in a completely just way among its stakeholders. In practice, this ideal world does not exist; the philosopher-accountant of infinite wisdom, per-fect knowledge and great integrity posited in Chapter 6 (Section 6.7.2) has yet to be born. In practice, when the state imposes the distribution function on the firm, it does this for its own specific ends, which often are not exclu-sively the achievement of justice and generally do not take into account the interests of other stakeholders. The information needs of the stakeholders other than the state are not generally met by the financial statements that are prepared in accordance with the distribution function imposed by the state. In order to meet their information needs, the firm has to prepare a second separate set of financial statements.

In Chapter 7 (Section 7.8), I argued that there are great social advan-tages if the amount of tax payable by a firm were to be based on the figure for profit that is reported to other stakeholders, including shareholders. This implies that all stakeholders should be provided with the same information—a single unique set of financial statements, which would be that imposed by the state. In my opinion the social advantages of such a single set of accounts are real and substantial. But this implies that the firm's income statement should be identical with its tax computation. The stakeholders (other than the state) would not be supplied with the information that they need in order to achieve justice. Hence a separate set of accounts is necessary. Regrettably the firm's financial statements would not be identical with its tax computation. I feel that the fault for this undesirable state of affairs lies generally with the state which does not give proper consideration to the demands of justice in framing its tax rules.

It is not impossible that the firm may be obliged to prepare more than one set of accounts that perform the distribution function. For example, the state may decide, in the case of a regulated public utility, that the computation of profit that is appropriate for assessing the balance of justice between customers and shareholders should not be identical with the computation that is appropriate for the calculation of the tax liability. In that case, the public utility would be obliged to draw up two different computations of its profit. Similarly, in the case of bonus payments to employees, there is nothing to prevent the firm contracting with one employee to base his bonus payment on profit calculated using current costs and contracting with a second employee to pay her bonus on profits calculated according to historical cost.

When, in accordance with the distribution function, the firm should take some action, the parties involved need to assure themselves that the firm in fact acts as required. In the case of the firm's tax liability this is straightforward, the state checks that it receives the appropriate amount. However, there are more complex situations. As explained in Chapter 6 (Section 6.3), the state's regulator may impose profit sharing on a public utility, demanding that the utility's profit (as reported in its last financial statements) should be divided according to a certain formula between its shareholders and its customers. This is essentially an application of the distribution function. However, the regulator also needs to check that the utility's customers have in fact received their due share of the profit; he does that by scrutinizing the utility's financial statements for the next period— an application of the reporting function. The rules used in drawing up the accounts for this reporting function must be the same as those used with the distribution function for the previous year's accounts. In particular, the utility's profit must be calculated in the same way (using the same rules and conventions), both in the previous year's accounts (which established that the utility's profit was too high) and in the following year's accounts (which demonstrate that the customers have received their due share of the previous year's excessive profits). The profit that is returned to the customers in the second year must be calculated with the same rules as those used for establishing that the shareholders' profit in the first year was excessive.

Hence a single set of financial statements serves two purposes: to provide information for future decisions and to check the implementation of past decisions. When a particular set of rules has been used in making a decision, the same principles have to be applied in checking that the decision has been carried out: the criteria used for controlling must be the same as those used for the original decision.

8.2.2 The Information Function

In the previous section, I argue that the accounts that perform the distribution function do not normally meet the information needs of stakeholders in general and that therefore the firm should prepare a separate set of accounts that perform this information function. In Chapter 7 (section 7.2) I argue that different stakeholders have different information needs and that, therefore, it is appropriate to provide them with different types of information. However, the differences should be limited to what is disclosed and not to the rules used to value assets and calculate profits. Hence the principles that are set out in Chapter 7 apply equally to all accounts that fulfill the information function.

8.2.3 The Reporting Function

In section 8.2.1 above, I argue that the accounts that perform the distribution function for a particular period should also perform the reporting function for an earlier period. I consider that the same principle applies for the information function. Hence the same accounts that perform the information function for stakeholders should also perform the reporting function. But the reader may well remark that the suggestions, set out in chapter 5, for the form and content of financial statements that report the justice of the firm's activities, seem to have little in common with the principles set out in chapter 7 that should be followed in drawing up financial statements that fulfill the information function. The reason for this apparent inconsistency is that the principles that are set out in chapter 5 relate almost entirely to the content of the financial statements and, in particular, what topics should be covered. The principles that are set out in chapter 7 are those that should be followed in establishing the numbers to be reported in the financial statements. There is no inconsistency between chapter 5 and chapter 7. The accountant, in drawing up the information asked for in chapter 5 should follow the principles set out in chapter 7.

8.3 ARE THE FUNCTIONS EQUALLY IMPORTANT?

The reporting function is an essential complement to both the distribution function and the information function. Hence the reporting function is of equal importance as these functions. However, the question arises as to whether the distribution function is more important than the information function. I have argued that the influence on justice of the distribution function is potentially stronger and more direct that that of the information function. Hence, in an ideal world, the distribution function would become the determining influence in causing the firm to act justly. But such an ideal world does not exist. In the real world, the distribution function governs the firm's behaviour in respect of a limited number of distributions of which the most important is the tax payable to the state. Apart from a few specialized applications, such as the regulation of public utilities, the great majority of the firm's distributions are not determined by the distribution function. Hence, in practice, the information function is the more important.

8.4 FINAL REMARKS

In this book I have intentionally sought to be controversial with the aim of stimulating my fellow accountants to think more profoundly about their discipline. I suspect that many will not agree with my basic argument, which may be summarized as follows:

1. Society's fundamental problem is not how to produce more goods but how to distribute them justly and fairly. Clearly people may have differing opinions on this point, but surely all reasonable people would accept that distribution is an important matter which has been neglected by accountants.

2. A person's moral responsibility towards his fellow men (and her fellow women) is not limited to obeying the law and keeping his promises. Again opinions differ. But this is the conclusion of many of the distinguished philosophers (much cleverer than me), whose views are analysed in Chapter 2. So certainly it seems reasonable to explore the implications of this viewpoint.

3. The firm has a moral responsibility to consider the welfare of all its stakeholders. Many accountants reject the stakeholder theory of the firm, because they consider that the firm's responsibility is limited to maximizing the wealth of its shareholders. But there is much evidence (summarized in Koller and Heskett, 1992) that even shareholders benefit when firms adopt policies that are based on stakeholder theory.

Hence there are good reasons why accountants should consider seriously the implications for their discipline of adopting the objective of distributive justice.

Notes

NOTE TO THE ACKNOWLEDGEMENTS

1. Ordelheide (1994).

NOTES TO CHAPTER 1

1. The *Oxford English Dictionary* defines 'paradigm' as 'a conceptual or methodological model underlying the theories and practice of a science or discipline at a particular time'. For example, prior to the writings of Copernicus in the sixteenth century, the paradigm on which astronomy was based was that the earth was the centre of the universe and that the sun, moon, and stars circled the earth.
2. In this book, I follow the usage of economists and use the word 'firm' to denote any form of business including companies and corporations.
3. The IASB states that its conceptual framework deals with general purpose financial reporting by business entities in the private sector, which is essentially the field of this book.
4. For example, in a survey reported in Frey (2008), people were asked, 'Which of the following best describes how happy you are—"not too happy" (score 1), "pretty happy" (score 2), and "very happy"' (score 3). In this survey, the average score was 2.17, that is, rather happier than 'pretty happy'. In many studies, these subjective assessments were backed up by more objective methods, such as asking an outsider to give her impression of a person's happiness.
5. The conclusions of the latest research on happiness are well summarized in Frey (2008: Chapter 2).
6. Statement on the FAO's web-site: www.fao.org/hunger/faqs-on-hunger/en/#c41481, accessed on 27 October 2009.
7. FAO (2004: Table 8.1).
8. See FAO (2008: 8). The United States Department of Agriculture's estimate is rather higher: 2100 kilocalories per day. However, both estimates lead to similar conclusions.
9. See FAO (2009: 11).
10. See Mathus (1976).
11. The text of the UN's report may be consulted on the panel's web-site, www.ipcc.ch.
12. For a more detailed analysis of the arguments presented here, see Hossay (2006), Meadows (2005), Nadeau (2003), Henson (2008), and Jackson (2009).

13. In fact the theorem (which assumes numerous producers and consumers) does not apply to George and Henry. However the arguments against neo-liberal economics that are presented in this section apply equally well to a situation where this condition is not fulfilled. For an explanation of the theorem see Feldman (1998).

14. The neo-liberal economic theory of distribution is not completely devoid of moral elements. According to the theory, the share of total output that a worker receives is equal to the contribution that he makes towards its production—see the next chapter, Section 2.3.4.

NOTES TO CHAPTER 2

1. An alternative term is social justice. As used in this book, the two terms have the same meaning.

2. There are several different definitions of distributive justice. Roemer (1996: 1) defines it as 'how a society or group should allocate its resources or product among individuals with competing needs or claims'. Bojer (2003: 7) defines distributional justice (I am uncertain whether the slight difference in the term is significant) as 'justice in the distribution of economic goods between the members of society'. Phelps (1998: 887) defines distributive justice as 'justice in the economic relationships within society: collaboration in production, trade in consumer goods and the provision of collective goods'. I believe that my proposed definition is consistent with these.

3. Rawls (1971/1999: 257).

4. This definition is based on Nagel (2005).

5. Mill (1859/1991: 14).

6. See the discussion of happiness in Chapter 1, Section 1.5.

7. The benefits of equality are well analysed in Chapter 5 of Hamilton (2003).

8. Nozick (1974: 151).

9. Locke (1690/1980: Chapter V).

10. Nozick does not actually cite this example. However he has a rather similar (and amusing) example of several Robinson Crusoes on adjacent islands, one who is well off because his island endowed with rich natural resources and the other destitute as his island is bare. Nozick argues that the richer Robinson Crusoe has no moral obligation to help the poorer Robinson Crusoe (Nozick 1974: 185). He also makes it clear that, where a person's options are restricted by the action of another, who had the right to act as he did, then the choosing the limited option is voluntary and in accordance with the principle of justice in transfer.(Nozick 1974: 262–64). By contrast, Milton Friedman believes that the sole owner of the well should not be permitted to sell water at an exorbitant price. As he is a monopolist, he should be subject to government regulation (Friedman 1962/2002: Chapter II). This case illustrates the difference between Nozick, the rigorous theoretician, and Friedman, the pragmatist.

11. Nozick accepts that, for the well-owner to charge for water, he must be entitled to own the well. For example, if he dug the well himself, he would have a good title according to the principle of justice in acquisition, and, if he purchased it from the person who had dug the well, he would have good title according to the principle of justice in transfer. However, if he simply found an oasis by chance, then he would probably not have a good title, as his appropriation would not leave 'as much and as good' for other people.

12. Nozick (1974: 169).

13. Nozick (1974: 163).
14. Nozick (1974: 160).
15. M. Friedman (1962/2002: 161).
16. Sternberg (1994: 80).
17. Sternberg (1994: 146). In fairness to Sternberg, she is writing about the distribution of the firm's wealth, not that of society. She does not take a position on whether society as a whole (the state) should help the single mother.
18. See Nozick (1974: 186).
19. Marx (1878/1974: 87).
20. This is generally interpreted as the highest average level of happiness in a society (total happiness divided by the population) so as to avoid the possibility of an increase in population being considered desirable even when it leads to a decline in the happiness of the existing members. With a constant population, there is no difference between the highest total happiness and the highest average happiness.
21. If the marginal utility of goods were constant, then the total utility curve would be a horizontal straight line and all distributions of the goods between George and Henry would yield identical social utilities. If marginal utility increased with quantity, the social utility function would be convex to the x axis with a minimum at point P. In that case maximum social utility would be achieved by allocating all the goods to either George or Henry. This illustrates the vital importance of the assumption of diminishing marginal utility.
22. This striking expression was coined by the Nobel Laureate Amartya Sen.
23. For a further exposition of the matter covered in this paragraph, see Bojer (2003: 24–26).
24. Rawls (1971/1999: 23). All page references are to the 1999 edition.
25. See Meade (1976: 20).
26. It has been suggested that the measure of cardinal utility developed by Von Neumann and Morgenstern in *Theory of Games and Economic Behavior* (1944) can be used to measure a person's utility. This claim is based on a misunderstanding of the Von Neumann and Morgenstern measure: it is an aid to decision-making under uncertainty and not a measure of a person's satisfaction. See Ellsberg (1954).
27. Rawls (1971/1999). Rawls entitled his book '*a* theory of justice' and not '*the* theory of justice', showing commendable modesty and respect for colleagues who advocated different theories. This is in sharp contrast to the arrogance of the IASB which proclaims that it knows *the* objective of financial reporting (see Chapter 1, Section 1.1).
28. See Roemer (1996: 163).
29. Hobbes (1668/1994: Chapter XIII).
30. Rawls (1971/1999: 4).
31. In a socialist country, the basic structure would certainly comprise the public ownership of the means of production. However, Rawls specifically designed his theory of justice for an economy run, more or less, on capitalistic lines.
32. Rawls (1971/1999) sets out these principles in two places: on page 53 and on page 266. The formulation given here is an edited version of the two. Rather confusingly, Rawls refers to two principles, but, as his second principle has two parts, there are really three principles. Also he lists principle 3 before principle 2. But, since he states that principle 2 is prior to principle 3, it is more logical to list the principles in the sequence given here.
33. See Rawls (1971/1999: 67).
34. This assumes that primary goods can be equated with utility.

35. Certain philosophers have argued that the nature of the life that the individual can lead is determined by not only the quantity of primary goods, but also their composition. Hence Rawls, in determining the composition of primary goods, is also imposing his concept of the good life on the individual; for example, in giving lexical priority to basic liberties, he is denying that the life of the well-fed slave is better than that of the hungry peasant. Rawls attempts to deflect this criticism by defining primary goods as those that anyone would want, regardless of her concept of the good life.
36. Rawls (1971/1999: 54).
37. For more detail of primary goods, see Roemer (1996: 165).
38. For example, how are 'the powers and prerogatives of office' to be combined with income? If Alfred (when compared with Ben) values power more than income, should the weightings in the index be identical for Alfred and Ben? On this point, see Roemer (1994: 165–72).
39. Rawls (1971/1999: 17).
40. Rawls (1971/1999: 11).
41. This is certainly the case if Crusoe experiences the same utility from fish as Friday from coconuts.
42. Cohen (2008: 7).
43. For a reasoned criticism of pluralism, see Section 7 in Rawls (1971/1999: 30–36). Rawls, in a rather disparaging fashion, refers not to pluralism but to intuitionism.

NOTES TO CHAPTER 3

1. The word 'firm' is used in the sense employed by economists to denote any form of business, including corporations, companies, partnerships, and sole traders.
2. There is generally a delay between the payment by the customer and the receipt by other people in the chain. This delay may be several years or even decades when a firm in the chain holds onto to its revenue and does not pay it out in the form of wages, purchases from other firms, and payments to capital providers. However in the long run, the money is bound to be distributed, say when the firm is wound up.
3. See Singer (1979: Chapter 3).
4. M. Friedman (1962: 133).
5. See Hasnas (1998: 24).
6. The term 'associations' includes firms.
7. Rawls (1977: 164).
8. Rawls (1977: 164).
9. Cohen (2008: 16).
10. This is a paraphrase of Hasnas (1998: 29).
11. Donaldson (1982) quoted in Hasnas (1998).
12. The concept of stakeholder is explained later, in Section 3.8.
13. Cited in Gray et al. (1996: 58).
14. A libertarian could argue that the argument here is based on law and not morals and that the state has no moral right to restrict the freedom of individuals to form associations, such as corporations. But even Friedman does not take such an extreme position.
15. Cited in Hessen (1979).
16. Even in respect of partnerships, British law grants certain privileges, such as the right to sue in the name of the partnership.

17. The concept of stakeholder theory that is presented here is a synthesis of the theories set out in Freeman (1984), Evan and Freeman (1993), Donaldson and Preston (1995), A. L. Friedman and Miles (2002), and Clarkson (1995).
18. Clarkson and most other writers on stakeholder theory refer to 'corporations'. I prefer the economist's term 'firm'. The difference is not significant, as almost all firms (other than the very small) are corporations.
19. See Donaldson and Preston (1995: 85).
20. I have wracked my brain for an alternative term. The best that I have come up with is 'beneficiary/victim' which is less misleading than stakeholder but most inelegant.
21. Mill (1859/1991).
22. For example, Freeman and Reed (1983). The GRI's Guidelines (see Chapter 5, Section 5.8) define stakeholders as those 'whose actions can reasonably be expected to affect the ability of the organization to successfully implement its strategies and achieve its objectives'. This definition is so wide that it includes terrorists.
23. Evan and Freeman refer to the 'corporation', but they make clear that these principles apply to all forms of business organization.

NOTES TO CHAPTER 4

1. Rawls (1971/1999) argues that, in a democracy, civil disobedience (deliberately breaking the law) is permissible provided it is undertaken as a political action with the aim of changing the law. In particular the action should be open, and the perpetrator should be prepared to accept the consequences of his action. It would seem that such situations are likely to arise only rarely with the managers of firms. See *A Theory of Justice*, Sections 55–58.
2. As argued in Section 3.8(a) of Chapter 3.

NOTES TO CHAPTER 5

1. IAS 1, paragraph 8.
2. When the firm has capitalized a part of its wage cost (for example when it used its own workers to construct a fixed asset), the depreciation of this asset is not an allocation of a payment to other firms. However such amounts are rarely material.
3. Presumably, as the state is treated in the same way as employees and shareholders, it is also a partner. Gray (1996: 195) points out a complication with the calculation of the state's share. The value-added statement reports the gross amount of employee's wages, out of which employees pay income tax to the state. The net benefit to employees is less than the amount reported, and the amount received by the state is understated. Furthermore, dividends are generally reported at the net amount (after deduction of withholding tax). This means that the distributions to employees and to shareholders are not calculated on the same basis.
4. It is assumed, for the reasons given in Chapter 3 (Section 3.9.2), that the contracts made with suppliers and customers are just and that the men's responsibility with respect to these stakeholders is limited to honouring these contracts.
5. See Chapter 2, Section 2.4.
6. The contribution theory of the just wage is discussed in more detail in Chapter 2, Section 2.3.4.

7. There is a principle, in both law and economics, that a person who suffers a loss as a result of another's wrong action should take reasonable steps to mitigate his loss. For example, if the fisherman can limit his income loss to €40 by switching his operations to another unpolluted lake, then the proper measure of the harm that he has suffered is €40.

8. See Gray et al. (1996: 40).

9. The closest that any country comes to requiring firms to publish a general report is the law in France concerning 'les nouvelles régulations économiques'. Appendix C gives a fuller explanation of this measure.

10. Cited in Buhr (2007: 66).

11. The results of the survey may be accessed on KPMG's web-site (www.kpmg.com) which is the source of all the statistics cited in this section.

12. The G3 guidelines may be consulted on the GRI's web-site: www.globalreporting.org.

13. GRI G3 Guidelines, page 11. © 2006 by Global Reporting Initiative.

14. World Commission on Environment and Development (1987: 43).

15. GRI G3 Guidelines, page 3. © 2006 by Global Reporting Initiative.

16. GRI G3 Guidelines, page 2. © 2006 by Global Reporting Initiative.

17. GRI G3 Guidelines, page 30. © 2006 by Global Reporting Initiative.

18. GRI G3 Guidelines, page 10. © 2006 by Global Reporting Initiative.

19. It could be claimed that the GRI's definition is narrower if emphasis is placed on the word 'and'—that stakeholders must both affect AND be affected by the firm. This interpretation would exclude people who have no power to affect the firm (for example indigenous people who are harmed by the firm's operations) which can hardly be the GRI's intention.

20. GRI G3 Guidelines, page 3. © 2006 by Global Reporting Initiative.

21. GRI G3 Guidelines, page 11. © 2006 by Global Reporting Initiative.

22. GRI G3 Guidelines, page 10. © 2006 by Global Reporting Initiative.

23. GRI G3 Guidelines, page 24. points 4.16 and 4.17, © 2006 by Global Reporting Initiative.

24. GRI G3 Guidelines, page 10. © 2006 by Global Reporting Initiative.

25. GRI G3 Guidelines, page 6. © 2006 by Global Reporting Initiative.

26. GRI G3 Guidelines, page 23. © 2006 by Global Reporting Initiative.

27. GRI G3 Guidelines, page 24. © 2006 by Global Reporting Initiative.

28. GRI G3 Guidelines, page 28. © 2006 by Global Reporting Initiative.

29. GRI G3 Guidelines, page 26. © 2006 by Global Reporting Initiative.

30. GRI G3 Guidelines, page 31. © 2006 by Global Reporting Initiative.

31. GRI G3 Guidelines, page 26. © 2006 by Global Reporting Initiative.

32. GRI G3 Guidelines, page 31, © Global Reporting Initiative (2006).

33. The protocol for LA3 specifically excludes benefits in kind.

34. Since 2004, the ACCA (the Association of Chartered Certified Accountants) has organized a competition for the best sustainability report of a British firm. In the very first competition, the two organizations that subsequently merged to form the Co-operative Group were both short-listed, with one of them (Co-operative Financial Services) winning the award for the best report.

35. Corporate Register, according to its web-site (www.corporateregister.com), is 'an independent, privately held and self-funded organisation based in the UK'; it is 'the primary reference point for corporate responsibility reports and resources world-wide'.

36. The full title is 'The Co-operative Sustainability Report 2007/8: Altogether Different and Making a Difference'. The date is confusing, because on the first page it states: '[U]nless otherwise stated, performance relates to the calendar year 2007.'

37. All references in this section are to the Co-op printed report.
38. According to the law, on the dissolution of a co-operative society, the reserves are not distributed to members but are transferred to another co-operative society.
39. Co-op report, page 61.
40. www.csrnetwork.com
41. See the Co-op's financial statements, page 78. In addition KPMG received £1,420,000 for taxation and other services.

Appendix A

1. World Commission on Environment and Development (1987), page 43
2. The GRI G3 Guidelines may be consulted on the GRI's web-site: www. globalreporting.com.
3. GRI G3 Guidelines, page 3, © Global Reporting Initiative 2006
4. GRI G3 Guidelines, page 11, © Global Reporting Initiative 2006
5. GRI G3 Guidelines, page 10, © Global Reporting Initiative 2006
6. For example, the GRI's definition of stakeholders includes competitors and terrorists who are specifically excluded in chapter 3's definition. Alternatively it is possible to claim that the GRI's definition is narrower, if emphasis is placed on the word 'and'—that stakeholders must both be affected by the firm AND affect the firm. Such an interpretation would exclude powerless stakeholders (such as indigenous people harmed by the firm's operations), which can hardly be the GRI's intention.
7. GRI G3 Guidelines, page 6, © Global Reporting Initiative 2006
8. GRI G3 Guidelines, page 25, © Global Reporting Initiative 2006
9. GRI G3 Guidelines, page 26, © Global Reporting Initiative 2006. Points EC7 and EC9 are on the same page.
10. GRI G3 Guidelines, page 28, © Global Reporting Initiative 2006. Points EN23 and En28 are on the same page.
11. GRI G3 Guidelines, page 29, © Global Reporting Initiative 2006
12. GRI G3 Guidelines, page 32, © Global Reporting Initiative 2006
13. GRI G3 Guidelines, page 33, © Global Reporting Initiative 2006
14. GRI G3 Guidelines, page 35, © Global Reporting Initiative 2006
15. GRI G3 Guidelines, page 30, © Global Reporting Initiative 2006
16. GRI G3 Guidelines, page 31, © Global Reporting Initiative 2006. Point LA8 is on the same page.
17. Since 2004, the ACCA (the Association of Chartered Certified Accountants) has organized a competition for the best sustainability report by a British company. In the very first competition, the two organizations that subsequently merged to form the Co-operative Group were both short-listed, with one of them (Co-operative Financial Services) winning the award for the best report.
18. CorporateRegister is an independent organization based in the UK. It claims to be the primary reference point for corporate responsibility reports worldwide.

Appendix B

1. All the statistics in this section relate to the year 2007. Therefore they do not provide an accurate representation of the current position of the Co-operative Group.
2. The full title is 'The Co-operative Sustainability Report 2007/8, Altogether different and making a difference'. The date is confusing, because on the first

page it states: 'unless otherwise stated, performance relates to the calendar year 2007'.

3. All references in this section are to the Co-op printed report.
4. The Co-operative Group issues financial statements which seem to be very similar to those issued by limited companies. They are stated to be prepared in accordance with the UK's Industrial and Provident Societies Acts and the applicable standards of the IASB.
5. According to the GRI guidelines, B+ indicates that the report discloses much (but not all) of the information required by the guidelines. The reference to 'B+ level' is puzzling as the Co-op's report discloses as least as much as the other reports which are marked A+; for example that of Shell. In fact, according to a statement on the Group's web-site, the GRI itself later checked the report and gave it an A+ mark. This suggests a difference of opinion between the GRI and the Group's auditors, who apparently have stuck to their original assessment of B+. Prima facie, this incident adds to the credibility of the auditors but raises doubts as to the quality of the GRI's assessment.
6. This table is contained in the printed report and not on the web-site.
7. The election process is indirect. The members elect the regional boards, who in turn elect the central board.
8. According to the law, on the dissolution of a co-operative society, the reserves are not distributed to members but are transferred to another co-operative society.
9. CO_2e refers to Carbon dioxide equivalent. Quantities of other greenhouse gases are expressed in terms of CO_2 with equivalent effect on global warming.
10. Co-op report, page 61
11. www.csrnetwork.com
12. See the Co-op's financial statements, page 78. In addition KPMG received £1,420,000 for taxation and other services.

Appendix C

1. Decree number 2002–221 of 20 February 2002.
2. See Alpha(2008)

NOTE TO CHAPTER 6

1. That is the position concerning accounts for the year 2009.
2. With very few exceptions, all major German enterprises are either stock corporations or limited partnerships (Kommanditgesellschaft) for which the distribution rules are virtually identical. A notable exception is Bosch which is a limited company (GmbH).
3. An English translation of this law is provided by Schneider and Heidenhain (1996).
4. If the supervisory board fails to adopt the accounts, the shareholders' meeting may do so and hence decide how much profit to retain. Since the shareholders may decide to distribute 100% of the profit and (for reasons given later) the supervisory board normally favours retaining profits, it is very rare for the management board and the supervisory board not to agree on the adoption of the accounts.
5. The corporation's constitution may specify a different percentage; for listed companies this may not be less than 50%.

6. In corporations with more than 2000 employees (1000 employees in the coal, iron, and steel industries), half of the members of the supervisory board are elected by the employees. The other half are elected by the shareholders. The employee's influence is somewhat weakened by the casting vote of the chairman, who regularly comes from the shareholders' side. In corporations in the coal, iron, and steel industries, the chairman is an independent person who is chosen jointly by the employee and shareholder representatives on the advisory board.

7. The financial statement involved is the balance sheet, as the corporation's profit is calculated as the increase in the value of its assets over the year, adjusted for withdrawals and inputs of capital.

8. The Income Tax Act (Einkommensteuergesetz) states, '[T]raders . . . have to declare at the end of the financial year the state of their business assets, which must be shown according to the commercial principles of proper bookkeeping' (cited in Ballwieser [2001: 1249]). The 'commercial principles of proper bookkeeping' are defined in the Commercial Code (Handelsgesetzbuch).

9. The Income Tax Act states, 'Options in determining profit which are part of tax law have to be claimed according to the commercial balance sheet' (cited in Ballwieser [2001: 1250]).

10. The interests of the employees are protected through their representation on the supervisory board (which has joint responsibility with the management in determining distributions) and not through the legal rules that govern the amount of distributions.

11. Often the fact that the enterprise pays little or no tax is hidden by the accountant's practice of providing for deferred taxation—a practice which accountants justify as necessary to give 'a true and fair view' and which the general public considers to be a device for concealing the truth that the company has paid little or no tax.

12. See Chapter 2 of Flower (2004) for a fuller discussion of these functions.

13. See Kay (1996: 147).

14. See Appendix B for a description of the practice of the British Co-operative Group.

15. Some neo-liberal economists assert that, in ideal conditions, the free play of market forces leads to the maximization of output. This claim cannot be substantiated. It is certainly correct that, according to the first fundamental theorem of welfare economics, perfect competition leads to a Pareto optimal solution, but there are infinitely many Pareto optimal solutions in any given market situation, each with differing levels of output. Furthermore the concept of the maximization of output is problematic. If it is taken to mean the maximization of the market value of output (which is the only logical interpretation when there is more than one good), the concept is problematic, because the prices of goods depends on the relative demand of different consumers, which in turn depends in part on the initial division of resources among consumers. Feldman (1998:892) presents the correct analysis: 'Economists have always agreed that if q^1 and q^2 are alternative net output vectors [that is, alternative output quantities that represent Pareto optimal positions] and p^1 and p^2 are the corresponding price vectors, then $p^1 \cdot q^1 > q^2 \cdot p^2$ has no welfare implications.'

NOTE TO CHAPTER 7

1. The first person to suggest that accounting principles should be set behind a veil of ignorance appears to be Gaa (1986).

2. See Flower (2004: Chapter 9).
3. Both definitions are to be found in Mahon (2008).
4. A full account of this case is given in Hastings (1977).
5. IASB (2006), paragraph QC18.
6. It is incorrect to argue that, because one can interrogate Bloggs, the statement 'Bloggs believes that the height of the Eiffel Tower is 320 metres' is objective, for how can one establish that Bloggs is telling the truth? However, the statement 'Bloggs says that he believes that the height of the Eiffel Tower is 320 metres' is objective, because one can observe Bloggs's utterances. Perhaps, in the future, mankind will be able to discover what is happening in a person's brain by observing objective phenomena, such as electrical impulses. In that case statements about a person's belief would be objective.
7. Aristotle (2004: 124).
8. Hill and Jones (1992) argue that 'much of the structure of law relating to business activity in society reflects critical points of conflict in stakeholder-agent relationships'. The term stakeholder-agent relationship refers to the idea that the firm's managers are agents of the stakeholders.
9. Even Milton Friedman, the arch-advocate of the neo-liberal theory of the firm, accepts that the firm's managers should not engage in deception or fraud. See Chapter 3, Section 3.3, for the full quote from Friedman (1962/2002).
10. The information needs of employees are considered more fully in Chapter 5, Section 5.6, and Appendices A, B, and C.
11. It is also in the interests of other stakeholders, such as employees and shareholders, that the costs of financial reporting should be limited as this increases the size of the surplus available for distribution.
12. The IASB's governing body was the IFAC (International Federation of Accountants), the body that represents the professional accountancy associations at international level.
13. For details of the composition of standard-setting bodies, see Flower (2004: 83–85, 140–43).
14. For more information on the Dutch accounting court, see Dijksma (1993).
15. Roughly 'who audits the auditors?'
16. Papas (1993) describes SOL as an 'independent self-governing body'. However, it was created by a law, the members of its governing body were appointed by the state, and the members of SOL who carried out the audits were employees and not independent professionals. Hence my designation of SOL as a government body.

Bibliography

Alexander, D., and S. Archer, 'On Economic Reality, Representational Faithfulness and the True and Fair Override', *Accounting and Business Research*, 33.1 (2003), 3–17

Alpha, *Les informations sociales dans les rapports 2007* (Paris: Groupe Alpha, 2008)

Anderson, E., 'What Is the Point of Equality?', *Ethics*, 109 (1999), 1

Aristotle, *The Nichomachean Ethics* (London: Penguin, 2004)

Bailey, D., G. Harte, and R. Sugden, *Making Transnationals Accountable* (London: Routledge, 1994)

Baldwin, R., and M. Cave, *Understanding Regulation* (Oxford: Oxford University Press, 1999)

Ballwieser, W., 'Germany, Individual Accounts', in *Transacc*, ed. by D. Ordelheide (Basingstoke: Palgrave, 2001), 1217–1351

Bebbington, J., 'Changing Organizational Attitudes and Culture Through Sustainability', in *Sustainability, Accounting and Accountability*, ed. by J. Unerman and others (London: Routledge, 2007), 226–242

Bojer, H., *Distributional Justice* (Abingdon: Routledge, 2003)

Bok, S., *Lying: Moral Choice in Public and Private Life* (London: Quartet Books, 1980)

Buhmann, K., 'Corporate Social Responsibility: What Role for Law?', *Corporate Governance*, 6.2 (2006), 188–202

Buhr, N., 'Histories and Rationales of Sustainability Reporting' in *Sustainability, Accounting and Accountability*, ed. by J. Unerman and others (London: Routledge, 2007), 57–69

Clarkson, M., 'A Stakeholder Framework for Analyzing and Evaluating Corporate Social Performance', *Academy of Management Review*, 20.1 (1995), 92–117

Cohen, G. A., *Rescuing Justice and Equality* (Cambridge: Harvard University Press, 2008)

Cooper, S., *Corporate Social Performance, a Stakeholder Approach* (Aldershot: Ashgate, 2004)

Cooper, S., and D. Owen, 'Corporate Social Reporting and Stakeholder Accountability: The Missing Link', *Accounting, Organizations and Society*, 32 (2007), 649–667

Dahl, R., 'A Prelude to Corporate Reform', *Business and Society Review*, Spring (1972), 17–23

Dick, J. C., "How to Justify a Distribution of Earnings." *Philosophy and Public Affairs* 4(3) (1975), 248–272.

Dijksma, J., and M. Hoogendoorn, *European Financial Reporting: The Netherlands* (London: Routledge, 1993)

Donaldson, T., *Corporations and Morality* (Englewood Cliffs: Prentice-Hall, 1982)

Donaldson, T., and L. E. Preston, 'The Stakeholder Theory of the Corporation: Concepts, Evidence and Implications', *Academy of Management Review*, 20.1 (1995), 65–91

Easterlin, R. A., 'Will Raising the Income of All Increase the Happiness of All?', *Journal of Economic Behavior and Organization*, 27 (1994), 35–47

Eatwell, J., and others (eds), *The New Palgrave, a Dictionary of Economics* (London: Macmillan, 1998)

Egan, M. L., and others, 'France's Mandatory "Triple Bottom Line" Reporting', *The International Journal of Environmental, Cultural, Economic and Social Responsibility*, 5.5 (2009), 2–20

Elkington, J., *Cannibals with Forks: The Triple Bottom Line of 21st Century Business* (Stony Creek, CT: New Society Publishers, 1998), 75–84

Ellsberg, D., "Classic and Current Notions of 'Measurable Utility'." *The Economic Journal*, 64(255), (1954), 528-556.

Evan, W. N., and R. E. Freeman, 'A Stakeholder Theory of the Modern Corporation' in *Ethical Theory and Business*, ed. by T. L. Beauchamp and N. E. Bowie (Englewood Cliffs: Prentice-Hall, 1993)

FAO, The State of Food Insecurity in the World 2008. (Rome: Food and Agricultural Organization, 2008)

———. *Summary of World Food and Agricultural Statistics 2004* (Rome: Food and Agricultural Organization, 2004)

———. *The State of Food Insecurity in the World 2009* (Rome: Food and Agricultural Organization, 2009)

FASB, *Exposure Draft: Conceptual Framework for Financial Reporting: The Objective of Financial Reporting and Qualitative Characteristics and Constraints of Decision-Useful Financial Reporting Information* (Norwalk: FASB, 2008)

Feldman, A. M., 'Welfare Economics' in *The New Palgrave, a Dictionary of Economics*, ed. by J. Eatwell and others (London: Macmillan, 1998), 889–894

Flower, J., *Global Financial Reporting* (Basingstoke: Palgrave, 2002)

———. *European Financial Reporting* (Basingstoke: Palgrave, 2004)

Frankfurt, H., 'Equality as a Moral Idea', *Ethics* 98 (1987), 21–43

Freeman, R. and D. Reed, "Stockholders and stakeholders: A new perspective on corporate governance." *California Management Review* 25(3) (1983), 88-106.

Freeman, R .E., *Strategic Management, a Stakeholder Approach* (Boston: Pitman Publishing, 1984)

French, E. A., 'The Evolution of the Dividend Law of England' in *Studies in Accounting*, ed. by W. T. Baxter and S. Davidson (London: ICAEW, 1977), 306–331

Frey, B. S., *Happiness: A Revolution in Economics* (Cambridge: MIT Press, 2008)

Friedman, A. L., and S. Miles, 'Developing Stakeholder Theory', *Journal of Management Studies*, 39.1 (2002), 1–21

Friedman, M., *Capitalism and Freedom* (Chicago: University of Chicago Press, 1962/2002)

Gaa, J., 'User Primacy in Corporate Financial Reporting: A Social Contract Approach', *The Accounting Review*, LXI.3 (1986), 435–54

Galbraith, J. K., *The Affluent Society*, (Boston: Houghton Mifflin, 1955)

Gray, R., D. Owen, and C. Adams., *Accounting and Accountability*. (Harlow: Pearson, 1996)

———, and K. Maunders., "Corporate Social Reporting: emerging trends in accountabiliy and the social contract." *Accounting, Auditing and Accountability* 1.1 (1988), 1–20.

GRI, *Sustainability Reporting Guidelines Version 3* (2006), available from the GRI's web-site <http://www.globalreporting.org>

Haller, A., and J. Ernstberger, Global Reporting Initiative — Internationale Leitlinien zur Erstellung von Nachhaltigkeitsberichten', *Betriebs-Berater*, 46 (2006), 9–41

Hamilton, C., *Growth Fetish* (Sydney: Allen and Unwin, 2003)

———. *Affluenza* (Crows Nest, New South Wales: Allen and Unwin, 2005)

Hasnas, J., 'The Normative Theories of Business Ethics', *Business Ethics Quarterly*, 8.1 (1998), 19–42

Hastings, P., 'The Case of the Royal Mail' in *Studies in Accounting*, ed. by W. Baxter and S. Davidson (London: Institute of Chartered Accountants in England and Wales, 1977), 339–346

Henson, R., *The Rough Guide to Climate Change* (London: Penguin, 2008)

Hessen, R., 'A New Concept of the Corporation', *Hastings Law Journal*, 30 (1979), 1320–1340

Hill, C. L., and T. M. Jones, 'Stakeholder-Agency Theory', *Journal of Management Studies*, March (1992), 131–154

Hobbes, T., *Leviathan*. (Indianopolis: Hackett: 1669/1994)

Hossay, P., *Unsustainable* (London: Zedbooks, 2006)

IASB, *Discussion Paper: Preliminary Views on an Improved Conceptual Framework for Financial Reporting* (London: IASB, 2006)

Ijiri, Y., 'On the Accountability-Based Conceptual Framework of Accounting', *Journal of Accounting and Public Policy*, 2 (1983), 75–81

Ijiri, Y., and R. K. Jaedicke, 'Reliability and Objectivity in Accounting Measurements', *The Accounting Review*, July (1976), 474–483

Jackson, T., *Prosperity without Growth* (London: Earthscan, 2009)

Kaplinsky, R., *Globalization, Poverty and Inequality* (Cambridge: Polity Press, 2005)

Kay, J., 'The Future of UK Utility Regulation', in *Regulating Utilities: A Time for a Change?* ed. by M. Beasley (London: Institute of Economic Affairs, 1996), 145–171

Keynes, John Maynard, 'Economic Possibilities for Our Grandchildren' in *Essays in Persuasion* (New York: Norton, 1930), 358–373

Koehn, D., 'Towards an Ethic of Exchange', *Business Ethics Quarterly*, 2.3 (1992), 341–355

Koller, J. and J. Heskett, *Corporate Cultural Performance*, (New York, Norton, 1992)

KPMG, KPMG International Survey of Corporate Responsibility Reporting 2008 (2009), available on the KPMG web-site <http://www.kpmg.com>

Lefebvre, C., and J. Flower, *European Financial Reporting: Belgium* (London: Routledge, 1994)

Locke, J., *Second Treatise of Government* (Indianapolis: Hackett, 1690/1980)

Mahon, J. 'The Definition of Lying and Deception', *The Stanford Encyclopedia of Philosophy* (Fall2008Edition),Edward.Zalta(ed.),URL=<http://plato.stanford.edu/archives/fall2008/entries/lying-definition/>

Malthus, T., *An Essay on the Principle of Population* (New York: Norton, 1976)

Marx, K., 'Critique of the Gotha Programme'. *Marx-Engels: The First Internationale and After*. (Harmondsworth, Penguin Books, 1878/1974)

Mayer, C., and J. Vickers, 'Profit Sharing Regulation and Economic Appraisal', *Fiscal Studies* 17 (1996), 1–18

Meade, J., *The Just Economy* (London: George Allen and Unwin, 1976)

Meadows, D., J. Randers, et al., *Limits to growth: the 30-year update*. (London: Earthscan, 2005)

Mill, J. S., 'On Liberty'. *John Stuart Mill On Liberty and other essays*. J. Gray (ed.). (Oxford: Oxford University Press, 1859/1991), 6–135

Milne, M., and R. Gray, 'Future Prospects for Corporate Sustainability Reporting' in *Sustainability, Accounting and Accountability*, ed. by J. Unerman and others (London: Routledge, 2007), 184–207

Monti-Belkaoui, J., *Fairness in Accounting* (Westport: Quorum Books, 1996)
Nadeau, R. L., *The Wealth of Nature* (New York: Columbia University Press, 2003)
Nagel, T., 'Equality' in *The Oxford Companion to Philosophy*, ed. by T. Honderich (Oxford: Oxford University Press, 2005), 266–267
Nozick, R., *Anarchy, State and Utopia* (Boston: Basic Books, 1974)
Ordelheide, D., *European Financial Reporting: Germany* (London: Routledge, 1994)
Papas, A., *European Financial Reporting: Greece*. (London: Routledge, 1993)
Parfit, D., 'Equality and Priority', *Ratio* 10.3 (1997), 202–221
Phelps, E., 'Distributive Justice' in *The New Palgrave, a Dictionary of Economics*, ed. by J. Eatwell and others (London: Macmillan, 1998), 886–887
Rawls, J., 'The Basic Structure as Subject' in *Values and Morals*, ed. by A. Goldman and J. Kim (Dordrecht: Riedel, 1978)
———. *A Theory of Justice*, (Cambridge,MA: Belknap Press, 1971/1999)
Rescher, N., *Fairness: Theory and Practice of Distributive Justice* (New Brunswick: Transaction Publishers, 2002)
Riahi-Belkaoui, A., *Accounting Theory* (London: Thompson, 2000)
Roemer, J., *Theories of Distributive Justice* (Cambridge: Harvard University Press, 1996)
Sakurai, H., 'Japan — Individual Accounts' in *Transacc: Transnational Accounting*, ed. by D. Ordelheide (Basingstoke: Palgrave Publishers, 2001), 1685–1805
Schneider, H., and M. Heidenhain, *The German Stock Corporation Act* (The Hague: Kluwer, 1996)
Shocker, A. D., and S. P. Sethi, 'An Approach to Incorporating Societal Preferences in Developing Corporate Action Strategies', *California Management Review*, Summer (1973), 291–304
Singer, P., *Practical Ethics* (Cambridge: Cambridge University Press, 1979)
Spacek, L., 'The need for an accounting court' in *A search for fairness in financial reporting to the public* (Chicago: Arthur Andersen. 1969), 27–38
Sternberg, E., *Just Business* (London: Little, Brown, 1994)
———. 'The Defects of Stakeholder Theory', *Corporate Governance*, 5.1 (1997), 3–10
Stewart, J. C., 'Ethics and Financial Reporting in the United States', *Journal of Business Ethics*, 5 (1986), 401–08
Stix, G., 'A Question of Sustenance', *Scientific American*, September (2007), 30–33
Stoloway, H. and M. Lebas, *Corporate Financial Reporting: a global perspective*, (London: Thompson, 2002)
Towers, D., 'The Wood for the Trees', *Accountancy*, February (2008), 16
Unerman, J, J. Bebbington, and B. O'Dwyer, *Sustainability, Accounting and Accountability* (London: Routledge, 2007)
Varian, H. R., 'Distributive Justice, Welfare Economics, and the Theory of Fairness', *Philosophy and Public Affairs*, 4.3 (1975), 223–47
Vidaver-Cohen, D., 'Taking a Risk, Max Clarkson's Impact on Stakeholder Theory', *Business and Society*, March (1999), 39–42
Von Neumann, J. and O. Morgenstern, *The Theory of Games*. (Princeton: Princeton University Press, 1944)
Wilkinson, R., and K. Pickett, *The Spirit Level: Why More Equal Societies Almost Always Do Better* (London: Allen Lane, 2009)
World Commission on Environment and Development, *Our Common Future* (Oxford: Oxford University Press, 1987)

Index

For Product Safety Concerns and Information please contact our EU
representative GPSR@taylorandfrancis.com
Taylor & Francis Verlag GmbH, Kaufingerstraße 24, 80331 München, Germany

www.ingramcontent.com/pod-product-compliance
Ingram Content Group UK Ltd.
Pitfield, Milton Keynes, MK11 3LW, UK
UKHW021608240425
457818UK00018B/443